Alasdair Gilchrist
IoT Security Issues

Alasdair Gilchrist

IoT Security Issues

First Edition

ISBN 978-1-5015-1474-6
e-ISBN (PDF) 978-1-5015-0577-5
e-ISBN (EPUB) 978-1-5015-0562-1

Library of Congress Cataloging-in-Publication Data
A CIP catalog record for this book has been applied for at the Library of Congress.

Bibliographic information published by the Deutsche Nationalbibliothek
The Deutsche Nationalbibliothek lists this publication in the Deutsche Nationalbibliografie;
detailed bibliographic data are available on the Internet at http://dnb.dnb.de.

© 2017 Walter de Gruyter Inc., Boston/Berlin
Printing and binding: CPI book GmbH, Leck
♾ Printed on acid-free paper
Printed in Germany

www.degruyter.com

To Rattiya and Arrisara

Acknowledgements

Much of the research in this book stems from Internet research based on published industry reports from Gartner, Cisco, Beecham's, Pew Research Center among many others. I would also like to acknowledge the many security resources available on the Internet such as Privacy International, OWASP, Microsoft Technet, and the Online Trust Alliance. Additionally, little of the section on Internet surveillance would have been possible to verify had it not been for the Guardian and Washington Posts published articles on the Edwards Snowden files and the Guardian's articles on the Investigatory Powers bill in the UK.

I would also acknowledge the efforts of Jeffrey Pepper and Megan Lester at De Gruyter for their efforts in publishing this book, as well as Stephanie Defrayne, Angie MacAllister and Scott MacAllister for their copy editing, technical verification and formatting help.

Contents

Part III: Architecting the Secure IoT

Part IV: **Defending the IoT**

Part V: **Trust**

Part VI: **Privacy**

Part VII: **Surveillance, Subterfuge and Sabotage**

Introduction

IoT Security Issues looks at the burgeoning growth of the multitude of devices controlled by the Internet, where product comes first and security second. In this case, security trails badly. This book examines the issues surrounding these problems, vulnerabilities, what can be done to solve the problem, investigating the stack for the roots of the problems and how programming and attention to good security practice can combat the problems today that are a result of lax security processes on the Internet of Things.

This book is for those interested in understanding the vulnerabilities on the Internet of Things, such as programmers whose primary focus is not the IoT, security professionals, and a wide array of interested hackers and makers. This book assumes little experience or knowledge of the Internet of Things on the part of its readers. To fully appreciate the book, limited programming back- ground would be helpful for some of the later chapters, though the basic con- tent is explained.

The author, Alasdair Gilchrist, has spent 25 years as a company director in the fields of IT, Data Communications, Mobile Telecoms and latterly Cloud/ SDN/NFV technologies, as a professional technician, support manager, network and security architect. He has managed both agile SDLC software development projects as well as technical network architecture designs. He has experience in the deployment and integration of systems in enterprise, cloud, fixed/mobile telecoms, and service provider networks. He is therefore knowledgeable in a wide range of technologies and has written a number of books in related fields.

DOI 10.1515/9781501505775-001

Part I: **Making Sense of the Hype**

The hype surrounding the IoT that consumers have been subjected to over the last decade is truly astonishing. We have been told that 50 billion devices will be connected to the Internet and communicating with one another, and that they will deliver untold of pleasures. An Internet of 50 billion devices all sharing data and collaborating will produce a lifestyle experience that was impossible to consider even a decade ago. We will have autonomous vehicles, drones delivering parcels, even drones as air taxis, bots answering contact centres and even the possibility of cyber-sex with virtual reality robots.

The problem is that we cannot just accept the hype as consultants, security practitioners and regurgitate this to our clients – we must keep an open mind and try to balance evangelism versus skepticism.

So, where has the promise of the Internet of Things gone astray? After all, we were promised a new world not so long ago, a world that heralded the connectivity of devices that would make our lives so easy and fulfilling.

Did the proponents of the IoT overstate their case? Did they perhaps believe that the IoT would escalate to a disruptive level, such as the smartphone and the tablet? Perhaps they did, but we are still not seeing that through future projections, which still look optimistic.

In this section, we will consider why the IoT has not grown exponentially as predicted, and why consumers are so reticent to embrace the technologies. After all, when we think in terms of securing the IoT, we need to understand why the public has not embraced a truly innovative array of solutions and products as they have other technologies.

Therefore, in this opening chapter, the consideration in regard to how consumers can analyze the hype and come to realistic terms with the IoT.

What the reader will learn is:
1. Hype is often misconstrued through evangelists vs. skeptics
2. 'Things' are very ambiguous and dependent on the definition of IoT
3. The public doesn't always know what they want or understand IoT
4. Companies and media are often technologically biased in surveys
5. Public surveys and results are contradictory
6. Poor enthusing examples of the IoT are holding IoT adoption back

DOI 10.1515/9781501505775-002

Chapter 1 – The Consumer Internet of Things

The Internet of Things, is a real enigma, not only is it such a vague term, covering all sorts of network capable connected things, which can be anything from a light bulb to a car to a home security system. It also appears to have almost unlimited scope bringing just about any modern consumer gadget or technical appliance, under its umbrella by virtue of its very loose definition.

Here are some common definitions:

> The **"Internet of Things"** (IoT) is a system of interrelated computing devices, mechanical and digital machines, objects, animals or people that are pro- vided with unique identifiers and the ability to transfer data over a network without requiring human-to-human or human-to-computer interaction.

From WhatIs.com:

> "The Internet of Things (IoT) describes the revolution already under way that is seeing a growing number of Internet-enabled devices that can network and communicate with each other and with other web-enabled gadgets. IoT refers to a state where Things (e.g. objects, environments, vehicles and clothing) will have more and more information associated with them and have the ability to sense, communicate, network and produce new in- formation, becoming an integral part of the Internet."

By Technology Strategy Board – IoT Special Interest Group

There are many more definitions of the IoT that can leave us bemused, but if we cannot agree on a definition then how can we secure it?

A Wave of Technology, or a Wave of Hype

The IoT rides on a wave of promise that its supporters claim will revolutionize our lives and the way we interact with the world, and what is more, this will happen within only the next decade or so. Indeed, depending on whom you listen too, some of the ardent IoT supporters such as Cisco, believe the IoT will be responsible for 50 billion (things) devices being online and connected to the Internet by 2020. Cisco does have a more expansive conceptual view where they include sources of data such as people, machines or even cows, in an agricultural scenario, within an Internet of Everything. There is no doubt we are seeing and will

DOI 10.1515/9781501505775-003

continue to see a significant industrial and agricultural increase in the role sensors and other IoT devices will play. But the consumer market continues to trail expectations.

Gartner and General Electric have major interests in the field; however, they are a bit more reticent and have a restricted scope of the IoT to sensors and devices. As a result, they are making a more conservative forecast of the IoT's short-term growth and financial potential. Hence they are speaking 20-25 Billion devices and 1.9 trillion new dollars spent by 2020.

These forecasts, regardless of the variance between the two sets of figures, are astonishing predictions. Yet, perhaps not; this may well be due to the ambiguous nature of these things. Initially, when we consider these new things it is typical to think of network-connected devices and gadgets such as wearable's, like the smart watch and the fitness bands. Some other, commonly identified consumer IoT devices are the smart thermostat, light bulbs and the smart TV.

Cisco and their fellow supporters of IoT, with some justification, claim that this wave of new consumer buying will produce trillions in new dollar spending across the IoT in the consumer, industrial, enterprise and commercial landscapes. Furthermore, in 2015, Gartner said that 6.4 billion 'things', might be connected and in use in the consumer IoT ecosystem alone by 2016. Furthermore, they predicted an acceleration of 5.5m devices per day joining the consumer IoT from 2016 onward.

IoT Skeptics and the Role of Security Issues

Not everyone in the industry however shares the common belief of the massive potential of the IoT. There are some in the industry that are becoming more skeptical as the years roll on and are even challenging how realistic even the conservative figures are. Remember, the IoT has been around since 2000 – actually a bit earlier – but has been hyped aggressively since 2010 and that is being generous. Gartner has had IoT on the peak of hype for several years now. Others agree the hype is at its peak, but that issues over lax security, concerns over privacy and loss of consumer trust will inhibit growth. There is also the mess of incompatible technologies and incomprehensible protocols that will also ensure consumers stay away. Many of the skeptics' claim the market will tumble down Gartner's trough of disenchantment, and will never reach anything like the implementation and financial forecasts, while others are slightly more optimistic believing in a much longer timeframe for adoption.

The skeptics do have a point; for even if we accept the lower forecasts of 20 billion IoT devices, installed and networked by 2020, this would require a tremendous amount of spending and installation effort over the coming years. Furthermore, what areas will see the greatest adoption and deployment? Recent surveys indicate that it will not be in the consumer IoT environment, which is contrary to much of the market's belief. Will it be in the enterprise, commercial or the industrial ecosystems?

The industrial IoT is the obvious area of adoption as it has had M2M for decades and the IoT conceptually at least is merely a slight evolution. Indeed, many engineers in operational technology mock the term IoT as being nothing more than the M2M (with hype) as they have worked with this technology under a different name for decades. From a security perspective, this is actually good news, because it means that at least one major sector of the IoT domain has the potential risk well-in-hand.

The Internet of No-thing

Some doubters will claim that most of the industry generated forecasts are based on mere speculation, are unrealistic, or are inclusive of the already vast number of existing sensors and devices installed in enterprise, commerce and industry. The term 'Internet of No-things' arises from the more challenging observations of recent survey results. After all, where is the demand for this popular disruptive technology in the consumer market?

Take a look around; in 2016 Gartner predicted – at the lower end of the scale – there would be 6.4 billion consumer devices installed and how many people do you know have smart devices in their home? Those that challenge the IoT forecasts and the popular surveys which paint a healthy IoT future believe that the vast majority of devices are indeed installed and active but they are in the industrial IoT and not the consumer environment, and hence the term, the 'Internet of No-thing' when addressing consumer IoT. Your new car, your new refrigerator, and a wide range of consumer devices have devices embedded that you likely do not even know about that add significantly to the existing and projected numbers. In these cases, the consumer may or may not be unaware of a price differential as a result of these technologies.

Supporting this assumption is a Deloitte poll that revealed a significant issue. It appears the public considers the IoT to be a catchall term used to describe any number of household appliances and personal devices, from cars to fridges, which connect to the Internet and can talk to each other. However, despite consumers saying they like the idea, the survey of more than 4,000 found high prices and skepticism prevailed over their initial desire for life- changing products. As far as the majority was concerned, they were not ready to buy as they doubted whether the technology had advanced enough, and that is preventing the IoT from really taking off.

Seven in ten shoppers told Deloitte they would not be buying any connected devices over the next twelve months and the only kinds of connected products owned by more than one in thirty households were smart TVs, entertainment systems and games consoles, although they discounted smartphones.

Just three percent of people had a connected security system, the same number as owned a smart thermostat. Only two percent had any form of home appliance, such as a fridge, cooker or kettle that connected to the Internet. However, in a more upbeat sign of the IoT potential, 40 percent of consumers responded that they would consider buying a smart device when they come to upgrading their current appliances.

The IoT would not be itself without another example of its inherent contradiction and paradox. Gartner's surveys in 2016 supports a contradiction to the theory of the Internet of Nothing, in recent polls among others, the results did suggest that the IoT had reached a tipping point in public acceptance. For just over 35% of the respondents claimed to have bought an IoT device in the last year (2015), which equates to just over $1/3^{rd}$ of the population, and 70% – which is over 2/3rds – intended to buy an IoT device within the next 12 months (2016- 2017) so at least the future looks bright.

Where are these IoT devices?

The mystery of this contradiction between public interest and lack of devices may actually be due to the way that different parties categorize IoT devices. After all, the figures could include the existing consumer products that they already own, such as smartphones, iPods, TVs, entertainment systems and game players such as X-Box and Play Station amongst others. However, these products were purchased several years ago before there was such a classification as the IoT, and well before the hype had people thinking of them as such. This is an important point. People buy products and generally not technologies; adding features to products has always been the edge that turns markets and the markets adapt quickly to change.

A possible reason for the lack of enthusiasm is that some IoT devices are hiding in plain view, take these Amazon tags for instance for ordering washing powder and other household consumables; these small consumer tags, for automated one touch re-ordering are easily overlooked, and as they insidiously invade our homes, could well go unnoticed. One product that would skew results significantly in any poll is the classification of the smartphone.

Why the ambiguity in IoT uptake?

If a smartphone is classified as a consumer IoT device, which in some surveys it clearly is, then of course this will skew results – similarly if we include people. However, many people if asked, 'do you own an IoT device?' may not consider themselves or their smartphone to be IoT. Therefore, some analysts have a tighter definition of an IoT device that may not include smartphones, humans, dogs or cows – and that would certainly move the figures in the other direction. Hence the massive ambiguity with regards the poll results related to IoT uptake and popular adoption.

An interesting note on the smartphone IoT debate is that there are several projects dedicated to turning your smartphone into an IoT device – if it isn't one already. These projects, such as Phonvert are taking advantage of the huge number of still capable smartphones, which are perhaps only two years old, that get discarded each year. These devices still have all their working sensors, like the camera, microphone, accelerometers, touch screens, Bluetooth radio and it seems such a waste to have them end up on a landfill site. Instead of throwing them away – Phonvert suggests 280 million smartphones were retired in 2015 alone without being recycled – why not turn them into IoT devices, such as a fridge cam, baby monitor, or a Bluetooth/Wi-Fi gateway and they supply the open-source software to enable this. Another bonus is that smartphones were designed with security in mind and that is not something that can be said of most consumer IoT products.

The Media and Marketing Hype

The media are extremely good at advertising and presenting new products to consumers through the TV and through other marketing channels such as Google and Facebook targeted advertising, it is how they make profit. The goal is to create a demand from customers who decide that they need these products, and to satisfy this projected appetite, vendors will pay to publicize their products. Therefore, adverts are awash over all media channels delivering the message of the potential capabilities of connected fridges, toasters or the smart kettle and how these will transform the purchaser's life-style.

Before the consumer leaps in though, they might be wise to look under the bonnet to see what they are actually purchasing. A risk assessment and cost/benefit examination of the consumer ecosystem would be advantageous. What is the IoT actually delivering as a benefit to the consumer that is worth them spending their hard-earned money?

Customer's do cost/benefit and risk assessments even though they might know it. Yes, they will not know the terms, but they do know the process. For example, when they purchase a Wi-Fi router they will almost certainly have been informed about the security issues. The threat is obvious, yet they will decide to implement or not bother with encryption or authentication. Why is that?

What tends to happen is that consumers do actually go through risk assessment and cost/benefit analysis, in that they use their experience, and history to evaluate the risk. For example, did having an open Wi-Fi or unauthenticated network connection actually cause them visible harm? They may well have listened to their technical friends and secured the Wi-Fi only to have found it a pain when hosting guests to a barbecue to go around and configure everyone's phone. Instead, they just switched of authentication and everyone was happy. After all, how many people can claim to be hacked and that attack rendered actual harm? This is of course not saying that they were not hacked, they most likely were, but it just wasn't harmful and the exploit invisible to them.

They may well be the most productive and virulent zombie within a botnet, but it is transparent to them. Furthermore, the fact they are a prized zombie (soldier) within that botnet may well be beneficial, as the botnet controller will make efforts to protect their asset. For example, a malicious piece of malware doesn't need to be harmful to the host; indeed, it can be beneficial to the host. It can be parasitic but also symbiotic, as the controller of the botnet will protect his assets from other Internet predators – the device will host the malware and the malware will do the host no harm, even protect it from other dangers.

This ambiguity with IoT security and value is where the marketing of di- verse IoT products really does become an issue. There appears to be large amounts of popular media hype, both positive and increasingly negative, that are throwing out contradictory messages. The positive hype of course is required to create a market, which enthuses the public, but it does contrast with a lack of fresh, imaginative and exciting products. This is noticeable in particular with consumer IoT when it comes to selling the idea of the automated smart home to the customer. It actually is disappointing to read or listen to presentation after presentation selling the concept of consumer IoT as being limited to a smart thermostat or a smart fridge. So why do manufacturers and their marketing teams never come up with more enthusing examples of the consumer IoT, rather than smart fridges, toasters and washing machines?

Lack of Killer Applications

The reality is that within the consumer IoT ecosystem there currently are no killer applications – as interconnected services that provide value – except for the smart home. Unfortunately, the smart home is currently a muddled mess of incompatible protocols, non-existent standards and competing immature controllers or middleware technologies attempting to cobble things together. The fact that even technologists find the architectures incomprehensible does not provide a reasonable and powerful use case to the public.

Let's face it, cobbling together a plethora of devices, using diverse wireless protocols, will require a non-standard or open source controller or an abundance of physical gateways to bind them all together and that is highly unattractive. An example of the current state of the consumer IoT in the home is the requirement for a hub or gateway for just about every appliance. This device (hub) is actually a protocol translator and aggregator, and this device is currently a requirement as it allows all the different manufacturers' devices to at least connect – albeit not communicate.

Some hubs have several inbuilt antennae or physical interfaces to support an array of radio or wired protocols, for example, Sigsbee, Bluetooth, 802.15.4, Ethernet, Wi-Fi, Z-Wave and Thread.

Now, Wink does this, and this is great for a technologist and an attacker, but for the average consumer this is just confusing. To this extent, just being able to install the devices is going to be such an onerous experience that it is debatable whether the security of the devices will play a part in tempering the consumers' appetite for smart goods. They will be just thankful that they were able to get the device to work at all. After all, there is a disconnect somewhere between the publics' perception of IoT security and the manufacturers.

There be Monsters

In a survey in March 2016, 66% of IT professionals stated that security concerns were the main barrier to them embracing IoT in the enterprise – now this is a theater where they are adept at securing diverse technologies, certainly since the adoption of BYOD – although it is getting more difficult. However, when consumers responded in similar market surveys held around the same time, over 70%

said they planned to buy an IoT device during the next year. But, why are consumers so ready to walk where IT professionals fear to tread?

If we cast aside skepticism for a minute and accept there are scenarios where a diverse range of IoT devices that intercommunicate and are interconnected via an intelligent IoT hub in the home can be wonderful ... well the potential is incredible, so let's think ...

Buying Secure IoT Devices?

One of the problems with the IoT is its vast scale of products, manufacturers and utility, therefore marketers cannot seem to get to grips with how to hone in on benefits for the consumer. Here are a few typical examples of IoT use cases that manufacturers or marketing houses push out to the public in order to sell the concepts and benefits of the IoT lifestyle... and they leave a lot to be desired.

1. *A connected fridge* – A standard fridge with added Internet and computer components which can alert the consumer to the current status of every product that might need replenishing and suggest or automatically make a reorder – It is little wonder that IoT is not proving to be disruptive to the consumer if marketing believes this to be a major benefit to the average consumer. Is this not just using technology for the sake of it? Why not just open the door? After all, for this to work every product would have to be fit- ted with a RFID tag that was capable of determining the best-before-date of the product, its current status and the usage rate of the product over a given number of days. What is more, the fridge is going to have to learn over an extended period of time the household's consumption rates for each product, which of course, could well vary depending whether it is a weekday or the weekend. In this basic scenario, there is plenty of data that the fridge will be required to transmit to the cloud in order to analyze the product quantities and the consumers' behavioral patterns. This data analysis is required to correlate patterns and forge workable knowledge that is function- al in making predictive ordering possible.

   However, over time, the fridge's cloud application could collect sufficient data to infer far more about the household than they might be particularly comfortable with. Especially, if the data collected was sold on to third-party marketing houses in order to target product advertising. Even if the data was not sold on, it still might be intercepted and provide an embarrassing loss of privacy, because many life-style issues can be inferred from the accumulation of eating and drinking consumption data. An example is if someone had an eating or drinking disorder. Furthermore, many medicines are stored under refrigeration conditions and the consumer may not want that information leaked out with the confines of the home. However, in more complex scenarios where the fridge is learning the eating and drinking patterns of each specific householder, in identifying an individual, then securing the data would be essential. As any data leakage, from a home that was not anonymized could be a major privacy issue. Lastly, as the fridge, most likely will have an embedded OS and computer components, it will be necessary to protect the appliance just like any other computer on the home network. This would mean at least protecting the fridge with AV software and firewalls to prevent, as in one notorious case, the appliance becoming a member of a botnet sending out spam emails.

2. *Smart lights* – This product is actually very popular despite the fact that a smart bulb is approximately twenty times the cost of an ordinary light bulb yet it is one of the success stories of the smart home scenario. It is simply an expensive light bulb that changes its hue and intensity depending on control from a smartphone app or going on the occupant's past historic usage and somehow inexplicably the occupant's mood. Now how does that work if several people are in the room? Are the bulbs going to start flashing during a dispute and aggravate the situation?

    Although, if the smart bulb can interface with a presence detector, it can also switch on or off depending on when someone enters or leaves a room, therefore, it could be an energy saving device. However, smart light bulbs, despite being one of the poster-products of the smart home, have checkered security.

3. *Bluetooth door lock* – This is another technology for the sake of it. A device that has the capability to recognize an occupants approach and automatically open the lock. How is this security improvement over a standard lock? The dangers with using radio frequencies to control sensitive devices are that they are very susceptible to frequency jamming. Bluetooth uses adaptively frequency-hops over 79 channels, which makes it less susceptible to this threat than other wireless technologies. However, it is still vulnerable to some commercially available wireless jammers and importantly, Blue- tooth eaves dropping tools. In addition, security analysts have exploited several makes of commercial Bluetooth locks using proven field exploits. There will be more about this later.

4. *Smart thermostats* – There is also the home thermostat, which learns the occupant's environmental preferences and can adjust temperatures throughout the house in order to make the habitat pleasant and save costs and energy. This is a good use of inter-connected devices if they could only

get them to work; as it is both sensible and based on sound energy and cost saving principles. One of the issues is that programmable thermostats can actually increase energy bills if deployed in an old building. The smart home is the best example of diverse sensors and actuators inter-connecting, communicating and co-operating through a controller, or a hub as they are more commonly called, in order to produce a holistic lifestyle experience. However, as there are so many diverse technologies and protocols typically deployed in a smart home solution, it is also the most difficult to secure due to the many diverse threat points.

5. *Smart TV* – A networked connected TV that connects to the Internet is an interesting idea that utilizes the capabilities of the TV to harness the additional functionality of the PC. However, by transforming a TV into an Inter- net-connected computer, it is also opening it up to all the same vulnerabilities and possible exploits. However, if the TV is similar to the other home network devices placed behind a router using a network address translation, it will be protected from the external threats out on the Internet. The configuration flaw that many home Internet connected devices have is that they actually allow incoming connection by default when they have no requirement to receive incoming connections. Outgoing connections are handled securely via NAT. If or when the device requires check-in to a cloud server to look for any firmware updates, it can do this from an internally initiated outbound connection to a manufacturer's cloud server. This might mean that a connection URL is hardcoded into the firmware and that can be a security risk. But as long as any local DNS servers are identified and secured and the home network is secure, this is not a major issue. However, to mitigate the rogue DNS threat there should be anti-virus and anti-malware software activated, up to date, and running across all capable devices on the network. Firmware attacks and hard coding are discussed later.

6. *Smart garage door* – These devices recognize the occupant's car approaching and opens the door but this requires inter-connectivity between the car and the garage door – in this use case there has to be some method of securely exchanging the identities of the car and lock mechanism to ensure proper authentication takes place before the garage door is opened. This could be by using low power radio protocols such as Z-wave, Bluetooth or ZigBee depending on the effective range required, but again this is not revolutionary but just as insecure. Worse, many garage doors have fixed frequencies that they operate on and can easily be hacked just by playing a sequence of frequency combinations. This is discussed later

7. *Smart car locks* – A car that recognizes the owners approach by the presence of a token or beacon, the cars computer opens the door, adjusts the seat position and drive-chain to the owners preferred setting and configures the infotainment system's setting to their liking. This is something that car manufacturers have been working on, amongst many other innovative ideas for a long time. However, it again will require strong authentication per- haps from a secured device such as a smartphone and close range technologies such as RFID or by using low power radio. However, both radio con- trolled car/garage and car-locking and control mechanisms have come under nuisance attacks lately again through radio broadcasts being so vulnerable to strong frequency jamming or replay amplification attacks. This will be discussed later.

The other issue with a high-priced item like a car relates to the effect on resale value of aging or poorly implemented technologies. If you bought a car in the last couple of years, 6 years from now you might as well have a built in eight-track player in it. concerns. Will car makers be required to recall cars that implement defeatable technologies? It seems unlikely as in the case of the eight-track player.

A breakfast system that on receiving the wake-up alarm sends signals to the kettle and the toaster that breakfast is ready when the consumer stumbles down to the kitchen – yes great, if you remember to fill up the kettle and put bread in the toaster the night before. However, these devices will likely have different radio technologies and protocols; so they will need to go through a controller (we will discuss controllers later) in order to communicate. Furthermore, in a family home, with say six people and one connected smart toaster and kettle, who controls these devices? You might find that a strange question, but recently a technologist working for the Guardian tried out a Wi-Fi enabled kettle and it took him eleven hours to get the thing to boil enough water to make a cup of tea. The problem was that the connected kettle required connecting to the home Wi-Fi router which wasn't very convenient and failed to work. Alternatively, it could connect directly to a smartphone, which did work, but getting the kettle to work via the smartphone was rather difficult and not something you would probably wish to try. Not, when all it normally takes is to flick a switch.

The IoT toothbrush, can detect tooth cavities and signals a request for an appointment to your dentist. This, like many health-focused use cases are attractive but is it really what the IoT is about? Can the individual not just be alerted and then they can make the decision to place a call to the dentist? This device is one of the most singular stand-alone devices imaginable. What will it connect to other than the hub controller and a messaging service? However, securing this type of device will mean restricting outgoing traffic through the hub controller and gateway router.

A connected-car can autonomously communicate to the brand's maintenance department to report among other things the status of over a hundred sensors within the car. Its use case benefit appears to be that if it detects a potential faulty component that requires servicing, it will book the car in for a service. This use-case has many security and privacy issues, which we discuss later in detail.

Making Things That Just Work

From the publics' perspective, they just want to buy a device that works. They do not understand the technology behind the IoT any more than they could explain the technology that makes their precious smartphone, TV or music player work.

All the public focused media hype is how the IoT will change the public's lifestyle, making their home smart and their life better by adapting their environment to be more efficient, labor and cost saving and convenient. This they believe will come about through installing IoT products. Little does the consumer expect that such technological advancements will require a smart hub for just about every IoT product. These hubs will connect to an array of intelligent sensors and devices that will somehow – intelligently – adjust their habitat to suit their mood and adjust the lighting and temperature accordingly. Of course, this will not be plug-n-play because we have security concerns but it will work at a price and great inconvenience. Eventually, the technology will change and when that happens, likely you will need to put your devices in the closet with your eight-track.

Now, if and even when this works it will be wonderful, but it is not something that the consumer, didn't have before.

Is this a consumer Internet of things?

What the IoT industry is marketing are single use devices or rather single scenario use cases that provide convenient services. However, most of these devices work in isolation and do not communicate or co-operate with other home devices, which is the point of the IoT. Therefore, they are not really, what we would define as consumer IoT, they are not really even smart products, as they simply have the capability to function as designed and have a connection to a network.

A more holistic, but also simplistic approach to marketing the benefits of the consumer IoT would be to have the car approaching the garage and the garage's external light sensor recognize its approach. The arrival of the occupier's vehicle is determined and the car and occupant's identity verified via identification, authentication and access control process. As a result, the external lights illuminate and the garage door opens while the device initializes a message to the controller. Subsequently, the smart home controller upon receiving the message disables the home security system and it responds by activating the door lock to allow the authenticated resident entry. In addition, the HVAC smart home devices receive a wake-up call to activate and switch on the internal lighting and set the AC or heating to the desired settings. Other home appliances can also be primed to be ready such as the kettle or to switch on the TV to the preferred channel or play a choice of music. The controller may look up a calendar and either send a signal to the cooker or microwave to heat up a prepared meal – or dial up a pizza and beer. This is what the IoT promises but so far fails to deliver because security issues are preventing it.

Skepticism, but the future looks bright

The McKinley Global Institute report issued in 2016 an estimate that by 2025, the consumer smart home market has the potential to generate around $23 trillion dollars. They believe that the impact of the smart home will come about through labor saving devices that help occupants clean, prepare food, do the gardening and look after pets. The strange thing here is how do labor saving devices generate money? They may save time and effort, there is no doubt about that, but how do the hours saved somehow convert into financial gain? Furthermore, they believe devices like robotic controlled vacuum cleaners and lawnmowers could reduce the labor hours spent by US consumers by up to 17%. Again, this is plausible, but how does it actually generate or save money?

However, McKinley do qualify those adoption figures, as they say automated home systems will depend on ease of use, dependable devices and secure systems. In order for consumers to adopt automation, they will need to be convinced that the IoT devices actually do save time and effort and that there will be a return on their investment. Presently, interoperability between devices is a major concern and these are issues that the consumers will need to see resolved before they buy into the IoT. Another issue is that the consumer will need to see how they can manage multiple devices through a single application or device – a smartphone for example.

McKinley's report did have many positives as it indicated that by using sensors and predictive algorithms, smart thermostats could conserve energy by detecting when no one is at home or in a room and control the environment accordingly thereby making significant savings. Additionally, the report suggested that smart thermostat's will learn about the consumer's usage patterns and adjust heating or cooling to have the home at the ideal temperature, which again in addition to creature comforts has financial benefits.

However, the potential cost savings from smart homes are not just about adjusting temperature and ideal ambient lighting. Considerable savings in energy and cost come from other connected devices such as washing machines and tumble dryers, which could run cheaper and more energy efficiently by getting information about the latest energy prices from grid providers. This would enable them to decide when it was more cost effective to run, for instance waiting until off peak or delay cycles during peak-energy consumption periods. This of course, relies on grid providers being able to supply energy prices that are accurate and to-the-minute – that is a symbiotic relationship during peak energy periods, but may be a long way off.

If Power grid companies were willing to supply this up-to-date pricing in a timely, reliable manner through smart meters, then IoT-enabled energy management applications could have a significant impact on monthly energy bills. Further, McKinley claims it potentially could result in an economic impact of savings of $50 billion to $110 billion globally in 2025. This would be achieved by preserving energy expended on energy greedy consumer devices such as washing machines, ovens, heating, and air conditioning. The smart home could also utilize the connectivity and intelligence of IoT devices to help further reduce electricity bills by ensuring that devices were active only when necessary.

As an example, McKinley states that Nest claims that its smart thermostats save 20 percent off heating and air-conditioning bills by turning on these systems only when occupants are expected to be home. However, additional savings are possible if power companies install smart meters and smart appliances, which have the capability to automatically shut down appliances during times of peak electricity demand. However, this can be a contentious issue. It may well be economical to run a washing machine during off-peak hours and to avoid peak-hours, if it is convenient. The consumer may even sign up for such a contract. However, it must be the consumer's decision; giving the power company the authority to make the decision to arbitrarily shutdown the consumer's appliances during peak-times is another thing entirely.

Consumer Trust – or Lack of It

Perhaps in the case of the smart home we are seeing more innovation, which is driving a more holistic approach where all the devices work together. We are beginning to see this with Google's Thread and Weave, Wink, and Samsung's Smart home among others. In these cases, all the devices intercommunicate, sharing a common understandable protocol and that should be the idea of the IoT. Indeed, that was the idea that all devices would or could intercommunicate and share data. However, that requires trust and that is in short supply between vendors let alone on the Internet, so the possibility of sharing data between devices even under the control of one entity (the home network) becomes difficult.

After all, why couldn't a power company share data with its supply chain; it would make sense as everyone could benefit from the aggregation of knowledge. Unfortunately, not every partner's agenda is in harmony. There are also security risks, after all a power company's network, as secure as it may be, can be compromised by lax security practices in a partner's network. This has been highlighted time and again that a major secure network has allowed extranet or shared communication between its own network and its partners, and been compromised by the partner, after all the strength of a network's security comes down to the weakest link.

Losing Control?

The weakest link in networks is not the main reason that the consumer IoT is perhaps not gaining the traction that the evangelists predicted. And, this has huge relevance to security. Consider for a minute all the proposed use-cases for the smart-home and consumer IoT in the previous section.

They are all about high end appliances and sharing data, an example being perhaps the consumer's fridge determines that there is no milk, so it makes an order for home delivery. There may also be a case that online a washing machine detects an anomaly in its spin cycle and sends the vendor a service call. Or perhaps, a consumer's car detects a potential problem, so its onboard computer contacts the service center over an Internet link to book a service to remedy a potential flaw. Similarly, the consumer may be brushing their teeth, only for an email to be sent to their dentist asking for an urgent appointment. The problem here is the devices are making the decisions, not you.

Another issue is that the IoT has, so far, not provided consumers with life changing options that suddenly embellished them with the tools that improve their life. Rather, they face the threat of losing control of their life.

There is no doubt that these smart tools would work well for the wealthy, single resident that can afford the benefit of such an automated life-style. If the BMW indicates a service is required, well take the Mercedes. After all there is always an alternative.

Obviously, some futuristic IoT products will capture the consumers' imagination. It does not take much to watch a Hollywood movie and see the leading man or lady living in an autonomous paradise. But, when we come back to reality we can never underestimate the stupidity of mankind's most popular but stupid innovation. This was possibly the TV remote control. The TV remote became no more that the rudest device ever to be put into the hands of the family despot.

The point being, that most of this smart home automation is dependent upon machine learning algorithms that analyze historical data of the occupant's behavior. Now in a single resident apartment that would work well, it would be fantastic to have everything tuned to their preference. But how does this work when there are two or more residents?

How do these control systems work in a busy family environment where people have diverse personal settings or get up and go to bed at varying times but continually squabble over shared resources such as the living room TV or the toaster? It is clear how this would work in a wealthy single occupant home or with families that have individual private space such games rooms, bedrooms and an abundance of kitchen appliances as well as a fully stocked fridge, such as in a large family house.

Moreover, in the average US or EU residence, especially in the UK where first time home ownership or even single occupier renting is financially prohibitive to the Y2K, let alone the millennial generation. These are the ones most likely to embrace the technology then how will this habitat optimizing devices work in their shared living areas?

This leads to the problem of how the system deals with conflict. For example; in a single occupant residence, the ideal IoT smart home scenarios are very attractive. The sole occupier can set his Nest to control the environment to their liking, and the lights will dim when appropriate or illuminate at the times it learns suits the sole occupier. Additionally, it will learn over time as humans are habitual by nature what music to play or even food to order. The system will learn the occupant's behavior almost as well as a dog can read their owner's body language and mood. It is possible that you may fall in love with the apartment as it knows your moods better than yourself. This is not so far from being realistic.

Imagine when the alarm clock triggers in the early morning and awakes the occupant. This will trigger a busy array of functions that immediately kick in, from switching on the shower to exactly the desired temperature and pressure too projecting the breakfast news, emails, messages or the stock market prices onto the bathroom mirror so they get up to speed as they shave or apply makeup. The breakfast will be initiated, the kettle boiling, the toast ready and the car warming up or cooling down, dependent on the climate, all in the rush to get on with their life.

However, in a family home the occupants may have vastly different expectations of a welcoming life-style environment, so if two or more occupants are asked to be present in the room or arriving in their cars at the same time, which profile does the controller use to set the environment? Worse is perhaps the breakfast routine; does the first one that awakes leap into the bathroom, dive under the shower that they expect is set to their temperature preference, and low and behold their choice of news headlines, topics and summaries are displayed upon the bathroom mirror. But what about the next one that scrambles out of bed, how will they be recognized and their profile loaded? is it such an autonomous system now?

Or just like before, most likely everyone will be squabbling over the controls – just like the TV remote – because the current active profile doesn't match their preferences.

Therefore, do we really need all these home control and automation functions in anything other than in a wealthy single person's home where they may provide all the convenience, creature comforts and be of real affordable benefit? Are these really lifestyle changing or even beneficial IoT tools, when the functionality is still so limited to a small segment of the population and the security implications so severe to us all?

Having remote access control, from outside the household is a different matter; that is the vast difference from the 80's and such. Here we can envisage both benefits and problems – when not secured properly – but not always as severe as they are relayed in the national news. Often we are fed news stories regarding IoT products that show them as being very weak and susceptible to cyber-criminals who could take control of the device at their whim.

Toys for the Rich

However, a large percentage of the population lives on tight month-to-month budgets. It is actually amusing to see how we survive at the beginning of the month, flush with cash we eat and drink well, as it is pay day. Similarly, the next week we eat and drink less well, but always to satisfaction. Hilariously, in the third week we are shopping for noodles, and the last week of the month we find ourselves rummaging around the waste bins for scraps.

This is why it is so difficult to understand how mere mortals survive on a monthly salary will adapt. As a result, they have to make hard decisions as to whether an early detection of unusual wear of a break pad requires immediate attention or that treatment of a dental cavity is more important that putting food on the family table. Moreover, how are they even going to pay for any of these IoT requirements, and where is the return on investment?

This is the point regarding the statement from the US Energy Information Administration, which estimates that currently only 37 percent of US residences have programmable thermostats to control heating and that 29 percent have programmable devices for running cooling systems. This is not as initially as poor as it sounds as 40% have manual thermostats and only 7 percent of homes have no energy control at all.

However, in 2016, still only 3 percent in the US, which also equates to the UK, own smart thermometers – only 3 percent.

Why is this? Well the US Energy Information Administration say that despite the consumer being very keen to lower their energy bills, the bills are so high that consumers will only invest sufficient money in an effort to lower the bills that they can reclaim within 6 years and the meridian is around $250. Currently smart thermostats are around $300 dollars if you DIY, but that is a major investment for a large proportion of society.

IoT isn't DIY

In the early eighties, there were microprocessor based control systems that were available to control the HVAC, open and close drapes, control the internal and external lighting even make the morning coffee and toast. Certainly, these were pre-Internet so were closed systems, but they were secure, and the Internet or even remote access via dial up modems was way in the future.

However, these were exciting products at the time, but they required some electronic and certainly some DIY skills to deploy them. The reason that they failed back in the 80's, or rather were not so readily accepted by the consumer as they arguably deserved, was, as today, the public are not hobbyists or DIY enthusiast as a rule. The public may want these smart home devices as the Gartner and Deloitte polls revealed. The consumers might be enthused by the marketing, and the potential cost and energy savings, but they are concerned about deployment. More significantly, today in 2016 the consumer is concerned about security, after all IoT security failures and scare stories regaling the lack of security and privacy inherent in the IoT fill the national news.

An interesting survey conducted by Deloitte discovered IoT devices are only acceptable to consumers that have a trusted partner company that they feel are competent to install the devices. DIY was not an option; the public went for companies that will be trusted – 34 per cent said they would rely on an energy firm, 28 percent on the tech companies or telecoms firms, and 10 percent on a High Street retailer. Just under three percent said they would be confident going along the DIY route.

This is hardly surprising because so often the consumer IoT is portrayed in high-level diagrams in glossy promotional brochures. These depict icons representing sensors distributed around the home, somehow interconnecting with one another and proactively adjusting the home environment or collaborating to perform some labor-saving tasks. This is conceptual and for technology peers it might be comprehensible, as they can perhaps envisage without detailed explanation how this will all come together. However, for the average consumer that struggles to configure their Wi-Fi access points to bridge to a gateway router, the level of abstraction is way beyond their understanding. Consequently, the consumer is extremely wary of buying separate and diverse components and trying to build this conceptual network on their own. They may well be interested in the technology, but they are awaiting these complex smart home solutions to be offered as a service, which will be delivered and installed by a trustworthy partner.

As an example, the US Energy Information Administration estimates that currently 37 percent of US residences have programmable thermostats to control heating and that 29 percent have programmable devices for running cooling systems. However, the McKinley report goes on to address the potential competition in the energy market, and they expect smart energy control devices to come down to price points where owners of programmable thermostats will convert to IoT-enabled devices. They also deduce more consumers will purchase energy-conservation tools. This is despite the fact that only 30 percent of residential homes bought such energy-conversation tools before 2016. The point is until the service providers – in this case, the electrical power companies – realize that it is a service they are providing and offer along with the service to in- stall smart home energy-conservation tools to residential homes; it just is not going to happen.

Is Security a Major Inhibitor?

There is also another major problem with early adoption of the IoT. Researchers are discovering security vulnerabilities regularly with consumer devices and the solutions tend to be to isolate and protect, but that goes against all of the original concepts of the IoT. After all, was not the vision for the smart home and the IoT in general having all these independent and heterogeneous devices talking and forming a trusted collaborative network? The vision was attractive at a conceptual level but this is only possible if all devices understand a common protocol and trust each other. Furthermore, how can devices share data if authentication and encryption is required over every link in the network? It would appear the vision and not just the security of the consumer IoT may already be broken.

To summarize the intercommunication between sensors and programmable applications makes the IoT a viable consumer solution, when delivered holistically and not just via single applications. However, getting all these functions and sensors to work in harmony is still a long way off, due to a lack of standards and dominant technologies. There are also huge security and trust issues when running heterogeneous networks that security and manufacturers have to overcome before devices can securely interact.

With IoT there are two distinct challenges, technological and security:
- Technological challenges relate to wireless technologies, radio frequencies, scalability and many diverse protocols amongst others.
- Security challenges arise from issues such as authentication, authorization, confidentiality, data integrity, availability, physical protection and end-to-end security.

In the next section of the book, we will consider the aspects of IoT security.

Part II: Security

The same basic security goals of confidentiality, integrity and availability that are tenets for all IT and data communications, related to computers and networks are also required to ensure the security of IoT. Despite this, the IoT has many further constraints and technical limitations in terms of power, compute, memory and storage, and even then there are issues with heterogonous networks as well as the ubiquitous nature of IoT.

The security challenges of IoT can be broadly divided into two classes: there are the broad technological challenges and there are also some specific security challenges. The technological challenges arise due to the heterogeneous, diverse and often ubiquitous nature of IoT devices, while the security challenges are related to the speciality, diversity, principles and functionalities of devices and the techniques and strategies that should be enforced to achieve a secure network.

Furthermore, the IoT introduces additional concerns to be addressed with respect to establishing security, and why we need to look to the past to secure the future.

DOI 10.1515/9781501505775-004

Chapter 2 – It's Not Just About the Future

Earlier we discussed some of the issues with public acceptance, security and the IoT as a technology. However, in this chapter, we will discuss how to secure IoT devices, or rather how to secure IoT networks.

What we will hope to put across is that there are many reasons that a security practitioner should not just focus on the device. The device is a single item in an ecosystem; therefore, every area should be covered, for example:
1. Learning from the past
2. Security by design
3. Read the Terms of Conditions
4. smartphone architecture
5. Looking back to past technologies to build networks
6. A confluence of new technologies such as radio and RFid
7. Basic IoT security practices

Security practitioners must take a holistic approach to an IoT device's security. They need to ask the right questions from the vendor. Not by asking, "is it secure?" No, IoT device is secure. Instead, they should be asking questions that relate to its intended working environment such as, why does it need to connect with other devices, and to the Internet, what information is it collecting and why, and where is the data going, and for what purpose? After all, that connected device, whether it be a smart wristband or TV, can possibly, and by design, be uploading data to a multitude of cloud destinations, and the consumer has no idea where that data is going or for what purpose.

Looking back to move forward

This is not a new problem, after the advent of the smartphone, a whole cottage industry started up producing mobile apps that provided the consumer with functionality that the vendors had not considered important. However, what transpired was that consumers would download from Apple or Google these cheap, sometime free mobile apps. What soon became clear was that many of these mobile apps were asking for permissions to access phone features that far exceeded their requirements to run the application. The consumer received through the mobile app manifesto a list of requests for permissions the apps required in order to run. The requests for individual permissions were displayed as a checklist to

DOI 10.1515/9781501505775-005

the consumer upon the application's download and each set of permissions had to be explicitly accepted before the app was allowed to run. The problem was that most consumers in their haste to run their new application just gave their permission to the app to control the camera, microphone, GPS, email and SMS access, without a second's consideration as to why for example a simple torch mobile app could possibly require such functions.

This is commonplace, and not just with mobile apps, how many people actual read the terms of conditions (TOC) when downloading open source or freeware software for example; very few. Indeed, the TOC can be highly ambiguous, only last year in 2015 Google and Oracle went into a legal battle over appropriate use of an open source license. Therefore, if these global giant's lawyers required a multi-million dollar court case to settle the dispute why should we mere mortals be expected to understand the pseudo legalize of the TOC.

Developers and manufacturers have understood that consumers do not read the TOC or certainly do not understand it, and they have known this for a long time so they hide away dubious practices deep within the incomprehensible legalese of the TOC. Perhaps, surprisingly, ransomware gangs or other opportunists have not been fully exploiting the consumers' explicit acceptance to the terms, which they gullibly surrender – or perhaps they are.

When the term the consumer IoT was initially coined, way back in the late nineties, no one other than the initial futurists probably expected it to become as pervasive as it is today. The visionaries and technology futurists at the end of the century envisaged IoT's potential and it was their first recognition of the vast interconnected potential that created the IoT vision. They had the perception that perhaps enabling technologies would mature to realize the IoT dream. They would have known that the technologies, which were still frustratingly unavailable or in their infancy at the time would be, required to fast track the concept of the IoT into reality.

Subsequently, even though the term has been high on the agenda in tech discussion for a long time, it wasn't until the late 2000's that the concept and potential for the IoT rocketed with many symbiotic technologies maturing and coming together to deliver realistic products and business models. Unfortunately, here is when security seemed to take a back seat.

Security by Design

Technologies such as the smartphone – a genuine IoT device – delivered the perfect human interface for controlling and managing IoT devices across the spectrum. Not only could the iPhone or Android equivalent interface with all the proposed things via its Bluetooth protocol support, it also embodied many advanced sensors and actuators. Furthermore, it became a ubiquitous device that people not only accepted, but also kept close to hand. This was a hugely important factor as getting popular acceptance from the public or the workforce to carry a human interface device whether it is an RFid security badge or a magnetic swipe card is difficult.

The importance of the smartphone and then shortly afterward, the tablet mustn't be underestimated as they provided the sought after human link to both the M2M and the evolving IoT worlds. They provided the ubiquitous bidirectional communication link between the digital and real analogue world that people wanted to carry.

However, the designers of the original smartphone – and then their competitors that came up with subsequent versions of the smartphone, had learned a valuable lesson from the PC and Internet era, that security was paramount and had to be built into the design.

Indeed, Apple produced the smartphone to be secure by design. It incorporated many advanced security techniques to protect it from malware and abuse. For instance, the key boot and operating system files were digitally signed, which provided safe boot. The phone would only boot if the boot-loader verified the boot and OS files were tamper free. Significantly, Apple also took the decision to make the phone a closed system; the phone would only accept downloads from verified secure applications hosted on the Apple Store. The decision to disable the ability to side-load or download unauthorized applications made the iPhone inherently secure. Furthermore, Apple's design ensured the separation of running applications by using a sandbox environment which prevented applications from communicating with one another. Isolating each application in its own sandbox prevented the use of shared memory or resources and kept them and importantly any malware isolated. As a result, Apple iPhones had an enviable record for security and if left un-tampered they were almost invulnerable to cyber delivered malware. This rather authoritarian approach to security was not universally accepted but it did not prevent the iPhone from becoming a huge selling consumer device.

Competitors following Apple's lead into the smartphone market, such as Microsoft with their own Windows Phone OS created a similar closed system impervious to Internet threats and malware. Google unfortunately with their open-source OS Android decided on an open approach, which did allow applications and software to be downloaded from unauthorized insecure sites or side-loaded via the USB. The results were that phones using Google's Android experienced an explosion of malware attacks that dwarfed the potential threats to Apple and Windows phones. Despite this Android phone still sold in vast quantities and even surpassed Apple in only a few years. Security it appeared was not always at the forefront of the customers' requirements. It would appear the freedom to download applications from any source was more important than the cyber-threats of malware. This perhaps cavalier attitude to security did much to kick start the era of the malicious mobile app.

Mobile apps suddenly became the latest application fad as developers' with sometimes little or no coding experience could mash them up quickly using freely available APIs and some glue code. What's more, the popularity, acceptance and usability of the smartphone accelerated, driven by the innovation and availability of these new mobile apps. Furthermore, the smartphones ubiquity brought about a revival in the stagnating fields of mobile data networks.

Data Mobile Networks

Technologies such as 3G data and mobile Internet had been around for several years, since the early 2000's, but had gained little public acceptance until the smartphone made mobile Internet a useable product. Prior to the advent of the smartphone, and 3G the user experience of mobile data had been poor. Typically, Internet browsing was provided by WAP, which provided the subscriber with very poor Internet browsing capabilities. Latterly more sophisticated phones could use HTTP browsers but the problem was that bandwidth and website designs rendered mobile browsing unusable, well to most.

However, with the successful launch of the Apple iPhone things were to change. Here was a phone, a device, that offered many consumer features such as a high definition touch-screen and an easy to use virtual keyboard. Furthermore, it provided capabilities and inbuilt functions that although present in earlier smartphone models such as the Palm Pilot caught the consumers imagination. The difference was it made these functions fashionable and usable. Suddenly, Apple had launched a device, that was truly disruptive, and that caught the imagination of the population. Apple's much lauded innovation for delivering the iPhone was not really innovative at all, many had gone down the smartphone road before, where Apple succeeded was that they delivered a usable device, a highly capable product, at exactly the right time.

The public acceptance of the iPhone, and latterly the Google based Android phones, is phenomenal as it resulted in an explosion in 3G data consumption, which had stagnated for over a decade. Previously 3G data offerings, which were available since the mid-2000s, delivered higher bandwidth and far more impressive throughput, than the very limited GPRS+ that had been available previously. However, the uptake on 3G was slow, making many service providers hold back on upgrading their networks. After all, it cost a huge amount of money to overlay a 2G GPRS+ network with a full 3G voice and data network.

The advent of the iPhone changed all that as suddenly the public had a device that was capable of showing web sites as designed and being actually as capable as a laptop to browse the web and social media sites such as Facebook, as a result the smartphone became ubiquitous. Consequently, during the late 2000's more and more consumers adopted smartphones not only to be able to be online and continuously connected, but to became part of a desired social media, a necessity that became also a social requirement.

The problem was, that although the technology (3G) had been around for a decade few had subscribed to its expensive data service plans. Now subscribers required data plans and inexpensive connectivity unheard of in previous decades. The mobile service providers responded immediately, where as previously they had been reticent to offer enticing broadband products to the public. There had been in the mid 2000's a voice centric approach with mobile communications and data was considered an afterthought. There was at that time, an old guard who remembered the early 3G era. They were fearful of building another service that no one wanted. Another concern was that data could cannibalize the network's voice based revenue through customers using VoIP.

Despite this earlier reluctance to embrace mobile data, the mobile operators now accelerated their research and development to increase their networks data bandwidth and throughput. Knowing that there was a real market for high capacity data networks the mobile and fixed line operators drove forward the next standards of data communications, 4G and LTE. Previously, 3G had taken a decade to be accepted, from early to late 2000 there was little interest, and many operators fell afoul of investing too early in buying the licenses and speculating on vast technical and capital investment to build these networks. BT the British operator almost went bust buying 3G licenses based on similar hype that we see today with the IoT.

However, the huge success of the smartphone, which we can consider an IoT device, turned all this on its head. Suddenly the smartphone and tablet were ubiquitous consumer devices, as were supporting Wi-Fi hot spots, and this forced communication service providers to readjust their strategy. The consumer demand for bandwidth and ubiquitous connectivity was overwhelming. Offered the potential gold mine of vast consumer consumption of data, service providers rushed to invest in the early builds for 4G mobile and high speed LTE IP data networks. Governments and the public demanded high speed broadband, some would suggest as a human right, to meet the population's insatiable demand for Internet connectivity on fixed and mobile devices.

A Confluence of New Technologies

In a similarly timed innovation, the introduction of the technology disruptive smartphone, *cloud computing* came of age and began to gain acceptance in the enterprise. Initially, security and trust were issues that stunted uptake but enterprises were won over through innovative products such as infrastructure as a service (IaaS), software as a service (SaaS), and platform as a service (PaaS). These innovative services allowed enterprises to move much of their non-critical infrastructure and applications to the cloud and make considerable financial savings as they only paid for the resources they used each month. This business model was extremely beneficial to SMEs that no longer needed to run extremely expensive data centers. However, despite these financial incentives large businesses were initially skeptical especially with regards data security, privacy and ultimately the concept of data ownership.

Where cloud computing had an almost immediate acceptance was with the financially limited and infrastructure poor businesses that could not afford the capital expense of computer rooms full of servers or the operational expense of managing them. The cloud brought this type of company unlimited, financially viable and available compute, storage and networking resources. Consequently, the small medium business and importantly the startups that would be the early pioneers in developing the first generation of IoT products raced to sign up and launch their applications with cloud providers such as Amazon. Indeed, many startup products that were born in the cloud have found massive social media success remain hosted in the cloud.

As a result, many startups decided upon the elastic cloud resource model that provides resources on demand yet curtails cost and capital provisions. For example, if an application could be hosted upon an elastic cloud infrastructure, then great, it was wonderful to launch the application and then scale for growth as and when required. After all what would the risk be with regards initial capital and operational cost? Growth would be dependent on success, but if additional resources were required these were the result of growth and hence success, then a cloud structure was perfect as it required no future capital commitments.

Furthermore, advancements in more mature technologies such as low power radio technologies and protocols along with sensor/actuator miniaturization played a major part in realizing much of the technology potential for the IoT.

However, having looked at all these underpinning technologies, why has this conflagration of a generation of dream technologies not driven the IoT further?

After all, currently in 2016, almost a decade since most of these underpinning technologies reached maturity but importantly, technologically and financially viable for startups and innovators, the consumer IoT remains only a vague concept without any real flagship use cases, products or killer applications? Certainly, there are popular devices such as smart watches and health and fitness bands but these alone are not going to become disruptive. Connected cars are another technology often portrayed in the press and gaining traction with every new release of a manufacturer's fleet. Though connecting cars to the Internet appears to be driven as much by the manufacturer than at the behest of the consumer.

Surprisingly, despite the range of innovative products launched by startups to try to capitalize on the available cheap components, sensors and radio technology finding a product that captures the public's imagination proves illusive. A product that provides real life style changing features and value is still notable by its absence in the consumer marketplace. This is odd because one huge success story during the early days of the smartphone was the meteoric rise in mobile applications. There was no shortage of innovative apps coming on the market at an additional cost to the consumer. The evidence suggests that consumers are willing to pay a premier price for innovative products if they understand the value delivered by the more expensive product however that just isn't the case with IoT.

It could be argued with considerable merit that we have seen innovative consumer IoT products that have brought value to the consumer. Certainly, they have if you consider being tracked by geo-location on your smartphone and delivered local taxi or restaurant details as being IoT. Products such as wearable personal health and fitness-bands are one example. Though smart light bulbs, TVs and thermostats, which have become the poster boys for the consumer IoT have failed to deliver that same utility due to the consumer not understanding the additional value delivered by the more expensive connected or smart product. After all a smart light bulb is typically twenty times more expensive than an ordinary light bulb yet they share the same basic function – to produce light, and anything else is merely gold-plating.

Basic Security Practices

From what has been learned from the past and from IT security it is possible to derive a few basic security best practices for the IoT.

1. Security should be enforced in IoT throughout the development and operational lifecycle of all IoT devices and hubs.
2. The software running on all IoT devices should be authorized and authenticated.
3. When an IoT device is turned on, it should first authenticate itself into the network before collecting or sending data.
4. IoT devices have limited computation and memory capabilities, firewalling is necessary in IoT networks to filter packets directed to the devices.

Updates and patches on the device should be installed in a way that additional bandwidth is not consumed and they should be authenticated.

Chapter 3 – Flawed, Insecure Devices

Previously, we discussed how networks could be inherently insecure and why this caused major security risks. It didn't really matter how secure a device was if it was installed within a weak insecure home network. In this chapter, we will move on to discuss flawed and insecure devices that come of the shelf and will be installed in weak or insecure networks, and what we can do about it.

In this chapter, we hope you will understand:
1. Why so many IoT devices go to market insecure
2. Why it isn't always the manufacturers fault
3. How to understand the IoT device production cycle
4. Why failure to secure products leads to reputational loss

Why are so many insecure devices on the market?

So, what is holding back the growth of the IoT, and it does appear to be stalling despite or perhaps due to the hype. The IoT's expected growth and adoption rate is no-where near earlier forecasts, despite the unprecedented hype of the last few years. A good indication is that in 2015-2016 there was for the first time a drop-in investment and interest from VCI's (Venture Capital Investment) in IoT startups. Furthermore, this drop-in investment and financial interest has coincided with the realization that the majority of IoT focused startups are unlikely to ever make a profit. Indeed, in many cases making a profit was not the intention, being acquired by a major player was the underlying business model. Depressingly, the same can be said regards cyber-security startups with VCI's taking a step back and now showing considerably more diligence when investing. This appears to be due to a lack of really innovative products and as a result many startups are merely copying or forking the same technologies.

A Manufacturer's Perspective

From a security perspective, the acquisition business model however had some very unfortunate consequences as far too many substandard products found their way onto the consumer IoT market. Many will opine that the rush to market and profit orientated business models are inhibiting the consumer IoT growth. This is because every flawed product reverberates throughout the market destroying consumer trust.

DOI 10.1515/9781501505775-006

However, to look at both sides of the argument we need to take a look at the industry from a manufacturer's perspective. To understand some of the issues that brought about these substandard connected products we need to appreciate the product's development lifecycle commonly deployed within agile startups. The problem with many of these startup products is developers' design these IoT devices initially as prototypes, undergoing rudimentary software development where the only design goal was to demonstrate a proof of concept and not actually a product deigned to be fit for public release. Unfortunately, business needs and financial constraints would push the product out-to-market before it was ready in order to catch a surge in public interest or to be first to market. This business drive for early return on investment and the shortest time to profit inevitably resulted in manufacturer's releasing products long before the design team had redeveloped, tested and verified the software, firmware and hardware. This seemingly self-destructive business model is not just about finance it is down simply to the way startups and manufacturers tend to develop software intensive devices.

The Device Production Cycle

Initially, the programmer concentrates on building a proof of concept model with software that proves that the device will function as planned and this is a very basic model. Then the software development team will strive to create a demo mock up with an API or GUI and ensure that the software works under almost any circumstances, meaning it will always produce the positive output regardless of the input criteria. This is of course important in demonstrations as nothing should be left to fate or the vagaries of Murphy's Law – anything bad that can happen will happen.

Should the project board accept the proof of concept model, the demonstrations go to plan, and then the project will get the green light. The issue here is that timescales change and so does boundaries of authority. Before the project may have been an IoT initiative now it will be under sales or marketing, with a natural shift in objective and motivation. Once the project is initiated, the programmers will start building a real version of the software that actually does work under the required software specifications and requirements (SRS) and does include security functions and features, which are appropriate to the application. Moreover, the software will work when it should and also fail when it should. However, the software design is an iterative process and typically, developers will work to an agile software development technique whereby a working model of the base specifications and requirements will be constructed. Subsequent iterations will add additional features and value to the product.

The attraction of agile development to a startup is that project value is created with continual iterations and at the end of each cycle there is a working model – a working prototype. The reason startups tend to use agile software development is that there is always earned value. What this means is that there will always be a working product at the end of each development cycle. Therefore, if the project management team terminates the project for whatever reason, say lack of funding, at least there will be a product to show for the efforts expended, which is the earned value. In addition, agile development requires at the end of every development cycle that the product is tested and demonstrated to prove its functionality. Furthermore, with agile development, the product can not only be demonstrated to be functional to stakeholders but it can be used as a base reference model for inspiring new innovations and importantly be quickly adapted to meet new requirements.

Software development in an agile market

Software development has changed rapidly over recent years and mobile applications or apps have accelerated this agile process. Today, software has to be developed quickly and be responsive to highly volatile market conditions. If a competitor launches a product with some new feature, the development process must be agile enough to quickly adjust and incorporate that feature into the next development iteration. This allows software to grow seamlessly and new features added as required without major change, unnecessary expense or timeline disruption. However, the temptation all too often is to fast track or early release the product perhaps when it is not yet market ready, with the intention to upgrade or fix seemingly minor flaws in the next development cycle and then include the patches in subsequent releases.

Now here is where we encounter a clash of cultures, objectives and motivations within the project team.

Clash of Cultures

The sales and marketing team will want the product ready as early as possible, by a certain date at the latest as they have after all to organize publicity and launch events in addition to the constant worry that they might be beaten to market and upstaged at the last minute.

On the other hand, the development team, which compromises all the software, firmware and hardware engineers, will be more concerned in testing, finding and eliminating bugs and ensuring the product works. Their concerns are focused on getting the product to work as designed so they will naturally be looking for more time to test the product.

Therefore, there is natural conflict of interests, with one team wanting to release as soon as is possible and another which will delay as long as possible.

This is of course where senior management must make a decision, and they do this based upon the business objectives. This does not necessarily equate to a rush to market and profit, by siding with sales and marketing. It is sometimes simply recognition that if left to the developers' there would be iterations of endless testing and bug fixing and the product might never be deemed ready for launch.

Developers and the Security Puzzle

Developers can and do face a host of problems when creating connected products for the IoT. Products will require a robust security model and require to be implemented on gateways and devices that support diverse protocols and technologies. Despite this, developers must ensure the security is robust as failure to provide sufficient and proportional levels of security will result in not only brand damage and ridicule but also data breaches of personal identifible information that could lead to action from the national regulatory bodies such as the FTC, or the FCC in the case of the U.S.

Gateways are hubs that connect devices and provide a translation service between devices that use different protocols or technologies together and to a central network. For example, a gateway can be something a like a smartphone that serves as a mediatory between a Bluetooth device and the cloud. The smartphone works as a gateway as it will accept data input from the Bluetooth protocol and forward it as either Wi-Fi to the home gateway router or directly to the cloud service via cellular.

Gateways can also be more complex dedicated products like the Winks that allows devices using Bluetooth, ZigBee, Ethernet, Wi-Fi, 6LoWPAN, Thread, amongst others to interconnect and it provides an uplink to an IP network. Gateways are also used to aggregate data from perhaps hundreds of low power or passive devices in a remote location for transmission across a single WAN link such as a Cellular network link. Therefore, the importance of securing the gateway is imperative as it can prevent hackers accessing the downstream devices and additionally it can protect against interconnectivity attacks. However, in order to secure the gateways and hence the devices, it is important that the gateway can identify each device as belonging to the network and this requires stringent authentication. A best practice is to use public key cryptography between devices and the gateway for authentication and for verifying the integrity of firmware updates. Ensuring files are always verified using their signature and to verify the hash values to check these files are tamper free is a major step towards protecting gateways and devices from malware and malicious or inappropriate firmware upgrades. There are already software frameworks available such as Eclipse Kura, which is good at securing devices and gateways. Another open-source product that can work with Kura is Eurotech's ESF. The ESF framework fills the gaps where Kura has only limited capabilities such as securing the gateway to the cloud services. ESF on the other hand can also enable remote VPNs, diagnostics and support cloud applications.

It is also a requirement of IoT development that solutions are stringently tested due to their inherent vulnerability, and possibility of misuse and this is especially important in things like connected cars, drones or even the humble washing machine. IoT testing criteria, documentation and methods must be developed to thoroughly test the solutions threat surfaces against appropriate attack vectors.

Testing IoT solutions differs from traditional IT applications due to three criteria, autonomy, connectivity, and momentum.

The first point is testing for self-sufficiency as IoT devices are by their nature autonomous. However, there is vulnerability that is introduced by a connection to the Internet and the opportunity to reveal and leak personal information makes the testing of IoT devices especially important. IoT devices operate with a certain level of autonomy whether managing a self-driving car or monitoring the heart rate of a runner, the data collecting power of the device is contained within the device itself only for a short time. Data is collected and stored temporarily on the device but it is soon shipped out to the cloud for storage and analytics.

Therefore, we must ensure that the design ensures that the device is capable of operating as intended even when not connected to the Internet. For some devices, this perhaps may mean that the device collects data and responds locally to certain logical triggers. For example, a heart rate monitor may trigger a signal to alert the user when their heart beat exceeds a prescribed threshold. The capability to collect, store and analyze data and then to recognize vital data points is a requirement of the physical device. The logic and processing of the data collected and the way the device responds is hosted within the on-board software of the device.

Connectivity testing checks the performance of the device. This is to ensure that the device is in a connected, disconnected or an intermittently connected state. This is important as many network connections are inherently unreliable. Unstable and unreliable networks are very common especially over long distance WAN links and when connecting remote IoT devices. Protocols must be tested and examined to ensure that the impact of network latency, jitter, packet loss and availability issues are recorded and understood. Furthermore, it is important to understand how delaying data uploads or system updates will impact the performance of the device.

Hand-in-hand with the impact connectivity has on devices is the measurement of momentum. Devices that are connected to the Internet, reacting to data and generating actions in response to that data will continue to influence actions even after a connection is lost. The extent of these actions is determined by the sophistication of the on-board software. Devices with limited on-board software may shutdown completely while more advanced devices may use the last server response and collected data to make decisions about what should occur next. Understanding how this momentum will drive actions in the field is a crucial element of testing.

Development of connected devices requires an in-depth understanding of security requirements, data needs and testing protocols. This information must be viewed in connection with the expected environment in which the device will be utilized.

Reputational loss

From the manufacturer's business perspective, the fact that the product works, that it does just enough to justify its claim to do what the customer expects is good enough to justify an early 'beta' release. However, the results have been a plethora of shoddy IoT devices entering the market that from a security perspective was just not fit for purpose. Examples of these types of premature release are in evidence in the national news on a weekly basis. Often we witness the latest major catastrophe and product failing in the trade or worse the national press, which are more often than not security centric. Products ranging from insecure baby monitor webcams, which are simply a remote audio/video monitor, to Bluetooth door locks and even high-end vehicles will be highlighted as the latest IoT security disaster. Typically, with headlines such as – 'IoT Security is Broken', 'IoT Security is Hilarious', or worse.

However, when we consider the evidence, it will point to a product that had little in the way of verified developed software and little if any security what so ever.

Typically, under further investigation it could be uncovered that the product more worryingly had been designed with no way to remediate flaws through remote upgrades. These devices worked, there was no doubt about that, hence their early release to the market. Using one of these products, a parent could connect and view their sleeping child from anywhere, a consumer could unlock the front door to their house, and a vehicle owner could unlock their car and drive away. The problem of course was that with little effort so could anyone else.

Chapter 4 – Securing the Unidentified

One of the primary issues when securing the IoT is in understanding what needs to be secured, why and how. Security is all about understanding the device, how it interoperates with others and interfaces with the network. Therefore, securing unidentified devices is impossible, and is something that needs ad- dressing.

In this chapter, we hope to explain:
1. How large scale devices can be identified
2. How devices can be authenticated
3. What sort of devices we need to secure
4. Why customers don't really care

Earlier, we stated that a smartphone was an IoT device, and it surely is as it is packed with sensors and actuators, for example a camera, a microphone, a gyroscope, a barometer, an accelerometer, a compass and NFC technology amongst others. The smartphone also comes with vast compute, memory and storage as well as an abundance of applications that would overshadow many laptops. However, most consumers would not consider an iPhone to be an IoT device. Not because of the smartphone's capabilities or lack of but simply because it was never marketed as one. Furthermore, a home office printer, a scanner, iPod or a TV monitor could also be Internet or network connected, and they too would be unlikely to be considered IoT by the consumer and therefore be overlooked by respondents in surveys.

The problem being with overlooking potential IoT devices is that you cannot secure something that you don't know about, and it seems that there are far more IoT devices at large in the average consumer's home and the consumer's life than we ever expected. Consequently, IoT security becomes very problematic simply because it is difficult to identify all the devices in the network, which have the potential to interconnect with one another. The problem here is that we may well overlook these common household appliances but network discovery protocols such as UPnP will certainly not and they will connect all these devices behind the scene. With TCP/IP as the backbone of the Internet and therefore of the IoT, there is the chance of exploitation. Therefore, it is essential that all the devices that have the inherent capability to join a network require identification and evaluation to understand the devices capabilities at the earliest opportunity, even before considering addressing individual product security.

DOI 10.1515/9781501505775-007

The Scale of the Problem

So how big a problem is the industry facing with regards securing the IoT? Initially, to attempt to quantify the actual scale of the problem, and the inherent risk, there is a need to look at the data available to us. In 2015, Gartner said that 6.4 billion 'things', might be connected and in use in the consumer IoT by 2016, this will be a rise of 30% from 2015. This seems unlikely, as this is significant growth. However, industry researchers go on to expand these figures to claim that the consumer IoT alone will add 5.5 million IoT connected devices every day from 2016 onwards resulting in 20.8 billion devices by 2020. These staggering quantities beggar belief. If these forecasts are even 1/3rd of what's predicted, then the IT security industry may have a huge problem on their hands.

What Type of Devices to Secure?

The scale of the security problem however is more to do with which type of IoT devices are we expected to secure? For example, there may be forecasts that 5.5 million new IoT devices will be connected each day to the Internet but what type of consumer IoT devices? If they are predominantly fitness bands, smart watches or other wearable devices that connect to a personal area network or via a smartphone gateway then this may well not be a huge problem. However, if there is a huge uptake in smart TVs, fridges, washing machines and toasters, then the magnitude of the security task is far larger. This is one of the security issues; with some IoT devices such as smartphones, watches and wristbands, their vulnerabilities are well understood and defined. How they can be protected within a network is also well understood. However, if 5.5m devices start to be installed every day the probability is that it is going to be devices that we have never even imagined.

Unplanned Change

In industrial, enterprise and commercial environments, within these specialist areas, security issues will be unavoidable but will be limited in their scope. The relentless march of technology will enforce change but it will be planned change, which will be made to accommodate new applications, system integrations, and operational processes amongst others. But these change processes are well understood and handled through mature risk management, cost/benefit analysis, change control and project management procedures and have been for years.

After all most security departments in industry, enterprise and commercial verticals will still have security veterans of the mid-nineties who had to deal with the Internet and virus explosion, also a few years later the Y2k millennium bug, then latterly the BYOD phenomena. These were similarly scaled issues that required processes and procedures to effectively address the seeming vastness of the problem. However, in those days they were dealing with current known threats but if we are looking so far forward into the future – the mid-2020s- then it is most likely a device and protocol that we have so far not even imagined that could be the one that trips us up.

The Consumer's View on Security

However, the experience, knowledge and historic procedures present in industry and enterprise are just not available in the case of the consumer IoT. With the consumer IoT, a manufacturer may well be supplying an IoT device to a customer to whom there may be little or no technical expertise available. Further, the customers' most likely do not have a concept of securing their home network let alone to understand the complexities of cyber-security--and why should they? Since when did it become a requirement for a consumer to have proficiency in cyber security and data networking in order to purchase and watch a smart TV, securely and what is more in the privacy of their home?

When, we look at the optimistic market forecasts for consumer IoT adoption, which is a positive indicator with regards consumer acceptance and appetite for IoT products. The results of the Gartner poll revealed a statistic that claim an average of 35 percent of the population had bought at least one IoT device in the last year. This is quite astonishing because what this means is that the IoT is growing rapidly, despite all the evidence to the contrary, with a 35 percent penetration rate in the market, this is very positive from a manufacturing and investment perspective.

However, from a security perspective it is much less encouraging because it means that the market is already expanding much faster than security controls are being developed and put in place. Indeed, the fact that there are increasing reports of cyber-attacks targeting consumer IoT products indicates that the cyber-attackers may have already left manufacturers, developers and the security industry at the starting line.

However, the security industry has not been lax, for in their defense, if we consider smartphones to be the most common consumer IoT device, which has an extremely high penetration level across all developed and developing nations then the security industry has been highly pro-active in tackling cyber threats. Furthermore, they have had to work in an extremely volatile market and protect consumer devices from malware and invasive mobile apps produced in the billions by vast, knowledgeable, highly imaginative and motivated attackers. However, in the consumer IoT, as we have already seen, it is not always possible to define an IoT product, its purpose, its environment and the related threats and possible vulnerabilities before it reaches the home let alone assess its security risk.

Where the consumer IoT becomes more perplexing and characteristically contradictory is that despite the horizontal scale, the width of the IoT's undoubted potential in interconnecting all these consumer products to deliver value there appears to be a less identifiable depth in the direct consumer usage or appeal. This might explain a recent survey in 2015 by Aquity Group, which revealed that 87 percent of the general-public claim to have never heard off or to understand the term, the Internet of Things. Indeed, in Beecham's survey in 2016 the results were that consumers simply didn't understand IoT devices and were not willing to pay for them.

To most IT or technologists this would seem unbelievable due to the hype that they have been subjected too, especially over the latter years of the last decade. However, we shouldn't expect technical terms and especially acronyms to migrate into the public domain just because they are ubiquitous and universally accepted and understood within the narrow confined fields of technology. The worrying part with this statistic is that the early adopters of the IoT must be in the 20 percent that did know what the IoT was, and so are perhaps technically aware, or already work in IT environments and are accustomed to the technical jargon. But if we are already seeing escalating security breaches in technology-aware homes, due partly to poor device and network security, then what does the future hold?

An example of this is the Amazon tags that we are beginning to see popping up around the house and they are becoming quite pervasive. It is now becoming quite clear though that the consumer doesn't actually know or care how these work.

Well here is how they work. The little button hidden away behind the product logo within the case spends most of its time sleeping, conserving battery power, but when pressed the device springs to life and activates a green LED. The activation of the LED is simply to alert you that it has received your instruction. Then, it looks around for a Wi-Fi device to pair with, typically your mobile phone, as it needs to communicate your order to the nearest store and have authentication and credit details to hand. It requires this as it has to send a message to determine which product you want to order, if indeed you wish to order. The tag then stays active only long enough to receive the confirmation of the order and then powers down. After confirmation of the reception of the or- der, the tag goes back to sleep as it is a low power device and leaves the mobile to communicate directly with the gateway router to fulfill the financial transaction. However, how does the dash button authenticate with the Wi-Fi gateway, in this example a mobile phone, that isn't clear. Sometimes, convenience does trump security.

Chapter 5 – Consumer Convenience Trumps Security

In previous chapters, we have discussed home security; however what we have not addressed is the consumer's acceptance of risk and their nonchalance to vulnerabilities and threats. In this chapter, we will address the way consumers care little for security, preferring convenience. However, convenience is not always the best solution. In turn we hope you will understand that Consumer convenience does not trumps security, and this is why.

1. Easy installation and operation
2. Plug n Play
3. No complaints no returns
4. Poor customer knowledge
5. Poor installation
6. Poor technology understanding
7. Applying best-practices

One of the problems with designing products for the consumer Internet and home-connected devices in general is the undeniable reality that customers' place convenience before security. And it is not just customers, the manufacturers and service providers have been aware of this phenomenon for many years now and in order to provide their customers with a good initial user experience they ship products intended to work out of the box. For the manufacturer, the retailer and the customer this is wonderful as everything just works as it should without the customer requiring any technical knowledge or skills. The biggest benefit for the manufacturer and retailer are there are fewer service calls or worse product returns and for the customer, the overwhelming benefit is that getting the device to work as it should is through an effortless straightforward plug-and-play type setup.

Plug n' Pray

A good example of this plug and play scenario is the Wi-Fi enabled gateway routers that a Communications Service Provider (CSP) supplies to a home customer. These devices are actually quite complex and technically challenging to install to ensure proper IP connectivity, let alone to deploy securely. The installation process of this

DOI 10.1515/9781501505775-008

device is relevant to the IoT as the gateway router is the customer premises equipment (CPE) gateway and as such, it is therefore, deemed by the CSP to be the demarcation point of the service provider's responsibility.

What that means in practice is that anything beyond the gateway router will be the customer's responsibility. Of course, the CSP has to draw a demarcation point to their service somewhere as they cannot be expected to be responsible for the customer's personal devices which are supplied by other providers or even competitors. However, the CSP wants to provide the customer with the best user experience it can while minimizing the number of service calls. Therefore, the way it circumvents many potential service issues is to provide a Wi-Fi enabled gateway router preconfigured for home use. The idea being that the customer can self-install the router as it has come with all necessary intricate configuration preinstalled.

Typically, the provider side of the router, the WAN connection to the service provider network will be pre-configured to connect automatically via a circuit identifier and password to the provider's network ensuring the customer receives an Internet connection as soon as they plug the cable into the wall socket. Similarly, the service provider will often leave the Wi-Fi and Ethernet LAN connections for the customer's home network to automatically be assigned an IP address via DHCP. The DHCP range of addresses will be from a private range typically in the 192.168.0.0 range which works within a private home network, but cannot be accessed from the Internet directly as these addresses are illegal on the Internet. Consequently, the CSP will configure Network Address Translation (NAT) on the router in order for the private addresses to be substituted for the single Public, and Internet legal, address configured on the WAN interface. Subsequently, in order to allow the Wi-Fi clients, the smartphones and tablets, to easily connect to the Internet, the CSP typically has only to configure the Wi-Fi with a default SSID and with a generic password or more often than not without any password at all. Worst of all though is that they configure UPnP (Universal Plug n' Play protocol) on the router.

The reason that CSP's will enable UPnP is that they want to get the user connected and working immediately, they don't want their customers who are often non-technical to have to worry about bizarre security acronyms such as, NAT, UPnP, WEP, WPA and WPA2, they just want the customer's experience to be as plug-and-play as possible. To compound the problem, the CSP often will jack up the Wireless power setting to its highest setting to ensure greater coverage, so that the customer's Wi-Fi enabled devices throughout the home can detect the signal and connect to the Wi-Fi router. Once again the track-record of this approach leads to lower service calls and fewer expensive truck rolls – home visits by engineers.

Easy install – no truck rolls

The goal for the CSP is that they want the customer to plug in their Wi-Fi router and simply point their home devices, such as their smartphones, laptops and other Wi-Fi-connected devices to the advertised SSID and everything will connect and work seamlessly. Other headless devices that do not have human interface such as a display or keyboard input device will learn the configuration via pairing with other UPnP enabled devices. Largely this strategy works for both the service provider and the consumer, hence the reason they persist with it despite it being against security best practice.

Customers also do like the plug-and-play approach, as they do not want to have to study user manuals or try to make sense of the scant instructions provided on the administration browser; they just want things to work, preferably out of the box in a plug-and-play fashion. Now remember, the UPnP protocol, this is where this self-discovery protocol comes into its own. UPnP is designed specifically to allow networked devices to discover other UPnP devices and form connections by exchanging basic configurations. The beauty of UPnP protocol is it works transparently behind the scenes to make the connections between other UPnP capable devices on the network without any user configuration – or even their knowledge. The connections between devices are established transparently by auto discovery and device inter-communication. This is fantastic for closed home networks as no experience or technical knowledge is required to set up devices, which can then communicate and share services. For example, UPnP is the protocol that will allow streaming audio or video protocols to work between devices. In practice, this means you can setup video streaming between your smartphone and TV using Real Time Streaming Protocol (RTSP) simply by clicking a menu option.

Convenient but insecure

Similarly, Babycam video monitors those devices that have been the objects of such negative security publicity lately. Well they also operate using Real Time Streaming Protocol and they will also utilize the connections established via UPnP to communicate with the parents' computers, smartphones or TV to share the video without any pesky passwords or authentication. This is because UPnP treats all other UPnP discovered devices on the shared network as being trusted. The problem is though if you still have UPnP activated as default on the gateway router then this configuration will allow incoming connections to the Video monitor from the Internet. However, the danger here is there is still no authentication required, so anyone can also connect and view the baby sleeping from the Internet, hence entirely understandable furor when parents discovered their video monitors were viewable on the Internet.

Now most parents, even technically knowledgeable ones, never considered the possibility that their video monitor could be accessible on the Internet. After all, there are billions of IP addresses out there even when narrowed down to a country or even an individual state and the consumer would have to be desperately unlucky for a hacker to find their particular webcam feed on RTSP port 554 – or so you might think. However, if an attacker limits their scan for the address range of a University campus or local service provider, then they could quickly scan and find open streaming video links – after all not all Video monitors are used for viewing babies.

Failing that, the cyber-attacker could just look up Shodan. This is a search engine for the IoT, and anyone can peruse Shodan's online catalogues of discovered video image feeds. In case you are unaware Shodan is a service that crawls the web and documents open ports and associated IP addresses, and in this case, would search and list addresses that are providing an unauthenticated video feed. Therefore, allowing RTSP video streaming out to the Internet with no authentication is a very bad idea. However, it doesn't seem to be sinking in, even after the Federal Trade Commission found TRENDnet in the US in 2014 was 'lax in security practices which had led to the exposure of the private lives of hundreds of their consumers on the Internet for public viewing' there are still estimated to be millions of such unsecured webcams easily discoverable on the Internet.

A point that we should understand here was that the FTC did not punish TRENDnet for being insecure and leaking the personal lifestyles of their clients out to the Internet. The FTC took action because of TRENDnet's persistence in claiming that their service was safe long after they knew they had a software fault. It wasn't the privacy leakage per se that TRENDnet were punished for, if that was the case, there would be barely a service provider financially solvent. Instead, TRENDnet were severely punished because it was the misrepresentation to their clients that they claimed to be secure, even though they knew they were not.

Many home networks are insecure?

The strategy of convenience over security may well provide the customer with a better user experience in the short term but it comes at a cost, the security to the customer's home network. This result is many home Wi-Fi networks being inherently insecure, not just through misconfiguration of UPnP on a gateway router but simply through the natural propagation patterns of Radio Frequencies as the Wi-Fi signal travels far further than the consumers are aware. Possibly in a condo or apartment block the RF signal is broadcasting too many neighboring residents or to public areas. If the Wi-Fi signal is not tuned down to limit its travel and range or the owner does not enforce strong authentication and the traffic is not protected by data encryption, which in our out-of-the-box scenario it will not be, then the Wi-Fi network is wide open to abuse.

Customer Ignorance

A Wi-Fi home network that has default SSID and either a generic CSP provided default password or no password at all is wide open for others to utilize the service. Now a decade ago or so, when broadband was limited and expensive, people were concerned about this bandwidth theft and war-driving exploits were a major concern to the more tech savvy consumer. That concern seems to no longer be an issue as bandwidth price has fallen and throughput has increased exponentially, so free Wi-Fi hot spots have become ubiquitous. Over the past few years, consumers seem to care more about convenience than security and we are seeing more and more poorly or unprotected home Wi-Fi networks.

The issue is that most consumers do not know about or rather care about Wi-Fi security, and why should they, they have purchased a Wi-Fi router as part of a service, and they expect the provider to ensure the service is secure. Little do they know that their new Wi-Fi network is broadcasting to the neighborhood offering a service anyone can eaves drop on. Furthermore, once an intruder joins the Wi-Fi network they effectively become part of the owner's home network, via DHCP, or UPnP, and gain unauthorized connections to not just the Internet but to all the home IP devices. Importantly, in some cases the network owner will be blissfully unaware of their circumstance or of the dangers of their unsecured wireless network.

The network owner may not mind a neighbor using their broadband bandwidth, however if they knew that the neighbors web activity – perhaps viewing extreme web sites, engaging in anti-social behavior, or perhaps participating in malicious cyber activity such as denial of service attacks – then they might rethink the situation. After all this type of activity could be traced to the home-owner's gateway router and ultimately their home – would they be so blasé about sharing their Internet connection then. In addition, the network owner will be typically unaware that their traffic is unencrypted, which is open to eaves dropping, and the threat of man in the middle attacks or the many other wireless radio vulnerabilities that the customer has probably never heard off.

We should not find this surprising, because the customer should not be ex-pected to be aware of cyber security, as they have requested a service that pro-vided Internet access within the confines of their home, so that they could con-nect their smartphones and tablets. They would probably be shocked to discover that the service provider had neatly sidestepped the responsibility for the security of their Internet service and thrust it upon them, the customer.

Chapter 6 – Startups Driving the IoT

Once upon a time, it was the Communication Service Providers that drove consumer and SMB technology as they dominated the market. The CSP's would as we have detailed earlier dispatch routers and other communication equipment to the home pre-configured. The result was that the consumer easily connected to the service and everything worked, the customer experience was wonderful.

However today it is not just the CSP that supply hardware and services, a whole army of startups are delivering products to the home. Most of which are insecure.

This is what we will learn in this chapter:
1. Check the Gateway configuration
2. Check capabilities of home devices
3. Check home IT installation knowledge
4. Check IT security knowledge

The previous chapter, examined home routers and Wi-Fi access points as they are very important to the security of the entire home network. If the gateway to the Internet and the hub for all home network devices is inherently insecure then every device on the network is going to be vulnerable to exploitation. The IoT of course exacerbates the problem of the technology knowledge gap between enterprise and the home because now we are witnessing a trend whereby it is not just the communication service providers that are driving the adoption of home networking we now have the manufacturers and vendors of all sorts of home gadgets driving the consumer IoT. The importance of this shift is that many of these manufacturers of IoT gadgets or connected things, have little or no security experience in radio protocols or cyber-security, so are ill-prepared to build secure products let alone advise the consumer.

The manufacturers are, like the CSPs' in our previous scenario, just wanting to provide a plug-and-play gadget that just works when the proud new owner takes it out of the box and switches it on. As a result, the manufacturers have strived to make the setup process as intuitive and automated as possible, typically relying on auto-discovery protocols, which facilitate the IoT device to find a network to connect to and then importantly detect a default gateway to the Internet.

Now, there are many reasons why the security-aware customer may not want the IoT device to automatically connect out to a mother-ship network in the cloud. An example, being that many home devices that are IoT capable are not bought specifically for that additional Internet feature, such as a washing

DOI 10.1515/9781501505775-009

machine, coffee maker or a set of bathroom scales. This is quite important because many products on the market today are being described as smart, such as
home thermostats, fridges, music and entertainment systems, even toasters and
light bulbs, which have a somewhat dubious requirement for always on Internet
connectivity.

Installing IoT Devices

In IT and industry, dedicated networks security and network administrators can
show due-diligence when installing IoT devices. The device will be thoroughly vet-
ted and its technologies and capabilities examined before the device is installed
remotely or within the borders of their networks. However, what about all these
employee wearable devices, that are out with the security and network administrator's control, such as employee smart watches, fitness bands and even athletic
shoes, how do these connected devices merge with the IoT security plan?

The danger is that all these undetectable user-owned networked devices
can synchronize with the employee's work desktop, and gain access to the enterprise network by accident in most cases, stealth at worst. What was once a
fortified closed ecosystem in the case of industrial networks is now open and
permeable, with potentially bi-directional data-leakages. In the enterprise and
industry, protecting against the threat of the insidious invasion of personal
connected IoT devices into the workplace is an onerous task. However, that
security responsibility and risk mitigation duty lies with a dedicated, skilled
and conscientious security or network team. The team use their knowledge
and skills to mitigate where possible the threat, or importantly to consciously
accept the risk – for example BYOD – but who is capable of performing this
duty in a consumer residence?

Security knowledge is lacking

What manufacturers and developers must realize is that there is a vast knowledge
gap between what they take as common knowledge and what the average non-
technical consumer understands. This is why there is such a major disconnect between installing technology securely in the enterprise and in the home. There
should be no expectation that every home has an uncommon level of security and
technical knowledge to understand the workings of these IoT devices.

Chapter 7 – Cyber-Security and the Customer Experience

One of the challenges with cyber-security is getting the user to understand the potential threats. Not so much now but many years ago people bought a computer thinking it would just work, it would be as intuitive as a calculator. Of course, nothing was further from the truth. Many years ago, a PC would arrive with Word, Excel, PowerPoint and craziest one of all Dbase. If the recipient turned on the computer, they would be faced by either a blank screen or page if using word or a blank spreadsheet if opening Excel. However, nothing was as daunting as Dbases flashing cursor. Yet people did find their way around these hugely uncooperative user interfaces, and went on to use the applications. However, today faced with a mass of wireless technologies and interfaces, the IoT is inexplicable difficult for the home user to understand.

In this chapter, we will try to explain:
1. What security technology they have at their disposal
2. Why the manufacturer has pushed security so it is now their responsibility
3. And why there is not a lot they can do about it
4. What they need to do to protect their home network
5. What can be trusted and how to understand security anomalies

Not so long ago in the early to mid-2000's, Wi-Fi home routers gained traction with the public and sales increased exponentially. Interestingly, enterprise would not touch Wi-Fi initially due to inherent security issues but the public loved the convenience as there was no wiring necessary and everything just worked. Almost immediately, security issues arose. Security practitioners and manufacturers were actually confused as to why residents did not secure their Wi-Fi. The manufacturers would mitigate their responsibility in the ensuing security breaches, by blaming the consumer for using the default security settings of WEP rather than using WPA2. The frightening thing was they were actually serious. They genuinely thought that everyone installing a Wi-Fi router would somehow understand the technology. This was of course folly, and could be demonstrated by the fact that even IT technicians installing Wi-Fi access points in the workplace through-out the 2000's had little understanding of radio frequency behavior, such as channel interference, RF propagation and antennae range and directions, let alone understand the security encryption algorithms.

DOI 10.1515/9781501505775-010

Therefore, even within IT, there are diverse levels of knowledge. Most technical people understand at a high conceptual level IoT, they may own IoT products and have a basic idea of how to secure their home network. Others may have a deeper understanding of the inner-workings of the product down to the way the radio technology and protocols work. Others, rarely, perhaps designers, may even understand how they interconnect with other devices, collect information, perhaps personal identifiable data, and then transport that data either in encrypted or clear text formats out to the cloud. However, should the manufacturer and developers of IoT consumer products expect this level of technical knowledge and competency from the consumer?

Pushing Security onto the Consumer

Furthermore, is it right to push the responsibility for security onto the consumer of the product. If the answer to either question is no, then what can the industry do to rectify the situation and provide consumers with better more secure products. This as we shall see shortly is not as simple as it may seem.

The problem that the industry faces with IoT devices is that they are not like other consumer products that are typically isolated, singular functional units. If for example, a manufacturer wished to produce a toaster. Then the design team will produce a toaster that conforms to national and if possible as many international electrical standards and safety protocols as they can. It would be absolute folly to design a product disregarding industry standards as it would almost certain fail to gain the necessary accreditation and safety certificates. This is because, the authorities need to verify that the toaster is not only fit for purpose but also passes stringent safety standards before it is allowed to be sold to the public.

Industry regulations and standards – where are they?

So, why are there no similar verification checks done on IoT devices? Can we not have IoT devices rated and certified by an independent expert body to verify that the product is fit for purpose and secure when used correctly. Well, the problem is that it is difficult to compare consumer utility items with connected devices. For example, with a standard toaster the certification process for its electrical safety is well understood, as is the way it operates under normal usage and so long as it meets the stringent requirements at the time of testing it will gain national trade certification. That vendor can then proudly display the certification badge on the product, whether it is a US or EU badge of conformity to best safety standards so the consumer can purchase the product with confidence. The consumer knows that when they plug the toaster in to the power socket that they are unlikely to be electrocuted and the one that ends up toast.

On the other hand, with an IoT device for example if we connect the toaster to the Internet, then the toaster is open to attack and this means that the criteria that determine whether it is fit for purpose, become very fluid and unpredictable. The IoT toaster's industry-standard certification label may attest to it to be fit for purpose – electrically – and this will give the consumer perhaps false confidence in the product. Having a certified security 5-star sticker on a smart toaster to proudly boast its apparent robust security is great for consumer confidence. It may well be secure, judged by the criteria specified and vulnerabilities know at the time of certification but that doesn't mean a lot when it could be found vulnerable to a zero-day attack and rendered almost useless as a product the next day.

The key point is that the industry should try to move away from trying to certify individual IoT products as secure – that simply will not work, as attacks make it a changing landscape. The scale and scope of the IoT is far too vast for any independent standards – even if there were such things – too possibly manage. Consequently, the security industry must realize that securing IoT devices is not an end in its self; they must secure the entire ecosystem.

The home ecosystem

In consumer IoT what we are getting even within the home private network is not an Internet of things – where all nodes communicate with each other – but an intranet where only authenticated and prior invited nodes communicate. To understand this, we must look at the trust model. Within a home private net work the trust model was that every device could and was capable of communicating with one another. Unfortunately, Wi-Fi is the predominant communication medium between hosts now in the home network. However, that requires authentication in order to have any sense of security, therefore only devices that are invited onto the network with pre-defined authentication credentials can join the group. Consequently, only authenticated devices can communicate with one another so the network is reduced to silos of trust or intranets.

For example, if Apple HomeKit devices, Google Thread and Samsung Smart home devices resided on the same physical private home-network then they certainly could communicate. If they could all talk TCP/IP, they could converse and even encrypt/decrypt data transfers up to the session layer. Packet streams would be exchanged and headers stripped and the data disseminated to the upper applications. There is no doubt they could exchange data efficiently and even translate it but the applications sitting above them would not be able to understand. Just like an Eskimo conversing with an Englishman they would have no idea what each other was saying.

The issue here is that if each group of devices can communicate within their own group their intranet, and devices that cannot authenticate cannot join the group then there is no Internet of things. We have simply built a network of diverse but more secure network silos.

This was the problem with Network Address translation (NAT) as it actually broke the concept of the Internet. Because NAT acted as a translation device and a gateway between private addressed devices and Internet hosted public addressed devices it effectively broke the concept of the Internet.

Remember the concept of the Internet is that of a flat open network where each device can freely connect and communicate with one another. However, just about every security countermeasure that is proposed to secure the IoT, effectively breaks it and segregates each functional unit from others, it is another intranet of things.

Having remote access control, from out with the household is a different matter, that is the vast difference from the 80's and such, here we can envisage both benefits and problems – when not secured properly – but not always as severe as they are relayed in the national news. Often we are fed news stories regarding IoT products that show them as being very weak and susceptible to cyber-criminals who could take control of the device at their whim. This is not of course true if the home network is secured – sadly most are not.

Security negativity

As the IoT is such a fashionable topic, both in business and industry, maybe the home, it generates much media attention. This is both a good and bad thing. It brings awareness to the public about the vast array of products, their features, the labor savings and how they can be used to improve the consumer's lifestyle or provide convenience, education or entertainment. The media will also if done responsibly bring to the attention of the consumers some of the inherent risks of deploying IoT devices within insecure home networks. Largely the media does this very well, but they are in the news business so they will also push out to the public the downside, which are the latest scare stories that emerge regarding security and privacy if they are deemed news worthy.

This is due to the way that the media works; they hype a celebrity, product or lifestyle product to the limit to sell copy. However, they realize that there is a point where the consumer gets jaded. Consequently, the editors determine that it is no longer newsworthy and then reverse the policy. This is unfortunately the swing or as Gartner terms it: the trough of disillusionment. What we are seeing with the IoT today in 2016 is exactly this. The media were evangelists for the technology only a few years ago as it sold articles, even the trade press. Now typically the media have reversed their position and are only interested in security exploits, loss of privacy and trust issues. As a result, we are now seeing more negative stories about the consumer IoT.

Security Anomalies

The truth is that IoT devices are not as susceptible or vulnerable to cyber-attacks as might be believed. Certainly, IoT devices have come under intense scrutiny and investigation and there is rarely a month goes by without some project releasing gruesome details of their successful hack. What we should keep in mind though is that many exploits are not actually cyber-hacks they are reengineering and that is a very different ball game altogether. In addition, we are also seeing dubious hacks that confuse consumers. An example of this type of ambiguous hack was the one performed on the Philips Hue (smart light bulb) system, which left many security practitioners, let alone consumers, a bit baffled.

What device can be trusted

Smart light bulbs are one of the smart homes most popular and user adopted IoT devices. This is most likely because they are easy to install and provide a basic function, adjusting hue and intensity of the lights via a smartphone. Additionally, some light bulbs come with speakers built in to provide music to provide ambience but these are more common in business public areas rather than the home. However, popularity and uptake can be a double-edged sword as far as security is concerned because the more devices that are installed the more attractive a target they become to attackers.

Now, who on earth would waste their time hacking a light bulb?

The answer is that many do, with motivations ranging as with most hacking from curiosity and mischief to down-right malicious intent. With the former it may be the work of pranksters switching the lights in all the rooms randomly on and off, simulating the work of a poltergeist whilst they have a good laugh watching the reactions of the bemused but unsettled occupants.

However, there are also very serious attacks that are launched against the humble light bulb. A common mistake with the consumer IoT is in misunderstanding the motives of an attack. The initial focus of an attack, in this case the light bulbs may not necessarily be the primary target, it may just be the first probing to establish a foothold in the home network, to provide the attacker with a virtual beachhead.

Consequently, attacks on these less capable devices are very common as they are harder as a product to secure due to their low cost and functional constraints. This of course makes them ideal targets for cyber-attackers looking for as easy entry method into the network. As a result, there have been several attacks on all the main light bulb products over the last few years. For example, Philips, Osram and LIFX have all been found to have vulnerabilities that have been successfully exploited.

However, not all hacks are equal some are easier than others, and in most cases the initial entrants into the market get hit hardest. This was the case with Philips, back in 2013 as market leaders in the field of smart light bulbs they were the prime focus for researchers and hackers alike.

The Philips hack used a malware script, created by Nitesh Dhanjani installed onto a PC on the same home network as the Philips Hue hub. The malware script when activated discovered the Hue on the same home network and issued a blackout command turning all connected lights out.

The attack itself doesn't seem too actually hack the Hue as such, rather it relies on hacking a PC or similar device on the same home network in order to launch commands aimed at the Hue hub controller. However, what does make this attack interesting was the consequences of the attack as not only do the bulbs stop producing light, which shouldn't be a problem because the Hue bulbs are simply in their standard off-state. Switching them back on again simply requires a command to be send to the controller. However, with this malware script the command to turn off was issued immediately after any light bulb received a command to power up. This rendered the Hue system useless as any command sent to the Hue was immediately contradicted by the malware script.

The interesting part: in commandeering a PC on the same network as the Hue makes the attack persistent and there is nothing the victim can do about it. Even if they go to the trouble and expense to change out the Hue hub, the hack will persist. Only if they disconnect the Hue hub and lose all control and connectivity with the light bulbs will the light bulbs become functional once more.

However, the Hue bulbs will not respond to app commands or be able to change color, they will be basic dumb light bulbs but at least they would work.

As we have seen, this exploit wasn't really so much a hack of the Hue as it was of a computer and the network. The Hue, by design, is based on open APIs and trusts local devices on the same network. This is a common condition with the consumer IoT that devices tend to trust one another without question. This unfortunately made the Hue vulnerable, but it is also what makes the Hue easy to use and easy to program. Therefore, was the Hue actually hacked as it was only doing what was requested, turning off when a trusted device issues a command. Indeed, had there been appropriate security in place on the PC, such as antivirus software, then the attack would never have worked.

The Hue designer admitted that perhaps not all Philips security choices were the correct ones, and there were issues that the company is looking into, such as the reuse of API tokens as opposed to issuing unique random keys, but such decisions have trade-offs. In this instance, each device that connects to the Hue would have to be authenticated by the bridge, as opposed to a single set-it-and-forget-it process during the initial installation. However, what did come out through the exploit demonstration was that the Hue, although vulnerable to other trusted devices was not directly exploitable itself.

Chapter 8 – Security Requirements for the IoT

In previous chapters, we have discussed IoT, home and network vulnerabilities. In this chapter, we will specifically address some of those threats and how they arise.

In this chapter, we cover:
1. Why security issues arise
2. Security and product confidence
3. Why manufacturing techniques go wrong
4. Why security overhead is often cut from design
5. And why cutting security is so detrimental to the end product

Why security issues arise

Building end-to-end security into IoT design is a lofty goal but one manufacturer's must aim for to ensure an acceptable level of trust in their products. The problem is with IoT is that it is an aggregation of many technologies, which makes the threat map and attack surfaces far larger. This is another key point regards IoT security – developers and security practitioners must meet the requirements of handling the nuances of IoT security issues through accumulated experience in a variety of technology disciplines. Security practitioners will only be confident and qualified to address IoT security issues if they have the relevant skills securing all the evolutionary technology steps that have arrived at the security conundrum that is the IoT.

The IoT hasn't just appeared out of nowhere; it is in fact an evolutionary process building upon the major technologies that underpin its functionality. Therefore, to understand IoT security a practitioner will need to know desktop security → application security → network IP security → firewall & web security → Wi-Fi & Mobile device security → Radio technologies & protocols, → Operational Security technologies and protocols → Cloud (API & web services). Therefore, it is a daunting task and little wonder things go wrong when there is no due diligence in the design phase of the product. Indeed, without designing security into the product as a fundamental feature then the product is being designed to fail – but despite this many hugely embarrassing and reputational damaging incidents regularly make the national news. The industry doesn't seem to learn from their mistakes, so why is that?

DOI 10.1515/9781501505775-011

Security and product confidence

It is doubtful whether many IoT companies deliberately set out to create faulty or insecure devices, despite what many will claim as an irresponsible rush to market. This is particularly evident now as IoT is such a popular topic and any security exploit of the device would be sure to gain prominent publicity. The Federal Trade Commission in the US has been handing out punitive punishment to manufacturers' that misrepresent their products. Indeed, such is the gleeful reporting of a successful product's exploitation in the media, it is hard to understand why manufacturers keep coming up short with regards securing their devices.

To play the devil's advocate, in the manufacturers' defense, the consumer IoT landscape with regards devices or home gadgets are priced within only a barely viable range of profit margin. Therefore, the manufacturers must optimize the sales opportunity, and get to market quickly and get to profit as soon as possible. The problem though is that they are not the only product on the market there will be many competitors, perhaps not initially but 'me too' products will be bound to follow. The entry into the market of competitor "me too" products makes pricing problematic as new entry competitors will undercut the incumbent market leader's price just to get some market share. This of course elicits a retaliatory response, which creates a cycle of price cutting which actually is in nobody's interest and this is termed a 'race to the bottom'.

Me-too manufacturing

One common problem, which the industry has identified and struggled with for decades, is the low price point that consumers are willing to pay for computer products, an example is the much-maligned video monitor, which sells for around $50 tops once market forces have played out. At this price point, there is precious little profit margin. So, the development team will simply follow the market leaders in a 'me too' rebranding of an ODM's (original design manufacturer) product.

However, for a business commissioning a brand new innovative product it doesn't need to start out that way. Despite this, the business will know that the financial barriers to prevent the competition copying the product and idea is remarkably low, so they need to buy as much time in a blue water harbor – the time in the market with no significant competitor – as possible. One way to achieve this is they can spend on security, because they should try to build into their product security and privacy controls that may present a barrier to entry to competitors. If they can develop sufficient software and privacy controls to secure the product, then they might make copying of their idea a bit more difficult and hence expensive for their competition.

The real issue is that in the consumer IoT market, building distinctive innovative products is extremely difficult. For when a manufacturer identifies a potential market for an IoT product, which is in this example a streaming video camera that can be designed, produced and marketed as a video monitor. Then they source the individual building block components, such as a web cam, a microphone and sound card and a Wi-Fi radio. Then they house these commodity-off-the-shelf components into an esoteric but aesthetic housing perhaps sporting a cartoon or something similar and the product is as good as ready to go to market.

However, despite all this effort the product is simply a mash up of COTS (commercial of the shelf) components, the value of the product is simply the idea or rather its proposed use. It is after all a webcam with a Wi-Fi card attached, what makes it interesting and potentially marketable is its proposed use as a video monitoring device for care-givers. However, as it is made from commercial of the shelf components any competitor can quickly copy the idea and have their own version with perhaps a different case and graphics out to market in a matter of days. Consequently, the time in the blue water is very short as the barrier to entry for the competition is so low.

Cutting development costs

Consequently, manufacturer's feel they have to price their products aggressively and as that means tight profit margins then some savings have to be made in the cost of goods. When companies start to look to making savings in cost of goods or the bill of materials, then there is only so much they can save on components as the competition are most likely using the same items and sources to build their product. Therefore, they look to take shortcuts in product or service development costs and specifically areas and features that can be trimmed without noticeable effect with regards the products functionality, such as development overheads. The usual suspects in this case are trimming the development team, multi-tasking team responsibilities where feasible, the re-use of code, plug and play firmware and skimping on quality and security.

Security is not an extra

A further major concern is an unfortunate misunderstanding that has arisen within IoT design. Manufacturers have come to believe through their experience and perhaps market research that the consumer isn't willing to pay a premium for security and privacy. They mistakenly read that to mean that consumers don't value security and privacy – that is a serious error in judgment. What the consumer was really saying was that security and privacy should be a given, and not an extra.

This basic misreading of the consumer's position meant that manufacturers did cut corners with security, as it is expensive, and as they believed perhaps rightly so, added little to the marketability of the product. The customer wasn't willing to pay for it so why put it in to the product.

This is understandable, as the pressure from top management downward will be to get the product out the door and earning market share – the target being to get the time to profit to a minimum. That unfortunately, also usually means keeping the cost to manufacture the product to a minimum. However, there may be other motivators at play, often it is not even about the money, the chief motivator may be mainly about getting the company's name out there in the marketplace as an innovator or market leader in that field. Get the media excited and get the CEO onto the news tonight.

The risks though of cutting production costs and going to market with an insecure or substandard product are huge, and not limited to just that company but to the whole market sector. Today, in 2016 the public is rightfully skeptical about the dreaded Baby Cam Video monitor after the huge negative publicity regards their insecurity and loss of privacy that was revealed on prime-time news. It also appears it is not just the public that has serious privacy concerns, earlier this year a self-published photo by the Facebook CEO appeared on social media. The notable feature was that on his laptop situated on the desk behind him he had placed tape over the webcam camera and microphone. Now if he is concerned by loss of privacy due to lax security, shouldn't we all be.

Loss of product trust

Similarly, the loss of consumer trust affected the producers of Bluetooth enabled door locks. They received a major public backlash due to the revelations on national news that their products were insecure and in some cases easily circumvented – a truly damaging accusation for a product that's only function is to be secure.

The failure of the Bluetooth lock products was not due to the actual technology deployed but the poor implementation by several manufacturers. However, the failure of the guilty or negligent has tainted the entire IoT Bluetooth lock market.

The same damage of reputation and loss of consumer trust affects the manufacturers of every product not just the flawed. This is regardless of the market. However, for the producers of IoT devices, where consumers are still naïve and trusting of the manufacturer then failures can be catastrophic to the business as that trust is lost forever. For example; take the consumer backlash regarding the privacy invasion through insecure webcam products and worse the hack of the talking Barbie dolls that caused such mass publicity and consternation when their security flaws hit the national and international news. If the manufacturers still believed customers did not value security and privacy, well they now had a resounding answer.

The companies responsible for these flawed products will claim that they are victims of unrealistic security analysis that were disproportional to the intended use of the product. However, that is a bit disingenuous in many cases when little or no security measures were in place or even undergone rudimentary penetration testing before the products release. However, in the case of the talking doll reputable security agencies did perform extensive and diligent security assessments and were satisfied to the toys appropriate security. This of course begs the question just how much security is enough.

Designing appropriate security

Here we have to show some understanding, as security is complex. If we consider the interactive Barbie doll exploit as an example of enough security proving to be insufficient. The initial 'hack', was not a cyber-hack performed remotely, it was re-engineering or reverse engineering trick. The initial researcher took the doll apart uncovered the PCB and started probing the electronics to read the firmware, the memory and debug the PCB code via the UART – is this a proportion realistic threat after all the PCB board is just a toy costing $75. The researcher then revealed that unsurprisingly he had uncovered recorded messages and personal details that any child might have spoken to their imaginary best friend – the Doll.

This is not a cyber-hack, it required a researcher to rip apart a toy and analyze an electronic circuit board. Now, if we consider a security tenet:

$$Risk = Impact \times (Probability/likelihood\ of\ occurrence)$$

The likelihood of occurrence can be expressed in terms of the frequency of occurrence, such as once in a day, once in a month or once in a year. The greater the likelihood of a threat occurring, the higher the risk, so how likely is it that your child's toy will be re-engineered?

Then where was the risk? The researcher required considerable time, motivation, skill and also to physically get hands-on control of the child's doll. What is more he destroyed it to all intends and purposes, then used an oscilloscope to perform electronic analysis of the computer PCB, perhaps using the UART or J** debug ports, to extract stored data from the integrated system memory chips.

Now how many people are capable of doing that, it is not a trivial task and to what purpose? Would the researcher be able to hand that doll back to the child without them knowing he had ripped it apart and then occasionally return to rip it apart again to steal the subsequently new stored conversations?

Yes, it is a hack and very skillful one, but on a threat scale from one to ten, as a cyber-threat it is not really going to register. It is like worrying that your iPhone could be lost and the texts and contents decrypted by the mysterious firm that hacked into the iPhone for the FBI. Yes, it is feasible but highly improbable!

However, in this case the manufacturer of the doll did not get off so lightly, as a few weeks later someone did perform a full cyber-attack on one of the dolls, though not the same one, without any physical contact at all and the fall out was devastating, but this again was down to a mixture of poor cloud and home Wi-Fi security. Now that was cyber-hacking as the perpetrator performed the task remotely and that is perhaps why we should be concerned. The real external threats matter, not someone who has hands on control of our 'Things', and not someone who has trusted access to our home and possessions – but perhaps that is the flaw with the consumer IoT. The security hype has driven the levels of paranoia beyond the reasonable, proportional and cost-effective levels of security that are the key tenets of security.

Chapter 9 – Re-engineering the IoT

It was not long ago that we considered threat surfaces to come through email attachments, drive-past browser attacks, cross application or malware delivered as download links. These were the days when we could think our tablet, smartphone or laptop was safe from attack if we followed basic security best practices. Unfortunately, that has all changed, with the IoT we now have strange new physical devices, such as toys, cars and drones that we need to protect that do not run antivirus software. As a result, we now have attackers using electronic engineering techniques and tools to extract passwords and previously secure authentication details out of chips from a PCB.

In this chapter, we will investigate why this has come around, and how these new electric warriors manage to circumvent security:
1. Electronic hacking
2. Firmware hacking
3. Evaluating the cost of security
4. Device vulnerabilities and flaws

One of the problems that the IoT is facing is that alongside the market hype, which creates industry and public interest, is this accompanying nemesis of poor security. In industry and enterprise scenarios, operational and IT engineers are not too concerned about IoT device security as they are prepared to build into their networks the protection required to defend the vulnerable IoT devices. Manufacturers are also aware that professionals will use their products within secure networks so they build in proportional levels of security, such as where possible, authentication and encryption to provide confidentiality, integrity and availability, the three basic tenets of IT security.

Despite this, the IoT has come under unusual threat vectors, not just from cyber attackers but more importantly, those that like to physically rip something apart and snoop around the electronics. Here is where there is an issue with IoT security. Many of the devices that we hear about in trade papers and the news are not cyber-hacked, or not at least as how the public understands it. The hacker, instead of being some ethereal masked criminal lurking out on the ether instead has been inside the house sitting with a cup of coffee and with his hands on the device, disassembling the product, and probing the electronic circuit board.

So, where can manufacturers draw the line at what is appropriate, cost effective and realistic security? Just how far does a manufacturer of a consumer smart TV with Wi-Fi and Ethernet have to go to honestly say they took all reasonable,

DOI 10.1515/9781501505775-012

appropriate and cost effective measures to secure the TV from inherent threats present in the environment in which it was designed to work. An example of this is a smart TV situated in the living room of a family home. The TV may have Internet and all sorts of PC functionality. It will have Wi-Fi and Ethernet but it is going to be relatively secure so long as the home network is secure.

A cyber-attacker out on the Internet cannot directly access the TV as it has a local network private address, which is not legal out there on the Internet. Additionally, when it transmits out to the Internet, its own private address is swapped for the gateway's public IP address and that ensures its privacy. That however does not mean it is safe, it could be a victim of a drive-past exploit where the victim browses a website with an embedded JavaScript file, which will automatically run and infect the browser. There are many other web style exploits such as cross scripting, SQL-injection, amongst others that can contaminate an innocent PC's browser – or in this case a TV.

However, not everyone nowadays goes via the Internet; some, it appears, like screwdrivers. If this is the case, then the attacker will most likely strip down the device and start probing for the UART pins. A UART in case you are unaware is simply a PCB's serial port, which purpose is to communicate with programmers, developers, and engineers to debug the inner workings of the PCB firmware. The UART is an essential hardware port on the device's PCB it has to be there. The problem is that the UART is a very simple port, it is serial, RS232 but with only three pins TX, Rx and Gnd. Consequently, an analyst probing for the UART pins, even if they are disguised as they often are now, can easily find them.

An attacker that has full hands on access to a device can rip it open and access the PCB and subsequently the UART pins. When the analyst connects to the UART pins and using a serial terminal emulator such as Hyper-Terminal or Putty, they will typically get a Linux shell prompt. If they are lucky, it might already be a root privileged prompt – remember this is an engineer debug tool – If not it is usually trivial to escalate privileges to root and gain control of the device.

Once of course, the analysts have gained root privileges, they effectively own the device and can do whatever they wish, such as change admin passwords and allow root access from remote locations so that the analyst can control the device remotely.

However, we must remember that the initial hack was only possible because the analyst had hands-on access to the product and was able to dismantle it, along with the time and motivation to hack its embedded OS. Additionally, they might have been working under favorable conditions that did not require them to have to reassemble the product, without a trace.

Another technique favored by IoT device hackers are firmware attacks. Every, smart IoT device will have some Linux OS firmware embedded and that can be a prime point for attack. However, hacking firmware is by no means a trivial pursuit it is extremely complex.

Comparing Apples and Oranges

Of course, these product attacks can be hard on the business, sometimes it can be fatal, and in mitigation, the company responsible for producing the talking doll had no experience of the complexities of the security issues that they were facing. However, they were well warned, especially with regard their privacy TOC, yet they decided to proceed with the product anyway. So, they really deserve little sympathy. The manufacturer's partners ToyTalk certainly should have shown due diligence when designing the product. By connecting the interactive doll to a cloud API, the developers perhaps should have shown more awareness. After all, the developers had experience in integrating toys with voice recognition and machine learning applications from third party cloud service providers. They might feel that they are just as much a victim of a security failure as the consumer because the cloud-based services are out with their control and even the reach of their own risk assessment.

A second problem, and here the manufacturers do have a case, is that consumers will not seemingly pay for added security and privacy – it should be a given. The result is that manufacturers are severely limited when make their products at lower price points with reasonable and appropriate security. They add security features that are as appropriate to the products intended use and what they can afford to spend in a product in the $25–$50 consumer range. At these price points, the amount of security that can be built into a device is severely limited.

Sometimes the media, even the trade media, who should know better, lambast manufacturers of consumer IoT for not having enterprise class security built into their IoT products such as a toy. That is wrong on several fronts; firstly, enterprise products like Cisco and Juniper routers are found to have security issues, as well as allegedly direct connivance with intelligence agencies – sometimes highly embarrassing ones such as the discovery of unauthorized code that had gone undetected for years in Juniper's software. Also, around 840,000 Cisco routers were found to have a flaw vulnerable to the Equation Groups exploit against VPNs and Cisco PIX Firewalls. This flaw again had existed for years, and worse it was suspected of existing for many years, but was only admitted by Cisco, after the hacker group Shadow Brokers released the attack tools it had stolen from the NSA on the Internet. Secondly, that comparing enterprise class security with consumer IoT device security is like comparing a $50,000 apple with a $50-dollar orange.

The Bluetooth lock saga

Manufacturers and startups in particular are rarely the inventors the public think them to be. More often than not they are simply innovators that find a good use for someone else's products or typically an innovative use for a device they can make cobbling together a few mass-market components. A few examples are the Bluetooth locks, which in mid-2016 were revealed to have numerous flaws in the way manufacturers deployed the Bluetooth protocol within their products. To illustrate the failing of these products, examine the research carried out by Anthony Rose and Ben Ramsey on hacking Bluetooth locks.

Research carried out by Anthony Rose, an electrical engineer and Ben Ramsey discovered that 12 out of 16 Bluetooth lock that they tested opened when wirelessly attacked. The locks — including models made by an array of manufacturers had security vulnerabilities that made their exploitation either easy or in some cases moderately difficult to exploit.

However, although these devices all used Bluetooth the issue is not with the protocol, but in the way it is implemented. Sometimes the flaw was in the mobile app rather than in the lock. However, the researchers discovered that four of the locks actually transmitted their user passwords in plaintext to smartphones. This is a ridiculous vulnerability that indicates that the manufacturers were clueless regarding wireless communications or were not even attempting to implement any form of wireless security. Presumably the developers thought Bluetooth was impervious to wireless sniffing, as it uses an adaptive frequency hopping technique over 79 channels. However, that is not the case as frequency-hopping is more for avoiding RF interference on specific channels rather than as a security measure. Transmitting the passwords in clear text makes those vulnerable to a Bluetooth sniffer which can capture the wireless communications packets decode them revealing the clear-text passwords.

If that wasn't bad enough, the locks sent the password twice during the same communication and the researchers discovered that simply altering the second iteration of the password, they could change the password thereby blocking the lock's owner. Additionally, the owner was truly locked out because the only way to reset the password was to remove the battery, but to get to the battery the lock had to be open – so at least thy had got that bit of security right.

Not all the lock manufacturers were foolish enough to send clear text passwords over Bluetooth and most did encrypt the user password for their Bluetooth transmissions between the mobile app and the lock. However, some of these locks didn't seem to have any sequence or session checking measures to prevent replay attacks. Therefore, the researchers were able to simply capture the transmissions between the smartphone and the lock when the owner opened the device. Then they could later replay the transmission and the lock assumed it to be a new transaction and opened.

Furthermore, one lock manufacturer boasted of its robust security in its advertising claiming that it used a patented custom encryption of similar grade to the military. However, those claims were disingenuous to be kind, as the patented custom encryption was simply XOR. Also, the lock was found to be vulnerable to a "fuzzing" attack which is when the researchers sent random data to the lock to see how the software responded. They discovered that by changing one byte in the encryption string that the lock entered an error state — and the lock opened.

Some locks were harder to open as they used a cloud app to generate the passwords; however, by staging a man-in-the-middle attack on the traffic flowing between the lock and the cloud servers via the smartphone app, the researchers discovered it.

A predictable "nonce," is a numerical value used to generate encrypted strings. The nonce is supposed to be random, but the nonce function of the lock under analysis simply incremented the previous value. Because of that, the researchers were able to impersonate the legitimate user and open the lock.

Device vulnerabilities and flaws

Having, their products hacked and then held up for public mockery must be hugely embarrassing for the manufacturer, the developers, the CEO, the investors, stakeholders and even the customer who must feel stupid for buying such rubbish. Therefore, it is almost inconceivable that any technology company producing IoT products would not be driven by the basic first principles, security by design and privacy by design. To find that some are still driven by profit before reputation and quality products and are in it for the quick buck is still deeply disappointing.

Flawed firmware

However not all companies are snake oil salesmen, many are genuine but just trying to exist in a very volatile habitat. A problem when manufacturing, remodeling or rebadging ODM devices, which depend on other device manufacturers (ODM) components, is the reliance on the ODM's firmware. If the ODM equipment is using outdated or flawed firmware, many use old versions of embedded Linux, then the product will be flawed from the start and these flaws may well go undetected through the product's software testing. This is one of the reasons that we see not one but many manufacturers devices fail security vetting when a type of device is shown to be insecure. A good example of this was with the Bluetooth locks; once security analysts discovered Bluetooth vulnerabilities and then successfully exploited one brand, the analysts could reuse the exploit successfully on several brands that were tested. This was because most of the brands used the same ODM components and firmware. This is one of the dangers of the 'me too' approach, where a business sees a successful initial launch of a competitive product and feels they must respond ASAP. Then they may reverse engineer the product and launch their own brand. Yes, they may be following the leader down the path to riches but it can just as easily be to ruin.

Code re-use

There is a final issue and that is the reuse of code. As IoT developers continue to produce new products and essentially try to deliver new product differentiation, the amount of embedded software, which developers are recycling within IoT products, is growing exponentially. The habit of reusing code in order to save time is commonplace. As a result, the products functionality is becoming more dependent on the firmware and software embedded within the product and less on the hardware components. Manufacturers' are striving for smarter, and more intelligently connected products, which are rich in features and able to support applications at lower costs and this has led to a proliferation of flaws across multivendor products. Moreover, it has also led to vulnerabilities spanning all sorts of new technologies, applications, and devices.

Code re-use is an emerging phenomenon in the software development industry, especially within the consumer IoT, industry, medical science ecosystems and many more. Presently, there may be approximately over 12 million lines of code in an Android phone, and a modern car may have over 100 million lines of code. Developers, then have the challenge to produce original software fast enough, and securely, without a prohibitive increase in cost or cut and paste open source code. The current solution seems to be to reuse as much code as possible. Yet achieving these cost and time saving goals often proves to be difficult. Ideally, a developer would be able to access trusted code libraries and reuse code from those open source libraries as building blocks within the application. Unfortunately, this only works if those building blocks can be verified to be free from security bugs or problems that affect the reliability, safety, or security of the device.

The issue with open source

A common misconception with regards open source software is that it will be secure as many have used it even in enterprise and telecom class equipment. The rational being that the code will be secure as a 1000 eyes at least have studied the code and found no flaws. Of course, this is wishful-thinking because perhaps myriad of eyes have cast a glance over the code but not from a security perspective. This is why the hugely popular OpenSSL project, which is integrated into enterprise applications, telecom grade routers and even industrial systems managed to evade security code verification until 2014 when the Heartbleed vulnerability was discovered.

The issue with Heartbleed was that when the analysts that discovered the flaw pointed it out, it was so obvious that few could understand how it had gone hiding in plain view for over a decade. The consequences of the Heartbleed vulnerability were vast and it received huge media coverage due to its potential for circumventing encryption in all sorts of supposedly secure transactions going back over a decade. Furthermore, 13 million e-commerce and financial websites were traced to being vulnerable to the Heartbleed flaw. This sort of news breaking on the news does make consumers sit up and question the security in place when carrying out financial transactions on the Internet. However, what is far more disconcerting from a security perspective, is that three years after the Heartbleed vulnerability was identified and information as how to remediate the flaw by upgrading to later OpenSSL releases was made available over the Internet. There are still around 5 million ecommerce and financial sites identified as being vulnerable to Heartbleed simply because they have not upgraded their version of OpenSSL. This might seem ludicrous, but we have to remember that many commercial websites were built years ago and the original coders have long since moved on leaving behind a seemingly working secure ecommerce site. Their successors who simply administer and operate the website may have no idea that their website code is still vulnerable.

This can be a major issue with open source software and code re-use as developers feel comfortable using highly regarded code and assume because everyone else is cutting and pasting the code, even the web giants are using the code, that it must be secure.

However, that is a wrong assumption to make; typically, other developers are using the same tactics and blindly re-using the same open source code, believing the same thing. Therefore, if attackers or researchers do discover a flaw within the re-used or open source code then it will likely affect many products on the market.

Chapter 10 – IoT Production, Security and Strength

Consequently, we can see that the manufacturers of IoT products have several difficulties and do have some mitigating circumstances for not producing robustly secure products at low price points. However, it is their brand name on the box, so it is in their interest ultimately to ensure life-cycle software support is built into the design–a way to upgrade over the air–in order to support the product so that it provides lifetime security.

Having said that we come to yet another IoT contradiction, what is the life cycle of a consumer product costing $100 or less? Is it actually realistic to expect a manufacturer to support a product for three or more years if it is no longer generating revenue? The manufacturer after all want the consumer to buy the latest product and even purveyors of expensive smartphones costing $700 to $1,000 dollars will stop providing firmware upgrades after only a couple of years for that same reason. Businesses are there to make money and that is generated from sales from fresh products and not from free after-sales support for retired products.

This actually creates a much larger issue as IoT products may be retired, or come to market and be well received but the manufacturer goes out of business, or possibly gets acquired within a year and the product is swiftly dropped. This creates a real security dilemma in that there is possibly going to be many zombie products still active within home networks that the manufacturer is no longer able to support as well as products that are long past their expected lifetimes that manufacturers are unwilling to support and their presence creates real security risks. One solution that the industry throws up is that there should be a kill switch, so after three years – the projected lifetime of the product – it should no longer function.

How is that feasible? This is where security analysts and developers come up with theoretical solutions to problems, which cannot possibly work in the real world. Would an IT enterprise or industrial buyer, purchase a device, regardless of whether the device was a $4 proximity sensor or a smart TV costing say $1000, with a deterministic three-year lifetime?

In the IT enterprise environment, buyers will typically purchase equipment with a five-year life cycle, and that is how business budgets and refreshes cycles work. In industry, the refresh cycle is much longer perhaps 10 to 20 years refresh cycle due to the cost of the machinery. However, the safety is that they know that

DOI 10.1515/9781501505775-013

the equipment can and will keep on working well beyond those short time limitations if necessary – not just die on a predetermined anniversary of their birth.

Ironically, manufacturer's sometimes also make products just too well, Cisco routers for example, would run and run for many years without any reset or human intervention. Microsoft Windows XP is another example; it was ubiquitous and heavily adopted in both the home and business. Therefore, as these products were so good, there was no immediate rush for the consumer to upgrade to the latest products as the version they had were reliable, easy to support and trusted.

When Cisco and Microsoft tried to retire their popular products, there was and still is consumer resistance. After all these products delivered everything the customer required, they had no wish or inclination to upgrade to another product. However, what if Cisco and Microsoft had suggested a new product even better than the last, full of bells and whistles, but hidden away in the TOC was a declaration that the product came with a kill switch after 3 years – would anyone of bought it?

Manufacturing IoT Devices

One of the misconceptions that many consumers and indeed even professional IT security practitioners make is that they assume that the smart shiny new ergonomically designed IoT product that they have just purchased was designed and built by the company whose brand adorns its packaging. They feel perhaps that it is a good, trusted brand that will have quality and assurance controls, so this is a product, which they can have faith in. In the world of modern consumer electronics, that is a risky assumption to make.

To understand why, we have to consider how modern electronic consumer products are made and this is relevant to security in the IoT particularly. The first stage in electronic product manufacturing starts with the printed circuit board assembly. This is where the PCB is assembled, populated with electronic components and tested. The PCB will contain typically an EEPROM (electrically erasable programmable read only memory) chip and this is the foundation on which the developers start to build the software stack.

The integrated circuits through require software drivers in order to communicate with the hardware and software stacks, whether that be Linux, Windows embedded or RTOS and these are no different functionally from the drivers we need to load to get PC peripherals to work they are just working right down at the microprocessor and chip level. These are highly specialist software products and are produced by companies such as Marvel, Texas Instruments, Broadcom, Intel,

ARM and AMD amongst many others. The software that these independent companies with their own teams of software developers' produce are called BSP (board support packages) and these device drivers provide the link between the hardware and the software stack. Device drivers contained in the BSPs are the first level of software within the stack and when combined with the PCB produce the foundation building block of the IoT device.

ODM design

The next stage will often include Original Design Manufacturers (ODM) and these are third party companies specializing in creating software stacks and supplemental components such as SDKs (software development kits), UI (user interfaces), drivers, admin web portals, as well as mobile apps amongst others. The ODM will integrate the Operating System (OS) as part of the software stack and this will typically consist of Linux or RTOS, and be supported by a framework, such as HomeKit, Alljoin, RiOT or OpenWRT, which will enable more agile but also a uniform development, which is important for consumer IoT electronics, which require a rapid time to market.

The overall role of the ODM is either to make the software stack to the customer's (the Brands) Software Requirements and Specifications (SRS) for perhaps a new innovative product but more typically they supply an off-the-shelf software-stack with some modifications. The reason for this is that ODMs specialize so if the product requires real time media streaming for example another ODM will provide that work and the required drivers. What this means is that there can be, not one, but many ODM's being hands-on through the software production phase. From a security perspective having several, maybe ten ODMs hands-on to the products software development would require strict SDLC project management to prevent security issues slipping between the gaps.

Therefore, what are the security issues here? Well, SODM services and products enables brand companies to produce goods without them having to have manufacturing plants and supply chains and all the vast overheads that can entail. By out-sourcing the software production of the stack to third parties enables the brand company to price their product more competitively. In addition, ODM's enable rapid development and production which in the consumer electronic world is important as getting to market early, and to profit quickly, is vital for products within boisterous new markets. However, where security issues arise, is it is not just the brand customer that has fierce competition for product pricing. The ODM also operate in a market of small margins driven down by an abundance of small software houses all quoting for the same work. This is one of the reasons that many of these ODMs are located in China and South Asia, as costs are inherently lower and hence why they can produce lower quotations for the work.

Now here it is important to recognize that low quotations and prices does not necessarily equate with poor quality. However, saying that, if brand companies decide purely on price then they contribute to the race-to-the-bottom mentality of ODM's cutting prices to obtain contracts. Cutting prices can only be feasible if corresponding costs are cut in order to maintain any sort of profit margin. ODM's locked in the highly competitive market are therefore on almost permanent cost cutting programs. This can often lead to Q&A issues but more relevant to us in security design, which will be omitted and pushed further up the stack for someone else to deal with. After all building in security features will cost extra in time, effort and material. If an additional IC (integrated circuit) chip will cost 15 cents, then there is often no cost/benefit justification including it into the product, as in the market the cheapest price wins.

The next stage of production requires integrating the IoT device with the back-end cloud service providers. There are a few major players in this market Amazon, Google, Microsoft, but many other ODMs have their own clouds. The Cloud Service Providers (CSP) will produce APIs and SDK to enable the ODM developers to integrate the product with the cloud services and applications. The ODM's will typically also have their own APIs to their clouds. This can be a significant privacy issue because for instance in the case of data that is produced from a fitness band, that private information may not just be going to the main cloud provider, for example Microsoft Azure, which the consumer expects and accepts, but also to several ODMs' private clouds that they in most probability have never heard off.

The final set of hands on the development of the product is the OEM (Original Equipment Manufacturer) who places their Logo and brand onto the product and proudly markets the product as their own. The OEM is responsible for all the marketing and sales as it is their product which although it was not built by them it was commissioned and funded by them.

The OEM also manages the after-sales services although they will almost certainly require the ODM to make any necessary fixes to flaws or security deficiencies. Interestingly it is the OEM's brand that is at risk to taking the full public relations hit should the product fail to meet basic security standards and gets embarrassingly hacked. This does beg the question why the OEM does not make a more flexible approach to ensuring security is included in the design process from the ODM onwards.

A common response from senior and seasoned marketing executives and senior product developers, is all too often, a shrug and a smile, and indicate they would be delighted to build security and privacy into the design, but who will pay that extra $1 production cost per box?

However, this begs the question, why is it financially productive then to make kitchen utility objects Internet connected?

The tale of the Wi-Fi Kettle

A technologist, named Mark Rittman bought a Wi-Fi enabled kettle – why, we do not know. However, he spent eleven hours trying to get the appliance to work. A key problem as with most IoT devices is that they do not have software that enables easy integration with other household devices. The problem he had was that the kettle could not communicate with the home hub. Instead he decided to directly connect the kettle to his smartphone – really clever it only took eleven hours.

Push Vs. pull marketing

The reason that many of these new connected products are coming with Internet capabilities is due to the manufacturers seeing the benefits rather than demand from the customer. It is a classic case of push rather than pull marketing. In this case the manufacturer is pushing the Internet connected device to the customer as being fashionable and smart because it is in the manufacturer's interest. Why?

Well, it is because they now clearly see the benefits of firmware over the air upgrades. Additionally, they see the potential of the data economy so they can in addition to obtaining product usage information also collect information that can possibly have after sales marketing potential. Everyone it seems is keen to jump on the data gathering bandwagon. The primary reason, hopefully, is the benefits to the manufacturer in being able to securely upgrade its product at any time via an Internet connection is considerable and it is indeed a prerequisite of any modern IoT device. Being able to upgrade the software on a car, washing machine, tumble drier, or cooker, indeed on any device that is microprocessor and software controlled can save the manufacturer a fortune in the event of a flaw which would otherwise require a return to a vendor or home visit by a service technician to fix.

Consequently, the sudden surge in connected devices is rather more about the manufacturers desire to push the Internet connectivity rather than the customers' desire to pull, for these new connected features. Subsequently, in some cases the customer may not even know that the Smart on the label indicates its IoT capabilities and be unaware that their new Smart TV for example is sending back not just operational, and usage data to the manufacturer's preconfigured cloud but perhaps all the information it can extract from other connected devices within the home. Similarly, that if the smart TV has the capability to initiate a connection to the cloud, which of course it does have as it is acting much like a Trojan Horse, then the applications in the cloud can take control. The applications can then run commands, send data, perhaps even marketing offers, and extract usage reports regarding the length of times and type of programs watched, as well as daily viewing interests. Furthermore, they can extract this data whenever they wish and then sell this accrued knowledge on to advertising houses.

The direct advertising merchants may then use this marketing knowledge to bombard the viewer with targeted and invasive marketing much like Google Adds on our Internet browsers. Now, many people will reasonably say, 'well that is helpful, I get informed only of products of interest, and it means they can subsidize a lot of the services which I get for free, so I can't see the issue?'

There probably isn't a problem in a single occupier home, as it is a single source of data for the like of Google to analyze but what about in a shared PC or a single TV display in a family home? What we must understand is that behind NAT enabled routers Google and Facebook amongst others cannot distinguish between individual devices on the home networks so they broadcast 'targeted' adverts to every device in the home sharing the same public IP address. This failure in determining individual devices let alone the behavior habits of the user results in so called targeted advertising appearing on a communal TV, a shared PC or any other device and some of the directed adverts may be inappropriate for children.

However, far more disconcerting is that a malicious attacker may be able to exploit an unsecured smart TV to listen in via the always-on microphone and eaves drop on the families evening discussions or worse view the occupants' activities in the room through the camera. Interestingly, when we come later to discuss privacy, there is a common perception that privacy today is dead or at least a dated concept especially with the younger generation, but could you ever be comfortable suspecting that your TV was spying on you? (This is discussed in greater length in the Privacy section.)

Chapter 11 – Wearable's – A New Developer's Headache

The sales of personal wearables have grown increasingly over the last few years, especially to those with a keen interest in sport, personal health and fitness. With these personal health and fitness aids, the security concerns are more focused on the data collected, how it is securely stored in the cloud and how it is anonymized. The privacy of personal data is an important issue that manufacturers of this type of IoT wearable devices must take seriously. After all the intended purpose of wearable devices was to connect devices across a very short-range personal area networks (PAN). As such, these short-range communication devices were relatively secure. Nevertheless, when the data collected from the devices leaks to the Internet via an unknown connection to a gateway router there can be privacy issues. There are also issues with how the data in some cases is stored and accessed. Some manufacturers offer both public and private access modes to cloud data, so privacy can be major concern. In addition, it is extremely important that the consumer reads the TOC and the Privacy Policy to find out just what is actually happening to their data. In some cases, their anonymized data is being passed on to third parties but just how anonymized is data coming from a wearable?

The concern with personal data being generated from wearable wrist-bands for example is a real issue or should be, however many consumers don't appear to care. The reason for concern is the quality of data being passed through to the cloud and perhaps on to third parties might be a lot more revealing than you might think.

The wearable sports accessory or personal health band targets the young, fit and healthy athletic folk, which presumably have no problem getting of their backsides to dim the lights or adjust the thermostat. Here the emphasis is on the consumer's exercise regime, the amount of calories burned and the quality of the analytical assessment of the exercise undertaken. The statistical analysis will provide the consumer with a detailed report of the benefits of their holistic training program over their whole body – present cardio, vascular, aerobic condition. However, here we have even deeper security and privacy matters, after all the sensors are continuously monitoring the consumer's health, heartbeat, aerobic condition and exertion for as long as the device is active. However, that is not all it is collecting as it is capable of knowing and collecting far more, such as the wearer's sleep patterns, when they slept and for how long, even the quality of the sleep. Furthermore, it knows when the wearer got up, where they went after

DOI 10.1515/9781501505775-014

breakfast even the exact location via GPS, the route travelled, also the speed they walked or drove over the travelled route. But that is not all it is synchronizing with the wearer's other PAN devices such as their smartphone to collect data on applications used and the time spend on each, websites visited and even the music track listened too.

This vast amount of personal data is drifting off into the cloud. But does the consumer really question, for what purpose? Most consumers will not have thought to ask or bothered to read the manufacturer's privacy policy. The problem is that that data is not on the smart watch or wristband but now resides in the cloud and if the consumer is not careful it may well be sold on to marketing houses that will then use the knowledge to direct targeted advertising. Manufacturers' will claim that the collected data is anonymized when it is sent to the cloud, but that is perhaps disingenuous. The marketing house might not be able to extrapolate the consumer's identity from the data, for example the consumer's but they can identify the location of the devices and track them accordingly. Consequently, these direct marketing houses can build up a picture of the consumer's home location, their movements and direct relevant advertising to the consumer's device where-ever they may be. After all this is why they are buying the data.

A more worrying scenario is if law enforcement agencies or government departments could access the data generated via the health band. Here the implication regards privacy, which is a much greater threat as the wristband could actually work against the consumer. In such a situation, the consumer may not wish to provide information that they by law are not required to divulge. An example is if questioned by the police to their whereabouts on a certain date or time. The Police could possibly gain that information via data requests to service providers, regardless of the consumer's willingness to co-operate and divulge that information. Another example is with health insurance or work benefits, a consumer may claim to be unfit for work due to injury, yet the data from the band could well contradict that statement. Therefore, regardless of the moral or ethical questions the consumer should be aware that their privacy might well be compromised when they are wearing an IoT wearable device.

Furthermore, the fact that an IoT wristband is collecting vast quantities of personal fitness data, which you may not consider important unless you are a competitive athlete, can still provide sneaky information leaks. A classic example was the Internet meme, where a young woman wore a fitness band 24/7 as an exercise aid. Unfortunately, the data sent to the cloud from the wristband became publicly viewable and the data indicated that there were times when the woman was having sex. Of course, nobody could definitively say that the individual was having sex, she might have had a late-night exercise habit, but by studying the pattern of behavior, others could reasonably infer from the data, supported by geo-location and time of day, that the data suggested just that.

One of the major issues when collecting and analyzing large samples of data, which we will discuss further under privacy and surveillance, is that analysts can infer behavioral patterns from the seemingly innocuous data, willingly or unwittingly supplied and come to conclusions that fit their agenda. This is one of the major issues with metadata it can often be misinterpreted due to an analyst's bias. An example of this the way the NSA tracks targets using GPS or Cell Tower triangulation from mobile phones. What they often are looking for is who the target meets and they do this by watching what other mobile phones come into close proximity with the target. This of course can be totally innocent such as when the target goes into a café for a cup of coffee. Anyone entering and leaving at approximately the same time as the target is 'guilty by association' and they will be tracked as well.

IoT by stealth

The problems of IoT privacy have become far more insidious just lately as new products come to market that are capable of privacy intrusion. One product priced at only $20 is the size of a coin battery, very small and easily hidden. The purpose, as marketed by the company is that you hide the coin-sized transmitter into the seat upholstery or the glove compartment of a car, motorbike or bicycle. The device via its transmitter is then traceable using a mobile app with a Google map GUI to enable the owner to trace the objects location. This is a good solution for tracking valuable possessions. The manufacturer has come up with a consumer grade product, which enables a consumer to buy this simple button sized transmitter and secure their highly expensive bicycle or even stick it on their dog's collar or a key ring. However, as it is so small the device can be deployed almost on anything. It could be slipped into clothing or a wallet, as it was undistinguishable from a coin or button, and then the owner could track that device wherever it travelled.

The sales of this device are huge, but did anyone – or perhaps they did, going by sales – see the alternative use for the device, as not being just tracking valuable bicycles, roaming dogs, stolen cars, but perhaps an errant spouse or partner?

When we consider IoT security and just how pervasive connected devices have become we need only look at a modern car as a prime example. The humble family car of only a few years ago has been transformed into the connected car of today. Some security researchers have described the modern car as simply a computer on wheels. It is estimated that the typical family car can have as many as 100 intelligent sensors and actuators, some are assisting the driver such as servo controlled brakes, or are providing alerts and status indications for the dashboard but an increasing amount are beginning to perform autonomous control functions, such as intelligent cruise control. GPS has been around for many years but now we are beginning to see dedicated Internet connectivity via mobile telecom SIM cards and this is becoming more pervasive with each passing year. We will discuss connected and autonomous car in detail later, but just now, the point is that whether we like it or not our cars are becoming Internet connected, not through our desire or request. We can see this because it's not a pay-extra premier option; it's coming as a standard feature, which says a great deal about in whose interest Internet connectivity lies. Indeed, it is very difficult to get the vehicle supplier to switch off or remove this Internet connectivity. Often the sincere response will be that they can disable some functions but others are mandatory and required for safety reasons. It appears that this, as strange as it seems is true, and that modern cars are no longer capable of being driven without computer assistance.

More of a concern is some vehicles are coming with SIM cards that can accept incoming calls from the manufacturer, and this feature is not always explained to the owner. Indeed, one service option with On-Star back in 2009 was sold on the basis of a security suite of services whereby they could disable the car if it was reported stolen and they did precisely that and switched off a stolen car when it was being driven.

Another interesting thing about cars and their computers is that new cars in the US come with a federally mandated "black box", which is actually a group of microprocessors that monitor and control the airbags, or at least that used to be their primary function. Now these semiconductors known officially as an Event Data Recorder or EDR have been installed to record the cars telematics on at least fifteen crucial data points for post-accident forensic purposes. The EDR has been in most new cars for over a decade but is now legally mandatory in every new car built since 2014. The EDR logs data, such as speed, acceleration, raking, force of impact, whether air bags were deployed and whether or not you're wearing your seatbelt, amongst others, for use in law enforcement and post-accident assessment. However, there are 15 mandatory data points which must be collected but some manufacturers, depending on make or model collect a lot more as there is basically no aspect of the cars telematics that can't be measured, quantified, and logged.

Unfortunately, car manufacturers are under no obligation to reveal exactly what data points they are collecting and are surprisingly reluctant to publish details. The big question however with EDR is who owns the data and who has legal access to it. The problem being of course is that many parties want access to this data, from law enforcement, insurance companies to the car manufacturer and dealer themselves. Fortunately, EDR is difficult to access as it is only available through the car's diagnostic ports and required specialist equipment to extract and read the data. Unfortunately, that didn't last long and Bluetooth enabled dongles are cheap and available and can now be attached easily to the diagnostic port to access the data.

The EDR was developed for a purpose and its data was never intended to leave the car it would be stored locally and accessed only by authorized people. This is quite true as the way the EDR worked was that it recorded in a loop continually over-writing previous data so there was no real historical record. The same isn't true though of the connected car.

Car manufacturers embraced the idea of EDR and capturing car telematics in particular and have since 2010 been working on deploying more and more connected services in order to provide additional driver support and value and of course to get their hands on the car telematics. Just about every manufacturer how has a connected package of services, which have become more difficult to opt out of. In some cases, getting the car disconnected from the Internet is not an easy task and requires dealer intervention. The packages have driver value such as emergency and roadside assistance, infotainment options and many more attractive features. Of course, this comes at the expense of extracting personal driving data, which is transported to the cloud. Indeed, Ford has gone so far as to turn their vehicles into an Amazon Echo on wheels. The Amazon Echo is a device that has an always-on microphone that sits passively listening to your conversations and awaiting a command. Designed typically for use in the smart home it has many benefits but privacy isn't one of them and now it appears it has found a place in the car as well as the living room.

Once cars become fully autonomous, they will rely entirely on their outgoing and incoming data to function properly, indeed if you try to disconnect a connected car from the Internet today you will find that we are already at this stage. The point here is that again we can see the IoT is entering our lives insidiously, whether we are aware or not. Not surprisingly it is being introduced with innovation, value add services and a desire for data as the primary drivers with security an afterthought.

The consumer IoT conundrum

One of the major conundrums of the consumer IoT is in deploying devices securely into the home. In an enterprise, commercial or industrial IoT environment the demarcation point for security would not be an issue. There would be no argument, as it would be the network or security administrator's job to secure the network. Hence they would ensure that they showed diligence in evaluated the products capabilities and then respond appropriately to protect the installed device.

The responsibility for protecting IoT end-points and devices within the home network however raises another interesting point. A general security tenet in the enterprise and industrial worlds is that security should be proportional, cost effective and non-intrusive to operations or processes. It is therefore up to the network or security administrator to evaluate via a risk/benefit analysis the level of security required to secure a particular asset. This has serious implications in the consumer IoT environment as home gadgets may have physical constraints available for energy, CPU cycles and memory. Therefore, their security capabilities for running even reduced OS or encryption protocols are limited. Consequently, in the enterprise, industrial or commercial environments it will be the network or security administrator's job to ensure that other network devices such as hubs that provide connectivity will undertake that security burden and provide the IoT device with suitable protection. In the consumer IoT ecosystem there is often no one with that expertise or no security appliances to protect the IoT devices.

This is where it is important to understand that a manufacturer cannot design an IoT device to be resilient to an attack on the local network, especially if the attacker has hands-on access to the device. This is true of any connected device, any attacker with free access, the motivation, time and resources can defeat the security of any device. Therefore, it is important to keep in perspective the relative vulnerabilities of IoT consumer devices. Often reported security failings are only possible to an attacker with local network, or hands-on access when the device would be highly improbable to be vulnerable to remote attacks. For example, many of the scare stories we see on the news are proof of concept attacks performed on consumer devices that manufacturers did not intended to protect from internal network threats. Similarly, the manufacturers did not design the product to be directly accessible out with the local network, and as such, the reported vulnerabilities are either non-existent or disproportional to the risk.

Designing in Vulnerabilities

One thing manufacturers are guilty of is producing and shipping products with a catalogue of security issues. The most pervasive and easy threat vector for an attacker is the default username and password. Just about every consumer Wi-Fi router comes with the administrator credentials stamped on the bottom of the case or are easily determined from the Internet. In most cases these default settings remain unchanged so if the attacker can find the IP address they can login using the default admin credentials. This is how the latest malware is able to recruit so many IoT devices for botnets. The way the malware works is that it scans the Internet looking for Wi-Fi enabled routers, security camera and such as these devices are notorious for having lax owner security. Once they have determined a victim the malware will try a selection of well-known default username/password combinations to hack the device. The hack relies on the fact that very many consumer devices still use their default credentials and few are changed. By not changing the default credentials the consumer leaves the device wide open to local and remote web attack.

However, the dangers of default password are actually worse than many initially think, as changing the credentials will do little good in the case of an attacker with hands-on access. In the case of Wi-Fi routers and most other consumer devices they have a small recessed button on the back accessible with a paper clip to reset the device back to its basic factory settings. Therefore, if an attacker has hands-on control of a device then they can simply reset the router and then log in using the administrator default password. This is unfortunately a requirement as many people forget the login credentials and can no longer access the device to change the configuration or whatever. Therefore, the manufacturer has to provide a backdoor access in order for the consumer to reset any forgotten login details back to the defaults – hence the paperclip switch. Consequently, the manufactures' and security practitioners agree that once an attacker has physical control of the device the game is as good as over.

Earlier we highlighted cases whereby a consumer may be issued with a Wi-Fi router that has by default insecure security settings. Now the developers of consumer IoT devices may well argue that they supply the configuration option within the device to secure it adequately within the confines of the consumer's home. For example, if the IoT device is a Wi-Fi enabled toaster and it is used on an authenticated, secured and competently designed Wi-Fi network, with encryption then they would argue that they have applied diligent, reasonable and proportional levels of security with respect to appropriate threats and the worth of the asset. It is up to the customer to configure the device to securely join the home network.

However, the manufacturers might also claim. If their product is miss-used by being installed on an unsecured, unauthenticated, and unrestricted Wi-Fi network that propagates well beyond the boundary of the home then although their product would be able to join the open Wi-Fi network on its default settings, it is not their problem. They would argue any potential security breach is the customer's responsibility as they have failed to provide a secure home network environment.

Therefore, the manufacturer can always push their responsibility onto the customer, in much the same way that they do when selling children swimming toys or accessories. They would stand by the products capability if used within a swimming pool under adult supervision, but wave all responsibility if used in the sea, despite the fact their vendors are selling them at the beach and the product is decorated with images of dolphins, mermaids, clown fish and happy snappy crabs.

Despite this discrepancy, they do have a point for even if the manufacturer shipped a wireless router with say WPA2 enabled, which would require another default passphrase, and with clear instructions how to configure all the consumer's devices to use WPA2 – which is impractical – to use the default WPA2 credentials, would the consumer actually be any more secure?

Well they would in a way, because now on the secured Wi-Fi network the consumer's devices such as their smartphones, toasters and TVs, which are attempting to join the network would be challenged for authentication credentials such as the WPA2 passphrase. These devices simply would not be able to join the network without authentication and encryption correctly configured.

However, to install the product will be extremely difficult. Not only is it not an ideal solution it is actually no more secure, except from perhaps amateur attacks. Certainly, the data would be protected from casual snooping via eaves dropping. Unfortunately, any serious attacker would have enumerated the target device perhaps through port scanning to determine the make, model and OS via returned banner headers and then use the default WPA2 keys used by the manufacturer, which they would find on the web to decrypt the data. Subsequently, the solution would never stand up to any serious exploit. The problem of course is those lingering default passwords for both admin web access and now for WPA2 authentication and encryption will leave the device vulnerable and let's not forget that paperclip switch on the rear.

Passwords are the problem

Why are passwords a problem? Because they are especially inconvenient for sites that we frequently visit and very hard to remember for sites we rarely visit. Furthermore, by best practices passwords we are told should be complex, unique, difficult to guess, and randomly generated and consequently nigh on impossible to remember. However, there is an issue here, if we must have different passwords for each and every site that we need to log in to how are we possibly able to make them unique, easy to remember and without being guessable.

Consider for a second how every time you access a website you apparently do so without any authentication – an exchange of credentials – the site just becomes available and you have entry. This would be a severe security issue, so how do these sites manage access control transparently to the user?

It is done through a tiny software file located on the user's hard disk, this is why if you reformat or change devices you will be required to re-enter your original credentials. This is also the case if you reset your browser and select delete cookies including passwords. So, the password is contained within a cookie stored on the devices hard disk.

A cookie stores the user's login credentials and they are stored locally on the hard disk. What is more within this cookie, is all the web browsing history, sites visited and personal data that is then delivered to the relevant site as and when required.

Four main types of cookies

Session cookies are required to browse a web site or it would be a very poor experience as HTTP is stateless so every request would require the browser to re-enter their credentials and that would be a horrible experience. By using session cookies, the website and the user's browser exchange login information for the duration of that session.

However, there are also persistent cookies that survive longer than a single browsing session and maintain their stored credentials to enable users to revisit websites without having to login each subsequent visit. Persistent cookies are great for commonly visited sites where you do not wish to have the inconvenience of logging in every time, and were security isn't a major issue such as when accessing online media and news sites.

The problem is that within these cookies are the user's credentials and they are stored on the local device.

Another type of cookie is a secure cookie that encrypts its data and is used over HTTPS. Secure cookies expire at the end of the secure session so are ideal for secure sites such as online banking and ecommerce.

Finally, there is the third-party cookie, which isn't issued by the website but by a mechanism installed within the website by a third part typically a partner, affiliate or advertiser and we will discuss these types of cookies later under Privacy. However, for now it suffices to know that it is these third-party cookies that enable Google and Facebook to track people as they browse the web. This is done regardless whether the person subscribes to Facebook or uses a Google product or service.

Why are cookies important?

The main reason is that they contain the user credentials so if an attacker has physical access to a device they can potentially harvest the data and then spoof subsequent connections to the website. However, there are also privacy issues, for example on a shared machine, all the aggregated history and even the personal details of users can be seen. This of course is to be expected as one of the many purposes of the cookie is to help with filling out forms and such. The drawback can be on shared computers, for if another user was to browse to let us say Amazon all the currently logged in user's personal details, their name address, postal address and even their sales history and recent unfulfilled orders will be displayed.

However, here is the problem, commonly we accept this with shared home PCs where perhaps we do not have individual login accounts for each family member. In this situation then there will be obviously data leakage – but who creates individual accounts on a family PC – everyone just jumps on whenever they get the chance. Similarly, family members connect any device to the home network without a second thought. So, that begs the question, why we are so concerned with home IoT devices having weak security, and why worry about what the kettle is whistling to the toaster in clear text? After all, is it not all within the confines of the home?

After all is this even rational we have lived with computers for generations and social media for at least a decade so why now are we so concerned about the once treasured rights to privacy that we have so easily surrendered.

The simple answer is we cannot assume the attack surfaces for the IoT will be the same as for legacy PC hacks, threats and vulnerabilities. However, we can be assured that passwords will provide little defense. Everyone from early manufacturers of mainframes to developers of IoT devices recognizes the weakness, and hackers just love them. Yet passwords are still the favored method of authentication between not just humans and systems but systems to systems. So why is this when it is so clearly a weak link in security?

Hackers will claim with some satisfaction and justification that they can crack just around any password given the tools, motivation and time. However, it is not just them so can the government, police or anyone else suitably curious. Even using long strings of randomly generated alphanumeric codes for M2M authentication may seem unbreakable but in reality, they are still weak as the password has to be stored somewhere. Previously hardcoding passwords and URLs in firmware was sufficient as it was considered to be out with the threat boundary of cyber hacking. But not now as hackers are specifically targeting firmware by downloading the code to study and then uploading rogue versions in order to compromise the device. Even worse, storing the password into EEPROMS isn't even out of the reach of hackers. For hackers are now interrogating the electronics of target devices and harvesting the previously embedded and protected sensitive data such as passwords and encryption keys. An example of using electronic expertise to defeat security is the way a researcher defeated the Apple iPhone code that protected the iPhone 5. The way the iPhone data protection worked was not only was the phone data encrypted but it was protected by a pass-code. If an unauthorized user enters the code incorrectly ten times the phone automatically wipes all the encrypted data rendering the phone useless. However, despite the FBI paying over a reported million dollars to have someone hack into an iPhone 5 and allegedly for that price not even learning how the hack was accomplished. A computer scientist at Cambridge University in the UK, Dr. Sergei Skorobogatov managed to gain access to an iPhone 5c using electronics to clone the main memory chip of the iPhone. What he did was to clone the NAND chip containing the pass-code software, mounted a socket in its place to facilitate easily swapping the chip, and then simply worked his way through all the combinations possible. By changing the chip every six incorrect entries, to be on the safe side, he circumvented the lock out and deletes mechanism as he now had another six safe guesses before changing the chip once more.

It is beginning to be that nothing is out with the reach of suitably motivated people.

Chapter 12 – New Surface Threats

Hacking IoT Firmware

Hacking IoT devices is similar to hacking any other IT web site or application. However, there are many more attack surfaces, which we will describe in this next section. The obvious difference is the vast footprint of vulnerable devices – the diversity of things. In addition to this explosion of potential targets have also come increasingly large areas of surface to attack.

Previously security practitioners were reasonably comfortable with the traditional highly fortified bordered network, and then along came IP mobility and BYOD and that turned traditional security blueprints into waste paper. Consequently, more flexible borderless network architectures were required that could accommodate anywhere anytime on any device computing, and after an almighty struggle security came to accommodate this new business model. The IoT however has sprung another surprise, not just with its scale, its scope, the diversity of devices, but the vast new surface threats it presents. For example, as we will see later threat modeling is now an order of magnitude more complex and time consuming than previously, if done diligently. But the most interesting aspect of the new threat models is firmware and electronic engineering threats, as these are just way outside our comfort zone.

It shouldn't have come as any surprise when Kaspersky announced back in 2015 that they had discovered malware that targeted compromising the firmware of computers that would effectively be so persistent it could survive an OS reinstallation. This is because news of this esoteric attack vector had been going around since Snowden's revelations regarding the nefarious activities of NSA and their cousins GHCQ and their interest in compromising system firmware.

The benefits to hackers and governments alike, as there is no real distinction when they are involved in this type of activity, are to establish secret yet persistent and invisible control of a system. No anti-virus at the time was capable of checking firmware, which is unfortunate as it is the software that loads upon boot-up and effectively controls the OS and hardware driver loading processes. What is more because firmware had been overlooked as a potential attack vector in the PC ecosystem, many if not most manufacturers did not bother to encrypt or check the integrity of the boot loader firmware. Furthermore, there is lots of firmware on a PC or smartphone, every device has its own supporting firmware called drivers, which are also potential targets to hackers or snoopers making the potential threat surface even larger. In the IoT there is firmware everywhere, in webcams, USB devices, TVs, digital cameras and music players,

DOI 10.1515/9781501505775-015

it is ubiquitous as each electronic device requires firmware to operate. Because of the low price points, manufacturers and ODM suppliers do not cryptographically sign their firmware or have chips that could determine if it had been tampered with even if they did. Exceptions to this are smartphone such as Apple that have used secure boot for years to prevent such a potentially devastating attack. Off course an Apple iPhone has a price point that can make adding chips to verify the digital signature of the firmware files are correct before allowing them to load economically feasible. However, this is only an effective countermeasure on expensive products with sufficient profit margins unless the antivirus software vendors come up with an alternative solution. Despite this, even if the hardware manufacturers digitally signed their firmware updates with a hash that could be verified before loading onto the device would be a major step forward. However, that in itself is probably wishful thinking with consumer IoT as getting consumers to upgrade the firmware when required is considered an achievement asking them to verify the digital signature's hash value before downloading is probably asking too much.

However, saying that is unfair as most IoT early adopters are probably ahead of the field here as unauthorized firmware upgrades are available in forums online for most smart TVs. So how do these customized firmware upgrades come about?

The thing is that although customizing firmware sounds terribly electronic and difficult most developers will not go near the PCB lets alone the EEPROMS. What they do is simplicity itself; they simply download the firmware files from the manufacturer's website. Typically, the files aren't even encrypted and if they are it is using some very simple encryption such as Base64 which is broken in seconds. This seemingly insecure oversight is due to the CPU and other resource constraints on most low-end hardware devices, which prevents the manufacturer encrypting the hardware with something more robust like 16 block ciphers like AES. Once the developer has the firmware code unencrypted it is a case of customizing the code via editing -Though note this is by no means a trivial task to edit undocumented code but using an open source tool Binwalk does help a lot. Finally, the developer downloads the new firmware to the device. Of course, the preferred method is to simply download a customized firmware version from the forum that provides the changes and customizations you want and then upgrade the device.

Hackers of course are not looking for addition features so they tend to look for older firmware versions and to perform a retrograde firmware update particularly if there was a firmware version with known vulnerability.

However, what if the device's manufacturer has gone out of business and there is no website or active support forum. Then you have to get reverse-engineering the electronics to gain access to the firmware within EEPROMS on the PCB via the JTAG and UART debug pins. Locating these is usually not a problem on devices that are a few years old, however on modern devices 2015 onwards almost all reputable manufacturers have hidden the pins and disabled JTAG by default. However, it is still possible to reverse engineer the firmware even when they remove the markings from the chips.

Manufacturers' have been slow to react to this threat in a coordinated way however some are now starting to encrypt their firmware but again with only weak algorithms. Probably the most secure method is for manufacturers to take a more robust stance on firmware upgrades and prevent unauthorized access to write to the firmware. This could be done via an exchange of secret encryption keys held within secure chips on the device. Only authorized partners in possession of these secret keys could then download firmware upgrades to the device. This is probably the way things will play out but getting manufacturers to agree to this will take years. Therefore, for the foreseeable future, be prepared for more and more firmware attacks.

This potentially new threat surface is also not theoretical, there are already real world firmware attacks being carried out, and they are increasing exponentially as hackers realize the opportunity that they have been missing.

Possibly the most notorious firmware hack that has come to light was the work of the Equation Group using the hacking tools Grayfish and EquationDrug believed to have been developed by the NSA. These tools are designed to subvert the firmware of hard disk drives. By subverting the firmware of the hard disk drive the hackers can ensure that their exploit remains persistent even if the computer is formatted and the OS is reinstalled. By hiding in the firmware, the exploit module called "nls_933w.dll" was capable of reprogramming or reflashing the hard disk drives firmware, while remaining both stealthy and persistent. The exploit module was discovered by Kaspersky labs who realized that the module had other capabilities, such as being able to create hidden storage space on the hard drive where it could store any stolen data to avoid encryption.

What Kaspersky Labs discovered was that the exploit module targeted the hard drive disk controller's PCB, which is essentially a mini-computer, which includes a flash ROM (Read Only Memory) and firmware code for operating the hard drive.

When a machine is infected with either of the exploit modules EquationDrug or GrayFish, the module downloads from a command server the payload code.

Once it has the payload the module then flashes the firmware, replacing the existing firmware with a malicious version.

The Trojan exploit can survive software re-installs and even firmware upgrades. The only way to be sure to get rid of it is to bin the hard disk drive. The way that this worked was because hard disk manufacturers do not encrypt or digitally sign their firmware code. As there is no authentication check it means a malicious exploit module such as EquationDrug or GrayFish can easily re-flash the firmware without any checks being performed as to the veracity of the upgrade.

The strange thing about this hack was the way it worked as it didn't steal documents per se it hid them in service storage areas in the drive or in the unused memory in the ROM. Additionally as the firmware is active prior to the OS boot time it is possible that the exploit module manages to capture the encryption password during boot time and store it in the secure area of unused memory.

Probably more frightening was the fact that the module was capable of re-flashing the firmware of more than a dozen different hard drive brands, including IBM, Seagate, Western Digital, and Toshiba.

What this hack did make clear was the IoT was facing many more attack surfaces than say IT or Industrial Control systems and security practitioners would really have to review their methodologies, vulnerability assessments and threat models in order to defend against these increasingly large attack vectors.

The one thing that we have to understand is that IoT security does not equate to device security and this is why it will be so hard to evaluate an individual device's security level and after rigorous testing award it a certification as a robust and secure IoT device. Instead, it makes more sense to evaluate each device within its network habitat and then consider what external and internal factors are possibly affecting its behavior, performance and ultimately its security.

As an example, if we were to take an IoT white box device, unbranded and possibly even unidentified how could a security practitioner go about assessing the relative security capability of that device within its current network.

Now there are a few alternative ways to go about this; and there is no wrong or right way it is down simply to what works best for the practitioner. Some security practitioners prefer to use a list approach for example by checking the device against the top known vulnerabilities and looking to see if anything stands out. An alternative approach is to check known threats, such as those that have recently hit the news and then running an online vulnerability scanner against the device. A third, more thoughtful method is to question the purpose, functionality of the device and think what worst case scenarios could happen and then test these scenarios against the device to ensure these are likely to be improbable.

If considering the list, approach then the ideal place to start is the OWASP top 10 IoT vulnerability list as this regularly updated site lists vulnerability and threats specifically targeting the IoT. Furthermore, potential attack surfaces are mapped to vulnerabilities that are subsequently mapped to threats. This ideally is what we want to identify the actual attack surfaces that present themselves to an attack, because all these new and unusual attack surfaces that we may not be familiar with need to be considered when securing devices as diverse as the IoT things. However, even IoT systems will have some shared common attack surfaces that we must identify and make sure that we check thoroughly and do not overlook, as they are not the standard IT attack surfaces.

The way that security practitioners do this is to go through a number of logical steps testing the device against each major threat group at a time while checking of each attribute within each group as being either compliant or noncompliant.

A comprehensive list of attack surfaces that was presented by Daniel Miessler at Def Con 23 and he suggests that there should be the following attack surface classes with some of their individual attributes as shown below;

Access control
– Authentication
– Session management
– Implicit trust between components
– Enrolment secure processes
– Decommissioning secure processes
– Lost access-processes

Device memory
– Clear text username
– Clear text passwords
– Third part credentials
– Encryption keys

Physical interface assessment
– Firmware extraction
– User CLI
– Admin CLI
– Privilege escalation
– Reset to insecure state

Device web interface
- SQL Injection
- Cross-site scripting
- Username enumeration
- Weak passwords
- Account lock out
- Known credentials

Device firmware
- Hardcoded passwords
- Sensitive URL disclosure
- Encryption keys

Device network services
- Information disclosure
- User CLI
- Admin CLI
- Injection
- Denial of Service

Administrative web interface
- SQL injection
- Cross-site scripting
- Username enumeration
- Weak passwords
- Account lock out
- Known credentials

Local data storage
- Unencrypted data
- Data encrypted with recovered keys
- Lack of data integrity checks

Cloud web interface
- SQL injection
- Cross-site scripting
- Username enumeration

- Weak passwords
- Account lock out
- Known credentials

Third party back-end APIs
- Unencrypted PII sent
- Encrypted PII sent
- Device information leaked
- Location leaked

Update mechanism
- Updates sent unencrypted
- Updates not hash signed
- Source location writable

Mobile application
- Implicitly trusted by device and cloud
- Known credentials
- Insecure data storage
- Lack of transport encryption

Vendor back-end API
- Inherent trust of cloud or mobile application
- Weak authentication
- Weak access control
- Injection attacks

Ecosystem communications
- Health checks
- Heartbeats
- Ecosystem commands
- Decommissioning
- Update pushes

Network traffic
- LAN traffic
- LAN to Internet
- Non-standard
- Short range

Part III: **Architecting the Secure IoT**

The objectives of this section are to introduce IoT architecture principles, by explaining what an IoT design is, how it can be built and how it differs from closely related M2M designs. Furthermore we will examine why we build IoT as we do and what IoT actually means for architects. The section will introduce many of the new tools, techniques and protocols that are available, and how to utilize them within a modern IoT system-design. Finally, and most importantly as far as this book is concerned consider the security concerns and explain the risks that we can mitigate through introducing the concept of threat maps.

DOI 10.1515/9781501505775-016

Chapter 13 – Designing the Secure IoT

In this chapter, we will discuss why designing for the IoT differs in some respects to building traditional IT architectures. We will consider the scale, scope and communication challenges that present themselves and show how we can use IoT models to build proof of concept models. Further we will discuss the choice of communication patterns and when they are best suited to particular design situations. Additionally, we will look at some design first principles for the IoT.

What the reader will learn from this chapter:
1. Why designing the IoT differs from IT & M2M architectures
2. What tools and techniques are available for IoT
3. Understand the IoT communication patterns
4. How to build IoT proof of concept models
5. Understand the IoT design first principles
6. What makes designing for the IoT different?

Architecting the IoT presents some unique challenges and creates some problems that require a different approach in technique or in design perspective to solve them. Currently the IoT market is vast and growing daily. The available IoT solutions are also appearing at Internet speed. Only three years ago the prospect of building an IoT network supporting millions of devices, deployed around the globe, with each triggering and transmitting tiny messages to a common host for real-time data analysis and long term storage would have been an onerous and expensive task. Nowadays, there has been advancement in cloud services for both compute and storage. IoT deployments and services are offered almost worldwide by cloud service providers; therefore, architecting this type of network would be almost trivial in comparison to the same task back in 2013.

To realize just how advanced these services have become architects have to consider why designing for the IoT differs from traditional IT architectures. Also, they must consider why IoT differs even from industrial control systems of which IoT is very closely related. The IoT and industrial M2M (machine-to-machine) share many foundations, features and design principles. The major difference is as the name suggests in the case of IoT in its reliance on the Internet. This is not to say that M2M did not utilize the Internet, of course it did but it just wasn't a core design pre-requisite. Another, key difference is the scale of the IoT vision. With M2M the principle was to build interconnecting machines and systems for control, communication and machine-learning purposes predominantly within a closed secure network.

DOI 10.1515/9781501505775-017

M2M is not just about machine and process control or data collection through telemetry it also strives to analyze the data to provide better knowledge of the process. M2M therefore is not just telematics. Indeed, M2M also strives to deliver through analysis insight and knowledge, which provides the ability to adapt the process to improve the system.

The IoT in industry, or rather the IIoT (industrial Internet of things), expands on the M2M design philosophy by potentially extending the scope of the design from the closed network out to encompass the vast knowledge of the Internet. By encompassing the Internet as a source of data and intelligence, IoT expands beyond the limitations of M2M and is an open system. Furthermore, IoT consumes the vast amounts of resources that the cloud makes available in compute, network, storage and analytical tools. Additionally, IoT enables M2M to evolve to become less insular and allow strategies such as Industry 4.0 which strives to encompass not just the factory but the entire supply and value chains. The goal is to scale beyond the network efficiencies and benefits to encompass partners, suppliers and even customers, which provides opportunity to develop new revenue streams and profits.

Of course, the most outstanding feature of the IoT is that its scale is so vast covering industry, commerce, transport, enterprise, communications, retail, agriculture, health care, education, research, tourism, and just about every aspect of our lives through consumer products and services. In all of these diverse applications there is one conceptual purpose of IoT and that is to produce benefit through the interconnectivity of things – just about anything can be a thing – to produce insight from data which facilitates informed action. That is the overwhelming benefit of the IoT concept.

The IoT can create knowledge from everyday interactions from seemingly innocuous sources and useless data that is often seen as a waste product and ordinarily often discarded. Machine learning is an integral part of IoT and that facilitates distilling knowledge from raw data. However, IoT has also found much more mundane usage such as in logistics, in facilitating the transfer of goods and service from third parties via cloud service providers.

As a result, in the consumer market the IoT offers the potential to provide products that are vastly more affordable and capable that those installed on the device itself. The consumer device does not host the intelligence but the connectivity tools required to reach a cloud based application. Residing within the cloud is a shared repository of data and software for the consumer application that runs on almost limitless compute, storage and memory shared resources. This efficient usage of shared resources enables products and services that would not have been feasible to produce only a decade ago.

There are of course many differences as to the architectural approach to industrial or consumer IoT designs, the relative importance of high-availability, real-time performance, and management and reporting are just a few, but security and safety should not be amongst them. To ensure that sufficient planning and resources have been allocated to security and safety during the architectural design process it is helpful to review how IoT networks are designed. Furthermore, what services that is available and popularly utilized to provide state of the art functionality at feasible cost.

IoT from an Architect's View-Point

The scale of the IoT is not just in the number of potential devices connecting to the Internet it is also in its breadth the way it spreads over all those vertical segments that were listed earlier. In addition, within each vertical market is a further host of specializations and use-cases with vastly different design requirements. However, all these vast number of smart applications and use cases that have arisen also require supporting services and that drives further innovation and creativity.

Technology startups and the open source community provide tools and solutions. Hence what we are actually seeing is just the start, as each new popular use-case for IoT will generate a plethora of supporting devices, applications, tools and services.

Modeling the IoT

When considering the specific design that an IoT architect must take into account, the potentially huge number of devices initially springs to mind. This is simply because most IoT applications will require a huge number of 'things' to be connected. Fortunately, in most proof of concept (POC) models, the architect only has to deal with a manageable amount that are enough to prove the applications principle functionality. Unfortunately, in the real world POC's if designed too well have a nasty tendency to become the first iteration in the design production cycle. This can lead developers or architect to believe that their purely conceptual model is correct and will soon be winging it way into production and expected to support millions of devices. Therefore, at every stage in the design process the architect needs to consider 'how many things can this design support?'

Another area that has the capability to grow extremely quickly is storage capacity. In the proof of concept process, certain data sources and structures, may have been identified and even scaled and analyzed to calculate the storage requirements. However, the design requirements can change rapidly as the project moves from POC to actual design and suddenly many more stakeholders start to engage with the project and suggest their inputs. Identifying data types is a major issue as the architect must choose the correct type of storage and to do that they need to ascertain the type of data being collected and the original sources.

Capacity requirement changes come about throughout the project, even the products development cycle may change, especially within an agile framework. Where initially the data and data types were fixed and conformed to an SQL schema, fixed rows and columns, there could be a change in requirements for instance to scrape data from social media sites, chat, video and photos and data would then need to be stored in unstructured formats. Of course, storing multimedia data would necessitate a different approach to data storage, such as NoSQL (not only SQL).

Similarly, the amount and type of data has to be taken into consideration, and importantly the architect requires an understanding of what the client expects from this data. One of the nuances of the IoT is the devices are capable of generating vast amounts of data, most of which may be useless. For instance, a typical device may send out every ten seconds or so simply a hello packet to inform the host that it is still alive and kicking.

Similarly, the device, if it is a sensor may send back a simple reading for example, 'the Temperature is 30 degrees', but it will send this out every second depending on the sensitivity and requirements of the application within the design. The application may not require this data, it has been told thousands of times already, it may simply require knowing when a change occurs or a threshold reached. In these situations, the data may not be required to be sent across the WAN network to storage, it may not even be required to pass further than the local connected hub in the WSN (wireless sensor network) or the proximity edge networks.

Restricting the transport of unnecessary data can preserve bandwidth, mitigate many network issues regarding packet delay, jitter and packet loss and produce a more responsive and alert system. If no due diligence is shown regards the potential of escalating data traffic, then IoT can be very unforgiving. As more and more devices join the network all that data traffic can soon overwhelm network links certainly in remote locations using low powered and constrained devices.

Furthermore, transporting unnecessary data can waste more than just available bandwidth it can also provide noise and unnecessary delays and effort for real-time data processing and analytics. The more useless data crossing unfiltered across the wire or air, simply makes identifying and analyzing the signal from the noise more difficult and consequently more error prone.

IoT architects should work with the clients to ascertain what data requires to be forwarded, and what can be filtered so as to relieve network congestion. Similarly, which data is to be analyzed in real-time and which information can be stored and analyzed via batch jobs at a later time. After all there is despite its relatively cheap price in comparison to just a few years ago still a finite amount of storage space available, and it is neither efficient nor financially prudent to go wasting it storing data that just has no value.

Therefore, planning for sufficient amounts and type of data and where to store or terminate them is not so simple. There is also the question of how to transport them to suitable processing points, for example to the local, edge or cloud processing unit can be a very risky business. If the application proves successful then current bandwidth, processing and storage demands could become exhausted very quickly and providing more resources will become a perpetual and ultimately exhausting game of catch up.

IoT communication patterns

There are device communication patterns that are relevant to IoT architects, and these reflect the way the end-node devices work and the type of data they are generating. Typically, devices will be installed in order to perform one of a few functions such as, telemetry or for automated control. The function that the devices perform and their functional role within the overall system often determines the data flow and type of information they generate to the architect. Generally, there are four device communication patterns.

1. *Telematics* – This is perhaps the simplest form of unidirectional communications as the device, typically a sensor – a passive component – simply relays environmental conditions such as temperature or speed up to a connecting hub or controller. Often these sensors are hard wired as they have no radio components as their general requirements are to be cheap, small and passive.

2. *Inquiries* – This mode of operation works similarly and often in much the same type of situations and applications to the telematics mode. However, with inquiries mode, the communication channel is bidirectional, though the design envisages the majority of traffic flowing from the device, there is the capability for traffic flowing from an interrogating controller back to the device. For example, the device could work in either push or pull style of operation where the device either pushed data out from an embedded sensor

continuously or the application or the controller could pull the information it required, only when it needed. Furthermore, the inquiries mode of operation can also be used in deploying actuators as the bi-communication channel permits the controller to initiate actions, such as to shut down or start up a process.

3. *Commands* – This bi-directional mode of operations typical supports operations where the priority and volume of data flow is from the controller to the device. This style of operation is often deployed in control and monitoring scenarios where a device responds to control signals from an application or system, for example controlling a drone. The reverse channel is required for feedback and acknowledgements from the device to the controller.

4. *Notifications* – this in a single directional communication channel and as its name suggests is used to provide notifications to the device from the system or from external systems. It is typically used in designs were a device or a group of devices require to know the status or change of status from another application, system or group of devices.

When designing IoT networks another potential trap in architecting IoT systems is the vague security requirements. Fortunately, in most vertical disciplines such as commerce and health care, that is certainly not the case as there are stringent security compliance requirements that are auditable and punishment for non-compliance will be severe. So, onerous are the potential punishments for deliberate and willful non-compliance, the CEO (chief executive officer) and CFO (chief financial officer) can face prison sentences.

Unfortunately, in the consumer market, there are no legislations or industry standards. Furthermore, as the IoT has no formal national boundaries and is global in its theoretical and planned scale there are unlikely to be any in the foreseeable future. Therefore, with no legal restraints or industry peer pressure IoT products in the consumer market are in many cases coming to market with little or no security features build into the design. One of the reason this is so prevalent is that many devices are being produced by companies with vast technical knowledge but with little concept of security. For instance, they do have the knowledge and can see the rationale regards securing the device but not the system. Consequently, they will perhaps spend time and money on securing the physical product but not on any threat modeling that would highlight failures in the smartphone app, cloud, or the transport security. Therefore, IoT architects have by necessity to perform their own threat modeling for the entire system from end to end.

In the previous chapter, we covered IoT specific architectural issues, with regards; devices, storage, security, data size, and end-to-end integration. We looked at some of the issues and at some real-world examples of where the best laid architectural plans can become unstuck. In this chapter, we will move on to consider what first principles we can utilize to solve many of these IoT architectural concerns. For example, we will map techniques to problem areas and then look at each in turn.

First IoT design principles

The areas of concern with regards IoT architectures can be attributed to a few well-known areas of operation that we can categorize into five main groups. The relative importance of some of these categories will vary depending on the vertical market such as in Industry, Health Care or the Consumer markets. Therefore, the groups are presented with no particular order of importance or preference.

- *Addressing* – Regardless of the device, whether it be a $0.20 temperature sensor or a cyber-physical device, such as a robot costing millions of dollars, they will still need to be individually and uniquely addressed. Furthermore, they have to be addressed in another sense, which is to be communicated with either directly and if that isn't feasible via a proxy or for the data to be stored and collected when communications are possible. This is often the case in space exploration where devices may sleep for long periods until they receive direct sunlight to charge their batteries and power their radio transmitters. However even in extremely expensive, high availability networks there are addressability issues in the way information is transmitted that is efficient and that will allow the communication of information to be disseminated across a vast number of devices in a fair manner. For example, in the case of a financial trading system, all the client devices will have to get published financial-data almost simultaneously. TCP/IP would be simply to slow and unfair on the devices way down the list of order. UDP or multicast would be fairer as all devices would have a fairer chance of getting the information at the same time.
- *Scale* – the IoT architecture is designed to scale and as storage and data transporting capacity particularly can have heavy appetites for their respective resources IoT architects must provide solutions to these capacity planning problems. Therefore, to that end architects must build in the flexibility for the network to scale on demand.
- *Connectivity* – Collecting vast quantities of information can result in quality of service issues such as delay, jitter, packet loss and other performance issues

as a result of network congestion. Importantly this is an even greater concern how with the prevalence of radio network, which by their nature are half duplex communication channels. This means that although the traffic is broadcast on a shared media, over the air over a specific frequency and channel, and all devices will hear pretty much simultaneously, only one device can actually transmit at a time. Network congestion can more readily occur as devices must store data they wish to transmit and forward it when they get a chance to communicate. Similarly, in WSN remote networks where devices are constrained by a lack of power, irregular and unreliable communications media, or inclement weather – remember in the US and EU, power and communications are expected and demanded 24/7, but in the rest of the world that is an unlikely expectation that is rarely delivered.

– *Data Storage* – One thing common to most IoT architectures is they collect data and they do so very efficiently, and the more devices are added to the network the more data is collected and it grows exponentially with a graphical representation that resembles a reversed ice hockey stick. Growth of this magnitude can get out of control very quickly and overwhelm any spare capacity that was planned into the network. Furthermore, it just isn't feasible to keep storing more and more data unless it serves an identifiable purpose.

– *Devices* – The devices are typically the first thing that spring to mind when envisaging the consumer Internet of things and we thing about desirable objects like Nest thermostats, or the latest waterproof Fitbit fitness bands that can now we used in the pool when doing the morning swim laps. In the industry, the devices that come to mind more likely to be futuristic style devices such as the cyber physical equipment that control an automated production line or robots working within process stages along the production line.

In order to solve these architectural issues IoT architects can use some well-known design patterns, which conveniently map to each category as we can see below;

– *Addressing* – Publish/Subscribe method:

– *Scale* – Cloud hosting services: Hosted cloud services are one of the underpinning technologies that accelerated the IoT from a theoretically interesting concept into the fast-moving technology there is today. Cloud services were the enablers for many startup operations that have provided social media and IoT services, tools and products. The IoT and social media would be a poorer place today without these innovative companies that have provided so much value to the market through their products and services. However, few of these companies would have flourished or even been able to build and test pilot services had they not been able to use affordable resource available for rental from the huge cloud provider's networks. Paying for only the resources they used, startups no longer had to spend capital on over-provisioned networks, servers and storage, they could just way for what they used and the networks added resources well and only when they were required. As a result, the network, servers, and storage stretched elastically, growing by adding resources when needed to cope with a surge and removing resources when the demand fell.

–   *Connectivity* – Queues: The problem with architecting for the IoT is that it is difficult to guaranteed connectivity under all circumstances to all potential devices. To compound the problem the Internet market is world-wide but the prevalence of reliable and affordable communication technologies across even developed nations cannot always be taken for granted. In many parts of the world, the 24-hour power supply that many take for granted is not available, let alone Internet access or mobile telephony. However, even in industrial developed nations reliable and persistent connectivity will be an issue. For example, there may be sensors on packages in a Logistics IoT use case, which enable them to be traced along their journey. However, trains go through tunnels, through remote rural areas and around mountains that may well disrupt the sensors' connectivity to the mobile networks signal – albeit temporarily. In another use-case it might not be financial feasible or even necessary to have a permanent Internet connection for remote devices or gateways as queuing methods can ensure that data is stored and queued ready for sending once a connection becomes available. An example would be vending machines selling consumer confectionary and cold drinks. The profit margins possibly do not stretch to the cost of mobile monthly data plans or ADSL fixed line broadband, certainly the amount of bandwidth required by the application will not require this level of service. Queuing solves this problem by sending the data only when there is a requirement such as once a day to upload daily sales figures or immediately if a stock threshold is breached. The benefits of queuing are that the application can send when required so can make a very short call saving costs. By working this way many mobile networks have M2M service plans that are much cheaper than consumer data plans as they are designed with short call durations and very small bandwidth for transmitted and received data as the operational characteristics.

–   *Data storage* – Cloud storage: Utilizing a cloud storage service is the prefect elastic, flexible and financially viable solution to the problem of determining data storage capacity. This doesn't mean that capacity planning regards data storage can be ignored it simply means that it is no longer as dangerous as available storage will be made available if and when there is a requirement so the application will not fail or the system crash.

- *Device capabilities* – AMQP (Advanced Message Queuing Protocol) and MQTT (Message Queuing Telemetric Transport) are two of the newer transport protocols that are lightweight and designed to work on con-strained devices with very limited CPU, storage and memory and run from a battery and use low power radio technologies.

Chapter 14 – Secure IoT Architecture Patterns

In this chapter, we will dive deeper into IoT design and how we use modular functional building-blocks to construct an overall secure IoT architecture. We will discuss each functional area, its requirements and how we can fulfill them. We will learn how to pick and mix functionality blocks to provide the best technology for each purpose. Additionally, we will be introduced to threat models and how we can apply them to build security into the design.

What the reader will learn in this chapter:
1. Basic IoT architecture
2. Functional areas (device connectivity, event processing and data management, presentation)
3. Basic building blocks used to construct IoT
4. Threat modeling and building security into the mix

When considering the various building blocks typically used in IoT architecture, it can be helpful to reference the diagram (Fig. 1 – IoT Architecture). Not all of the building boxes may be required as it is often a pick and mix approach to select the functional units required. However, a brief description of the diagram and its individual functional units follows:

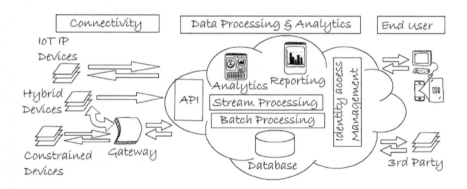

Fig. 1: IOT Architecture

DOI 10.1515/9781501505775-018

The devices and data source, are in a section of the architecture, which will be generally dictated by the type of IoT function. For instance, we need to consider whether it is a brownfield or green-field deployment. In a green-field (new) installation the architect may have more opportunity to dictate the type of devices and technologies but more importantly their connectivity and protocols. So for instance, in a green field enterprise IoT project they might be able select native IP devices that can directly support an IPv6 or the 6LowPAN stack. Alternatively, in a brownfield deployment or where device choice is restricted by availability of existing technologies and protocols, some devices may not be available with native IP support. In that case protocol gateways in the data transport section will be required to translate and aggregate the heterogeneous traffic from sources onto a common IP output.

In remote installations where reliable power and connectivity may not be an option for example in agriculture where IoT devices may number in the thousands and be deployed over hundreds of acres such as where sensors and actuators are deployed as irrigation units. Then the architect will require constrained devices designed for low power, hence low radio transmission and with low CPU, memory and storage to reduce price and preserve battery energy. Constrained devices will typically also require utilizing the hubs or gateways power to enable communication. Furthermore, in order to provide the connectivity via the passive access network to the IP driven Event and Data Processing units the signal will have to go through a translational process.

The design will have data transport building blocks, which will provide granular services such as an event hub, which is a type of dedicated service bus. As a result, there will most likely be services dedicated to heterogeneous protocols after all it might not be solely IP that is transported. In addition, there may also be requirements for other connector services for external data sources such as non-IP protocols such as Bluetooth.

Event and data processing

The building block of event and data processing provides the event handling and data processing and analysis functions that may be required in the IoT architecture. There will be for instance a data ingestion module which may be a publish/subscribe pattern, which will handle large scale data connections – 1 million publishers – in terms of numbers and aggregated bandwidth at the ingress – 1Gb per second.

Ingestion modules are designed for tiny transactions, messages of less than 1KB but they can handle perhaps a trillion a month. They may also handle the encryption/decryption of data and pass this through to an event handling module for rapid processing. The event handling modules manage the integration with other modules to provide IAM (identity and Access Management) a vital security mechanism, required to provide assurance of the identity and authenticity of the device and determining the devices role within the system and the devices explicit access privileges. The event handler also manages the flow of data between the storage and analytic modules as some data will require real-time streaming analytics whereas others will be stored and analyzed in batch mode at an appropriate time. Other key function modules are the provisioning API's as devices need to be on boarded, registered and configured for their role within the system and will be done via an external specialist system which will integrate with the IoT system IAM modules via APIs. An IT enterprise example of this type of provisioning and device management that may be familiar is the way security manages devices such as mobiles and tablets in a BYOD (bring your own device) environment. Here a Mobile Application Management System handles the functions of device provisioning and registration while integrating with the security IAM systems to enforce identity and access management.

The breakdown of each of these building blocks to granular services will depend on the design and application but some of the storage services may be decided based upon whether to use a SQL database, an unstructured NoSQL DB, or a table/blob form of storage. There may also be requirements to support external data sources.

The analysis modules breakdown into services such as open-source products such as Storm that manage streaming analysis and Spark that handles in-memory batch analysis on local Hadoop distributed data clusters. However, data analytic services are far more scalable when provided by cloud services especially for services supporting diverse analytical needs for machine learning, or services that support Hadoop's HDInsight and Storm. Therefore, the options may be to store data locally on Hadoop distributed clusters but scale the analytics to the cloud, a better alternative in a Greenfield deployment is to push storage and analytics out to the cloud. Then storage becomes trivial as cloud storage can scale from terabytes to petabytes and do this very cost effectively on demand.

In any system architecture, there has to be a way to view the current system status and run reports against historical data so the charts provide the information for data visualization, reporting and presentation. The vital services required for providing the reporting functionality come from the services that we build that are dedicated to providing real-time operational dashboards and management dashboards. It is this valuable information that can be aggregated and analyzed to produce business intelligence.

In the next chapter, we will discuss threat models, what they are and how they can benefit security practitioners. We will learn the principles behind the threat model and how we can benefit from using them during the design period to flag and map potential threats. Later we will learn how and when to create threat maps and to apply them within the development process. After considering the theoretical usage of threat maps we can then apply what has been learned to the IoT architecture framework that we developed in the previous chapter to identify threats and the boundaries of trust.

The Internet of Things (IoT) presents unique security, trust, and privacy challenges unlike more conventional web based solutions. Unlike traditional web applications where security, trust and privacy issues are well understood and are mitigated through well documented security best-practices. Also, these best-practices are designed into a mature software life cycle development. In contrast IoT concerns regarding security, privacy and trust are relatively new and not well understood by the software, firmware and hardware designers that collaborate to design IoT products.

Protecting IoT solutions requires designing security into the product from the very beginning of the products development life cycle. By introducing security within the conceptual architectural design provides the most effective method for securing every step of the process. Potential threats and vulnerabilities can be identified in the software, firmware and hardware and change introduced to mitigate these at an early stage, which is far more efficient, in terms of money, effort and development timeline.

Chapter 15 – Threat Models

In this chapter, we discuss Threat Models in detail, what they are and how we use them to provide secure designs. We will consider the design principles and stages of threat modeling and how we apply these techniques to the conceptual framework of the design to ensure that security is by design. Later we will show how to use the six-step approach to threat modeling and learn about more advanced IoT specific threat models and how to apply them to design frameworks.

In this chapter the reader will learn:
1. What are threat models
2. How to we apply threat models
3. The 6 steps to building threat models
4. Advanced threat models
5. IoT vulnerabilities & threats

Once the architects have proposed a conceptual framework for the design the next step is to use this blueprint as the basis for a threat model. A threat model is the starting point for introducing the product's security development lifecycle and evaluating the possible threats and vulnerabilities against the design framework. Only by examining each stage of the architecture, the proposed devices, interfaces, services and trust boundaries can we start to evaluate the security effectiveness of the proposed architecture.

What are threat models?

The purpose of a threat model is very straightforward, and it is simply a paper exercise to identify threats and vulnerabilities that an attacker might use to compromise the system. The greatest value derived by performing threat modeling is within the design stage of the products development lifecycle. Constructing a threat model early in the design phase forces the whole design team to buy into and engage in the product's security development process. By discussing and reviewing the system/products security requirements at the planning stage enables the team to reach a consensus of opinion. This may prove difficult but finding solutions and making changes at this stage, when all that requires is making a few icon changes in a drawing is far better than the alternative. By having the design team address potential security issues during the early design phase is

DOI 10.1515/9781501505775-019

extremely important as later retrofitting security into the product will be expensive if it is even viable. The potentially large number of devices in an IoT network could make reloading the firmware on every single device difficult; the disruption to the network intolerable and during these periods of instability even put the network at greater risk.

Designing a threat model

A threat model is a structured document that's purpose is to stimulate dialogue within the design team regarding the proposed security measures and their purpose as a holistic solution, however they do need to concentrate in specific areas. The key areas to concentrate on when threat modeling are the proposed security and privacy features, and any other features that should they fail cause a security or privacy issue as well as features that are at the edge of trust boundaries. These trust boundaries are designated points where data transitions from one data source or owner to another. At the transition point the data could be vulnerable to many types of vulnerabilities that threaten the three tenets of data security, confidentiality, integrity and availability. Trust boundaries are subject to specific threats and re prime points for potential attack, for example, escalation of privileges, tampering, spoofing, denial-of-service, repudiation and loss of confidentiality.

6 steps to threat modeling

Threat modeling is composed of six steps which are:
1. Model the system, in this case we are using the IoT architecture framework
2. Identify the attack surfaces or vectors
3. Identify trust boundaries
4. Enumerate the threats and vulnerabilities
5. Mitigate the threats and vulnerabilities or accept the risk
6. Validate the countermeasures

In the threat model diagram (Fig. 2), the simplified IoT architecture has been rendered into a threat model with the zones and trust boundaries highlighted. The four zones are the device, network, infrastructure and the interface. Having identified each zone in the architecture reference diagram, the task now is to try to identify attack surfaces within each zone and object or service – remember IoT security is not just about securing the device but taking a holistic approach to system security.

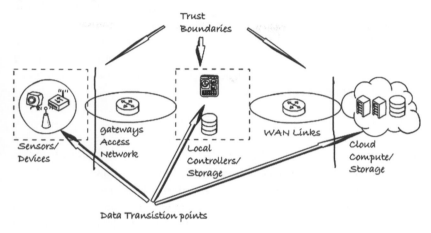

Fig. 2: IoT Threat Model

Now that the IoT security zones have been identified the next task is to remunerate threats and potential vulnerabilities within the devices, objects and services within each of the zones taking special case to consider data transition points at the trust-boundaries.

There are several techniques for doing this, some people use lists of known potential threats, other use lists provided by security forms or organizations such as OWASP, which produces a top-ten of IoT threats and vulnerabilities. Other security practitioners use their own formula based on knowledge and experience. The latter option is viable if the person has experience working in a specific area of IoT. For example, a security practitioner or process engineer working in a manufacturing plant as they can bring their detailed experience and knowledge to check for very specific threats and vulnerabilities not on the top ten lists. Whatever method is used the point is to study the potential attack vectors that an attacker may use to compromise an asset or the system. By becoming familiar with the common threats associated with each functional zone in the system, the security practitioner can gain insight and understanding as to how these specialized modules function and their inherent strengths and weakness.

Advanced IoT threats

Now that the security zones in the reference architecture have been identified, associated threats and vulnerabilities can be mapped to each zone.

Security vulnerabilities that exist today within the IoT are often different from traditional IT or OT systems. For example, one major group of threats that are new and specific to the IoT concern advanced physical threats, which relate to electronic re-engineering of the device.

Devices

- *Physical security* – the device must be physically protected from theft, denial of service, tampering, vandalism or physical re-engineering
- *Identity* – With IoT systems' especially those with remote devices such as field sensors it is imperative that the system can verify the devices identity via authentication and manage access control by role based access rules.
- *Data privacy* – data must be protected both at rest in the device and in transit this included within configuration files and local firmware and storage. This is a major difference to laptop and PC security where electronic hacking of the electronics on the PCB was never considered, despite in the case of a PC being far easier to access than many IoT devices. The target for those probing the hardware UART, ROM and EEPROMS is to discover encryption keys or sensitive hardcoded passwords and URLs. By compromising the physical security of the device and getting hands on access means it is probably only a matter of time until the hacker can compromise the security, typically by breaking the encryption which protects the data at rest and in travel.
- *Network security* – Threats and vulnerabilities that target devices over the air or wire are within the domain of network security. Network security is a vast and highly complex area but attacks normally are initiated through intelligence gathering such as by running port scanners or vulnerability scanners against the device. These scanners will look for open ports and services and check them against a list of known vulnerabilities. It is not unusual for devices to run very early versions of Linux or Android and these can return volumes of data on unpatched flaws and potential vulnerabilities.
- *Firmware* – Attacks on firmware again is a relatively new vector but doesn't necessarily require the detailed technical skills of electronic re-engineering. This is because not all firmware upgrades are considered to be malicious – though they certainly would not be authorized – as device user communities often post up hacked firmware that improves the functionality of a device,

such as a smart TV for example. However, any third- party firmware attack is a serious threat as it can cause denial of service and even destroy the device.

– *Firmware upgrade* – The threat of firmware upgrades is harder to define as if it is coming from the manufacturer then it can be just as troublesome as from an attacker. IT professionals will no doubt testify to the severity of problems brought about by authorized upgrades. For instance, a loss of power or Internet connectivity is enough to crash the machine causing damage irreparable over the Internet.

– *Data collection* – this is a major privacy concern that is becoming more prevalent in IoT as devices collect and generate a lot of data by design. Where and how that data is sent and secured are privacy vulnerabilities.

– *Backdoor* – The threat of backdoors is extremely worrying in the IoT as devices can be easily compromised and in certain industries such as health care and financial services, the loss of personal health or financial data could result in severe penalties. The danger with backdoors is that many are generated by malware but these are more easily discovered and eradicated by anti-malware software. However, there is no anti-malware software for many IoT devices and as many IoT applications run in secure sandbox OS, it would be ineffective anyway. The more challenging aspect of backdoors are those made during software or firmware development, or worse planted by governments or national security organizations – for they might never be detected.

– *SSL-certification* – SSL is still open to several threats despite them having received huge public media attention, many servers still are vulnerable to Heartbeat and Poodle and few handle pinning effectively which puts at risk encrypted data over the network.

– *Self-discovery protocols* – Another unintentional threat and vulnerability is how promiscuous many protocols are, an example is the UPnP protocol, which is wonderful for connecting devices in a trusted home network, the problem is through it trust anything attached to the same network without any authorization. Self-discovery protocols need to be identified and evaluated as to their purpose.

Networks

– *Low capabilities constraints* – denial of service techniques are the scourge of resource-constrained networks as bandwidth, CPU, memory and most importantly battery life can be overwhelmed preventing the device from working.

- **Port scan** – Port scanning tools are also free and easy to use when intelligence gathering prior to a network attack, to enumerate the network, retrieve banners and find listening services on open ports.
- **Data injection** – High quality Network analysis tools are available which are open source which allow attackers to capture and edit and replay packet streams by injecting them back into the packet stream. If some applications do not check or use sequence numbers, then passwords login attempts can be captured and then simply replayed without the trouble of having to decrypt the user login or password.
- **Lack of encryption** – Devices very often used to have no encryption of the traffic on the data transport level with HP finding in 2014 that as many as 70% of IoT devices they tested did not use encryption such as TLS.
- **BTF vulnerabilities** – Behind the firewall vulnerabilities are issues that are prevalent on the local network, such as unauthenticated pairing using UPnP, port scanning from malware on a compromised PC or worm infestations. The list of BTF vulnerabilities is large due to the trusted nature of devices within the local network especially in the consumer market.
- **Web proxies and hubs** – An associated vulnerability with using proxies is the Forwarded-For header can be used to spoof IP addresses under certain conditions. Similarly, the attacker may use Trace to see what is being sent to the server by the proxy and thereby gain understanding of how to copy the secret communications between proxy and server to bypass the proxy altogether. Some hub products support many protocols, such as ZigBee, Bluetooth LP, Zwave, Thread and others and this can result in an increased attack surface and in the case of threat modeling many trust boundaries to map and model.
- **DDoS** – Distributed Denial of Service attacks can be launched against networks of any size so an IoT network regardless if it was Industrial, Oil & Gas, or Enterprise would be vulnerable. On the flip side of the coin, poor security measures on devices are resulting in Botnets made up of IoT devices becoming more prevalent. Thingbots have been discovered that are up to a million-end-points with 96% being IoT devices. Lizard-Stresser has also been making the headlines with demonstrated capabilities to launch large scale attacks of 400Gbps without the use of any amplification techniques.

Infrastructure

- *Intrusion* – (IDS/IPS) Intrusion detection and prevention is always an important security tool as it detects anomalies, bad-signatures and malware on the wire, air or in hosts
- *Unknown backdoors* – Ports scanning software and vulnerability detection applications can detect open listening ports (backdoors) and alert the security practitioner to close them
- *Isolation* – Network security design is often determined by isolating areas to prevent access from less secure zones. Firewalls work in this way by isolating each of its interfaces and assigning them with a specific security level. By doing so traffic can only flow from a more secure area into a less secure area but not vice versa. This protects assets in secure areas such as secure database servers from insecure areas such as the Internet or web servers in a DMZ.
- *Outside agencies could have backdoors* – There appears little that can be done about this other than to run vulnerability software regularly and check port scans daily as it seems Government agencies have been very active in persuading, bribing or cajoling companies into opening back doors into their products. Many network companies have apparently aloud the NSA and GCHQ to place backdoors into their products especially when they are destined for foreign climes, seemingly in what they call "custom opportunities".

Interfaces

- *Active* sniffing – man in the middle attacks, fake DNS responses attacks as well as credential theft when data is transmitted unencrypted.
- *Distributed password cracking* – as its name suggests using many sources to brute force a password cracking attack on a subject
- *Hacking tools sophistication* – anti-forensic, dynamic behavior (anomaly), modularity (multi OS tools)
- *JavaScript drive past web attacks* – user and admin portals on IoT devices are typically very simple HTTP web sites with little in the way of security.

Part IV: **Defending the IoT**

In this chapter we will look at how we can address the problems of defending against threats, such as Trojans and all sorts of malware that can attack the IoT network. More importantly, we must consider how we will protect our network against zero day attacks. This is important as we have no knowledge of these particular threats and their specialist attack vectors so we must therefore consider all possible attack surfaces.

DOI 10.1515/9781501505775-020

Chapter 16 – Threats, Vulnerabilities and Risks

In this chapter we will explore the world of threats, vulnerabilities and the inevitable risks that are encountered in the IoT. We will highlight some known threats and vulnerabilities and where we can source up to date threat intelligence. Additionally, we will consider counter-measures and ways to mitigate risk and ways to secure device, firmware and software. Additionally, we will discuss alternatives to default passwords and possible alternatives.

In this chapter the reader will learn:
1. About the threats, vulnerabilities and risks for the IoT
2. How to get latest threat intelligence and countermeasure information
3. How to secure devices, firmware and software
4. Practical counter measures
5. Device firmware upgrades, their benefits and dangers
6. Alternative ways for authentication and identity management

IoT threats & counter-measures

One of the major problems with the IoT is that it should allow 'things' to interconnect people, computers, and all sorts of things, in order to share data, communicate information across a diverse area of interest. After all the purpose of IoT is to provide a mechanism that transforms the way we currently live by providing automation through intelligent machines to relieve us of mundane tasks. Unfortunately, the IoT has a rather severe backlash, in that it erodes our own skills to perform the tasks that we assign to machines.
–   Securing software, firmware and hardware
–   ***Rogue firmware*** – This is a major threat when we consider the IoT as many things are hardware devices, toys or home utility appliances so they are vulnerable to innovative attack vectors. They have weak surface areas that hackers can exploit for deep diving into the inbuilt electronics. Furthermore, the hardware firmware can be upgraded or downgraded to provide a hacker with a more vulnerable version of the firmware
–   ***Backdoors*** – Many IoT devices use Android as an OS and that is very susceptible to malware, indeed Google are pushing their stripped-down Android based OS "Brillo" for the use in IoT. Android is widely open to backdoor attacks via malware how Brillo will mitigate this risk remains to be seen.

DOI 10.1515/9781501505775-021

- *Malicious certificates* – SSL/TLS has been the security method of favor for a long time as it provided authentication and encryption. However, hackers have since also started to use SSL/TLS to hide their nefarious activities so it is no longer the safe option it once was.
- *Eaves dropping* – Eavesdropping on network traffic is certainly a viable hack if traffic is being transported in clear text such s over an unprotected Wi-Fi network. However, if the data is encrypted, then eavesdropping especially over Wi-Fi networks is no longer a trivial pursuit but very complex and so traffic should always be encrypted when traversing the Internet

However, probably the best and most effective ways to mitigate any of these security threats is to use file encryption, hashing and a secure boot process. By using secure updates, hashed firmware upgrades, and secure boot processing ensures only secure signed boot files are loaded. However, this does have drawbacks as it means there can be vendor lock-in and prevent the use of downloading open source supplements and applications.

A major issue with IoT devices was that those found to be faulty could not be updated over the Internet. Surprisingly, this was not just connected kettles, toaster and the like but very expensive things such as a Tesla car. Importantly, the Tesla car when discovered to have a firmware flaw was incapable of being upgraded over the air, instead Tesla had to ship out USB sticks with the software to get owners to upgrade their vehicles.

Obviously, building a product that cannot be upgraded over the air is a design failure, after all most devices within their life cycle will require upgrading with feature or security patches.

Despite this seemingly sensible logic it doesn't always work out this way. Manufacturers cannot always design their product in this way. The main problems are BOM (Bill of Material) and the physical flash size on the physical device.

One problem is that the firmware memory chip can only contain enough Flash memory for a single version of the firmware. What this means is that upgrading the firmware can be perilous. Should anything go wrong during the upgrade then there will be no way to back out of the upgrade and revert back to the previous version and can load two concurrent versions in flash storage for secure change control.

Some modern NAND memory chips can support two or more firmware versions to co-exist on the same chip, which obviously alleviates the danger of a failed firmware upgrade. Also, patches can be uploaded more securely but the cost in engineering is greater.

However, upgrades are very risky;

- **Loss of power** – Should the device, especially an IoT device lose power half why through a Firmware upgrade it could result in bricking the device.
- **Networks errors** – Again firmware upgrades can take considerable time and any failure or glitch on the network can cause the upgrade to fail.
- **Insufficient Storage** – some hardware versions just do not have the physical requirements to support the latest firmware upgrades which will result in failure and a bricked device.
- **Incompatibilities** – Not all versions of the same manufacturer's hardware, drivers or devices use the same firmware which leads to compatibility issues with hardware and software.
- **Lack of libraries or prerequisites** – Lesser known manufacturers or clones may not have available libraries, drivers or firmware available especially if they have been bought over or gone out of business.
- **NAND errors** – These are memory errors that can come about through data corruption, noise or poor signal quality.
- **Hash signatures and checksum errors** – Hash signatures would be highly beneficial to IoT firmware upgrades as they would ensure the integrity of the firmware package unfortunately not many IoT devices have the intelligence to verify the hash signature.

There are of course some practical issues as to why we do not wish to upgrade firmware except when really necessary. For example, a firmware upgrade on a chip that can only support one version of the software could crash irrevocably during a network or software glitch. To put the risk in proportion, 0.1% of failures could result in a huge number of devices being rendered unusable, and that is not something to be taken lightly.

There are also problems with Cyber suites, for example how do we communicate between devices securely? Moreover, if we are using TLS for securing the communications were the client and server have a common symmetric secret key how is the secret key going to be secured. After all we have seen previously how these secret keys can be implemented on low end devices with DTLS with minimum 16k ROM and 4K RAM but despite this electronic tampering with the devices chips can gain access to the keys and then past present and future access to communications.

An alternative is to use public keys however that is troublesome and very difficult when it comes to changing or deleting keys. However at least the devices do not share private keys so this method at least provides perfect forward secrecy so previous communications are safe and cannot be de-encrypted.

There is also X.509 certificates that we use daily on the Internet used in HTTPS and a chain of trust however certification revocation is difficult and time consuming. Also, the exact time is required which may be a problem for IoT devices. Remember many IoT devices; sleep to conserve battery power so may not synchronize their clocks accurately.

So how do we assign passwords or credentials securely at the time of production?

— With pre-share key generation, everything must be configured at the time of production in the factory and this could mean using some unique key perhaps derived from the MAC address of the device.

— Don't use big plain text lists s these are pretty easily enumerated and cracked.

— Don't use stupid formulas, gain they are probably easily enumerated and cracked.

— You also want to be able to rotate the secret key so not to fall victim to the next heart bleed, but this is where it becomes extremely difficult, forcing the changing of the secret key for a new version may prove to be even less secure depending on the password strength policy.

— Change the factory default credentials at time of first communication – this is a good best practice as it forces the secret key to be changed from the default but increases the complexity of installation.

Lightweight M2M bootstrap protocol – this is an excellent strategy and one that should be deployed whenever the physical constraints of the devices allows for it.

Chapter 17 – IoT Security Framework

In this chapter, we will discuss designing the protocols and communications into a design and how this can differ dependent on the devices and their function in the network. We will examine the existing protocols such as TCP/IP and Ethernet which are ubiquitous throughout the IT domain in communications, enterprise and commerce. We will examine why and how we should deploy them where possible within the consumer ecosystem and some alternatives when that avenue is not feasible.

The reader will learn in this chapter:
1. Common network protocols used in IT though not so much in IoT
2. When and why to use IPv6
3. The basic communication protocols for WSN (ZigBee, Bluetooth, etc.)
4. Understand messaging protocols
5. TCP or UDP, why the difference
6. Understand the protocol stack and where to use HTTP and Restful API

Introduction to the IoT security framework

When we start to consider security, privacy and trust in the context of an IoT network, it is necessary to first study the actual architecture. Network architectures vary dependent on their purpose, for example, an enterprise network differs considerably from a data center network, in both topology and architectural design. Consequently, when we consider security in an IoT context we have to study the architectures and frameworks that are commonly in use today. The rationale behind this is simply that IoT architectures have a different purpose than enterprise, consumer or cloud networks. Indeed, IoT networks can encompass features from all three, yet an IoT network will support different devices, protocols and purpose. Therefore, it is helpful to take a high-level look at the evolution of the IoT architecture, why the topology came about and how it differs in technology and purpose to traditional network designs.

Before we dive deeper into studying the security, privacy and trust components of an IoT network – and how they differ from those corresponding modules in a traditional enterprise network – we should pause to consider how and why IoT networks have evolved along a different evolutionary path. One of the unique qualities of IoT network architecture is its inherent ability to scale in order to accommodate the explosive growth that is expected.

DOI 10.1515/9781501505775-022

Estimates of the growth of the IoT vary considerably but all forecasts agree that there will be astonishing exponential growth in place by 2020. A commonly quoted forecast is that there will be around 50 billion devices or things attached to the Internet. Additionally, the main growth driver will not be due to increases in human population, as the number of connected devices surpassed world population back in 2008, instead it will be because of everyday consumer devices being connected to the Internet. Consumer devices, which previously were unconnected, such as TVs, light bulbs, HVAC systems, washing machines, cookers of all shapes and sizes and even cars will be amongst many other consumer devices that will be connected to the Internet. Furthermore, these smart devices will provide the means through mobile apps, and web service APIs to allow humans to interact, control and communicate with the devices remotely.

In order to drive and ultimately be able to support the industry's staggering growth predictions certain technologies have evolved at the right time and they act as both enablers for growth and aide technology adoption. The three main drivers are the advent of ubiquitous computing – which is the capability for lightweight operating systems and communication protocols to run on small computer devices with tiny amounts of memory or CPU. Additionally, we have also witnessed the rise in ubiquitous use of IP, which has led to the convergence of protocols to run over the top of IP rather than on proprietary transports. Moreover, the adoption of IPv6 in mobile telephone and carrier provider networks supports the deployment of IPv6 as the IP protocol of choice. Lastly, there is ubiquitous connectivity, which really is at the heart of the IoT. Ubiquitous connectivity is what differentiates much of the IoT use cases from earlier electronic and microprocessor solutions of the 80's. By having a rich choice of wireless connectivity options at hand, including Mobile, Wi-Fi, Bluetooth, ZigBee, Thread, and 802.11.4 amongst many others, designers are spoilt for choice as there are connectivity technologies to best suit, wide area (WAN), metro/neighborhood (MAN), local area (LAN) and personal/wearable (PAN) networks. In addition to coverage these wireless technologies cater for low power, constrained devices and even mesh networks which are often the best solution for wireless sensor networks (WSN).

However, just because there is a plethora of new and lightweight, energy efficient protocols out there to help us build IoT networks, it doesn't mean that designers must use them. In many cases, the designer will wish to build a homogeneous network where ever possible, using a common protocol stack throughout the network. This is the ideal case that designers and security practitioners work with in IP networks in the IT enterprise, data center and in mobile and communication service provider networks. In these use cases, the designer can simply work to an IP stack throughout, confident in the knowledge that every device and end node throughout the network, from the core to the edge will have the resources to support a full IP OSI stack. For instance, when a designer considers using, IPv6, TCP/IP and TLS as the network, transport and session layers they will know that device resources such as CPU, memory and energy will be available in abundance. Even in many networks labelled as IoT, this will still be the case, as enterprise and commercial deployments of the IoT will run over IT infrastructure, in order to leverage previous investment and to utilize the vast body of knowledge accumulated over the years supporting IP networks.

In these circumstances, where the IoT network is un-constrained and operates over a full IP stack, there is no requirement for new design or security knowledge and skills. However, in many cases especially in the consumer IoT and smart home/office sectors that is just not possible. The reason for this is that despite the best intentions of designers and security practitioners to build a homogeneous network that supports IP throughout, it just isn't always feasible from a technology or financial perspective. This is especially true if designers decide to utilize existing 'things' such as devices that run on Bluetooth or ZigBee as well as devices that can run lightweight or even full IP stacks. If that is the case, then designing a heterogeneous network is unavoidable as gateways and hubs will be required to interconnect and translate diverse protocols into IP for backhaul to the remote controller apps on a mobile or within the cloud.

Moreover, it is not just the device's specific protocols in the proximity network at the edges of the IoT be aggregated before being dispatched over the Internet. Here the nature, purpose and ultimate destination of the traffic will determine the preferred protocol. For instance, some traffic may be manipulated, processed and stored at the edge of the network; such is the case with fog computing so as to minimize latency. Other types of traffic may simply be passed out over IP backhaul and Internet pipes to application or storage servers in the cloud. In both cases the type, quality and reliability of the network links, with regards to metrics such as, bandwidth, packets loss, latency, availability, and jitter will be the criteria that decides that most appropriate technology and protocol.

In this next section, we will consider three common IOT protocol stacks which as an IT security practitioner you will probably not have worked with before. In Fig. 3 – Heterogeneous Networks, there are representations of homogeneous and heterogeneous network topologies within a generic IoT network.

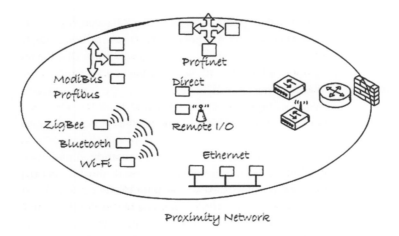

Fig. 3: Heterogeneous Networks

With reference to (Fig. 4 – TCP Stack) this is the full IP stack common in IT enterprise and commercial networks, each protocol within each layer of the OSI can be considered an optimal choice that matches the design criteria and the design constraints while delivering optimal performance and operational flexibility.

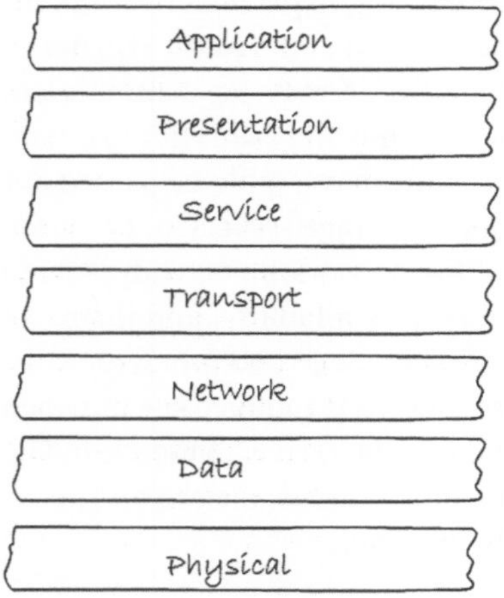

Application

Presentation

Service

Transport

Network

Data

Physical

Fig. 4: TCP IT Stack

If we briefly consider each layer of the full TCP/ IP stack in turn starting at the Physical layer, we will get a better understanding of why these protocols have been selected. The TCP/IP stack condenses the seven layers of the OSI model down into four layers, network access, Internetwork, transport, and the application layer, as shown in figure 4.

The network access layer typically consists of the physical and the media access layer, the most common MAC is Ethernet as it is utilized over many types of media such as copper wire, Wi-Fi, and optical cables in all sorts of short haul and long haul networks. Ethernet is ubiquitous and is very easy to interconnect with other networks as Ethernet frames typically encapsulate other native protocol datagrams or packets to allow easy transportation across an Ethernet network. At the destination, the Ethernet headers are stripped of the frame leaving a native packet.

Therefore, using Ethernet as the Physical and MAC layer is an extremely flexible protocol as it supports wired Ethernet and Wi-Fi which are the two most common types of network interfaces.

At the Internetwork layer, we are dealing with the choice of routing and networking protocols and this will typically IPv4 or IPv6. The IP suite contains several other network protocols such as ICMP (used in Ping), ARP (used in address resolution protocol) amongst others.

The next layer in the TCP/IP model is the transport layer, and this will determine the use of TCP/IP, a reliable protocol, or its unreliable version UDP. The use of the terms reliable and unreliable should not be misunderstood, it doesn't mean that TCP/IP is better than UDP, often that is not the case it depends on purpose and the type of network. What the terms relate to is that with TCP/IP packets will be reliably delivered to the destination even if the host network adapter has to keep resending lost or delayed packets. UDP on the other hand just send and forgets as it has no mechanism to handle lost packets. As a result, TCP/IP is ideally suited for batch transfers of bulk data over unreliable links as it can guarantee delivery, however resending lost or delayed packets is of little use in the context of real-time traffic such as VoIP and video streaming – resending delayed packets will actual make the situation worse. Therefore, UDP depending on the reliability of modern networks is often a better choice.

The application layer, in the TCP/IP model handles services such as HTTP but also encryption. HTTP 1.1 is ubiquitous on the Internet and is the basis of the web 2.0, web services and HTTP APIs. In addition, HTTP is also RESTful and as it is the default mechanism of web communications this means you have all the client and server resources and drivers available. Additionally, with HTTP encryption is available via TLS (HTTPS) so there is an automatic secure channel available without any additional design. Unfortunately, there are some drawbacks such as the significant overhead due to HTTP's headers and text based payload. In IoT design where end-points may have significant resource constraints HTTP's inherent overhead can be a very significant design issue.

Moreover, Http 1.1 is not without its problems as it is over 15 years old. As a result, a new version, HTTP 2 has been launched that will remediate many of the issues of HTTP, such as the header overhead and wasteful connections. These design improvements should go some way in elevating many of HTTP's shortcomings in IoT ecosystems.

Chapter 18 – Secure IoT Design

Following on from the network protocol design for IP networks in the last chapter, we will now look at more IoT specific protocols for publish/subscribe models best suited in wireless sensor networks (WSN). In this more technical discussion we will examine the most commonly deployed publish/subscribe protocols, why they are used and their advantages over alternative network patterns. In this chapter the reader will learn:

1. Why IP and HTTP are often unsuitable in IoT designs
2. About Publish/subscribe patterns
3. About the Message Queuing Telemetry Transport or MQTT
4. MQTT benefits and issues
5. How to secure MQTT
6. Alternative IoT protocols in WSN
7. The IoT stack
8. CoAP and 6LowPAN their benefits and issues

In the previous section, we took a brief overview of the TCP/IP stack as commonly defined in an IT enterprise. We saw some of the advantages to using tried and tested standardized protocols and some of the drawbacks. The conclusion is that for small scale, non-real time, IoT applications the current IPv6 IP model would certainly suffice. After all, HTTP can support RESTful APIs and TLS encryption, which makes it suitable for integration with application and cloud services. Furthermore, we can secure the traffic from the end node or device right through to the application.

Unfortunately, with this design there are issues with HTTP because of the number of TCP connections that are required to be opened – remember HTTP only handles one request at a time – and this results in potentially high levels of wasted bandwidth carrying duplicated data. HTTP/2 will hopefully remediate many of the shortcomings of HTTP 1.1 and having a standard homogeneous network stack throughout the network would be ideal from a security perspective. The importance of avoiding heterogeneous networks wherever practical is down to the number of translation points at gateways and hubs. Each point where a protocol is translated there is the underlying potential for insecure practices and vulnerabilities to be introduced. However, sometimes we have to introduce new – or not so new – protocols into the mix simply because they offer something special and that is the case with the publish/subscribe protocol, MQTT.

DOI 10.1515/9781501505775-023

Message Queuing Telemetry Transport or MQTT as it is now known is not a new IoT protocol it was initial created back in 1999 as a data agnostic publish/subscribe transport protocol, however it wasn't until 2016 that it became standardized by ISO. However, MQTT was not sitting idle in the intervening years awaiting standardization; quite to the contrary it was making a big impact in the M2M operational technology world.

MQTT's popularity in M2M came about due to its simplistic payload design. Contrary to other data transport and messaging services, MQTT allowed organizations a free hand to customize their own message formats, as a key design criteria was for MQTT to be data agnostic. Other notable design points were MQTT's lightweight which made it possible to run on clients or subscribers that had very few resources, such as CPU, memory and energy. All that was required for an array of devices to run MQTT was the capability to run the MQTT library, which requires as little as 3-4KB and connect to an MQTT broker. The libraries themselves were available for a number of operating systems, notable for mobile devices such as Android and iOS, but also for processor boards such as Arduino and Raspberry.

Several other features make MQTT suitable for IoT implementation, such as its low bandwidth usage and bi-directional communication, which makes it possible to operate behind NAT routers and gateways. This is feasible due to the client being able to initiate a TCP connection through a firewall – without opening any ports – with a MQTT broker. As the initial connection is from the secure side of the firewall to the insecure side the firewall will automatically allow the session request to pass through, and establish a NAT session which allows the return packets from the MQTT broker back through, thereby establishing a TCP/IP session.

However, that TCP/IP session is also one of its drawbacks as MQTT requires TCP/IP, which is not always available or desirable on IoT networks. One notable case is with WSN (wireless sensor networks) which consist typically of a vast array of very resource constrained sensors, which only have limited CPU and memory available. Furthermore, these WSN sensors often have to preserve energy in order to operate their inbuilt wireless chips so establishing and maintaining permanent TCP/IP connections to the MQTT broker is out of the question. For maintaining long term TCP sessions when the constrained device has nothing to communicate is wasteful of precious battery life which would be better preserved by putting the device into a sleep mode.

Consequently, recent development of MQTT has revolved around a new version of MQTT – SN (MQTT – Sensor Network) and this variant is designed to support protocols other than TCP/IP. Indeed, the purpose of MQTT-SN is to extend the MQTT style messaging to other network transport protocols such as UDP, ZigBee and 6LoWPAN.

In larger, more resource plentiful networks, MQTT has found a use as not just a messaging service as it is with Facebook Messenger, but also as a primary transport protocol in the networks of Amazon Web Services, IBM and Microsoft.

However, MQTT is also not without some issues, although MQTT-SN will likely remediate most of them. 1) MQTT in its original format is reliant on TCP/IP and a persistent connection to the MQTT broker. 2) The broker is the heart of the system so is centralized and must be in a high-availability cluster or fault-tolerant design. 3) MQTT brokers facilitate the conveyance of messages between those sending messages (clients) and those receiving messages (subscribers), and this is based upon the message's topic. The way MQTT handles this is by constructing a hierarchal string to route and filter messages to the appropriate subscribers.

A string will look like this: IBM\MQTT\Client\Topics.

There is no problem when topic strings are short such as with the example above but as the hierarchy grows the topic string can become too long. Another minor issue is that there is no message aging so that messages that have no subscription or are not collected can remain in the message store forever. However, these are minor issues that do not directly concern security.

Where security is an issue and a quite significant one is with the complete absence of any of its own security features or functions. MQTT was designed without any security in mind, and even now, after 15 years it still lacks many of its own security features. Many of these missing security attributes can be mitigated by using additional security standard protocols such as TLS to encrypt the underlying TCP connections. However, that makes MMQT no better or worse than HTTP, which is also a socket-connected protocol that uses TLS to encrypt its TCP connections. Additionally, when using MMQT as a messaging protocol there is also a conflict of interest when encrypting the TCP connections.

As mentioned, the MQTT protocol does recommend the use of TLS for secure MQTT implementations, and there is a reserved network port (port 8883) for this purpose. With regards MQTT security, TLS provides an encrypted communication channel over which MQTT messages are sent. The way this works is that before the MQTT channel between the publishers → broker → subscribers, is established TLS uses a handshake to pass certificates (or keys) from the publisher to the broker, but also between the broker and subscribers. If the certificate/key exchange is successful then TLS creates a secure encrypted channel, if not, the connection is aborted.

The downside of using TLS and other methods of encryption for that matter is that they can add significant overhead to the process. Remember the claim that security was omitted from the design to keep the footprint light, which is one of MQTT's major plus point on resource-constrained devices. For example, a MQTT client library can have a compiled size of just 3–4 KB. However, a TLS handshake alone can consume that much memory resource, without accounting for the encryption overhead on the individual packets. For many resource-constrained devices, this added workload can simply consume too much in terms of CPU, memory and storage resources.

The huge increase in resource consumption is during the initial TLS handshake where a client initiates a secure communication session by starting the TLS Handshake. The MMQT Client and server then agree on the TLS version and the Cipher Suites to be used for securing the channel. This process is very costly in terms of CPU and bandwidth as can be seen in Fig. 5.

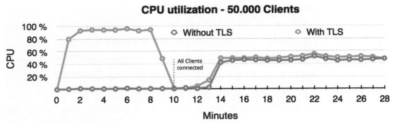

Fig. 5: MQTT Overhead

TLS also has additional overhead for each MQTT message that is sent. This is dependent on the cipher suite used for the connection, so the TLS overhead at runtime varies. Block Ciphers typically cause more overhead compared to Stream Ciphers in terms of traffic (due to padding). The runtime overhead in terms of CPU is also higher, when compared to standard TCP, since crypto-graphic operations are involved.

However, secure MMQT has a major advantage over HTTPS, in that there is an interesting aspect regards TLS overhead. Once clients are all connected to the broker, (Fig. 5) the client can send and receive messages without any additional handshake overhead – or rather only negligible additional overhead. This is because the MQTT client only needs to establish a connection once per session – in contrary to protocols like HTTP, which needs to re-establish a connection on every request. The slight increase in resources consumed by TLS per connection is because TLS needs to allocate additional buffers, so RAM consumption is slightly higher per MQTT connection.

There are ways to mitigate the issue of TLS connection overhead and that is to try to restrict a TLS handshake (connection setup) to one per MQTT session, use long-living TCP/IP connections with MMQT or to use Session Resumption. TLS session resumption techniques allow the reuse of already negotiated TLS sessions. TLS session resumption works when the client attempts to reconnect to the server, perhaps it has just awoken and needs to communicate. Instead of renegotiating a new connection via a full handshake the client and server reuse an already negotiated TLS session used previously so the client and server don't need to do the full TLS handshake again.

There are two session resumption mechanisms – but these are not always present in the MQTT libraries:

Session IDs: The server stores the secret state together with the Session ID. When the client reconnects, it provides the Session ID and the session can be resumed.

Session Tickets: The server's secret state is transmitted to the client and is encrypted with a secret key only the server knows. The client sends this ticket back to the server when reconnecting. If the server can decrypt the contents, the session is resumed with the state contained in the secret ticket.

As we saw earlier security in MQTT is very limited and has two levels the first being that MQTT will allow a user ID and password to be transmitted at connect time, thought this is in clear text, and the broker allows authorization to be based on those credentials. The second level of security that is supported is the ability to secure the underlying TCP/IP connection – all versions of TLS up to and including 1.2 are supported. Additionally, there is also the possibility to use Client certificates (X.509), which can also be leveraged to help the server broker authenticate clients. However, the important thing is that MQTT does not have security in the design, as it was designed to be as lightweight as possible, so security practitioners will have to evaluate the security of the MQTT network, especially the broker and find a way to provide the mechanisms that will ensure the confidentiality, availability and integrity of the protocol.

IoT Network Design

Wireless technology plays a major part in the growth of the IoT because it frees the consumer from the tedious and potentially damaging act of having to run cables to devices, especially when we consider the use case of the smart home. After all microprocessor based kits were available in the early 80's that could control, internal and external lighting, opening and closing curtains/drapes, garage doors, as well as programmatically control the HVAC amongst many other so called smart functions of the IoT. These microprocessor controllers were in their day the equivalent of the Nest thermostat, with sleek ergonomic design and state of the art LCD displays. The problem was that they required running wiring throughout the house and that put most people of the idea. IoT designers today are free from that onerous practical constraint; they only have to worry about dreaming up a practical use for connected fridges, toasters, slow cookers and food processors.

Additionally, it will not just be the consumer Internet that will benefit from pervasive Internet connectivity; business and industry will also benefit and they have the advantage of clear use cases as they have already adopted the Internet connected approach to augment their existing machine-to-machine (M2M) operational technologies.

M2M operational technologies are at the heart of industry such as health care, aviation, manufacturing and logistics, to name just a few. M2M is not new it has been around for decades. Examples of M2M technologies developed out with the IoT are vehicle telematics, robotics, augmented reality, radio frequency identification and location based services. These have all been major operational technologies within the context of industry, logistics especially has benefitted. However, M2M has tended to have a very localized scope with companies wary of allowing their prized assets connectivity to the Internet and all the inherent dangers that goes with it. As a result, M2M has evolved securely within the confines of traditional highly defensive barrier networks. These heavily fortified networks isolate the assets from the outside world and often even to the company's own business IT network.

The IoT approach is a game changer with regards securing the technology assets as it not only removes the fortified barriers protecting the operational networks but actively promotes interconnectivity of real world devices and machine to human interaction with critical assets by leveraging the ubiquity of the Internet. However, in order for that to be possible network and process planners must be able to convince businesses that interconnectivity of devices and communication and storage of any data produced will be secure both at rest and in motion. However, there are other differences between an IoT network design and that of a typical enterprise. For one, enterprise traffic tends to be south-north by definition with traffic from users heading towards servers or the Internet located at the very top of the network architecture. The IoT however, has different traffic flows with much of the traffic flowing east-west over WSN and between interconnected devices via gateways and controllers. There are of course traffic flows leaving the network for cloud storage and analysis, but in industrial, enterprise and even consumer IoT deployments it is important to place these services as close to the traffic source as possible to enable fast response times and low network latency. For instance, if the IoT network is sending data back to a cloud service for real-time analysis and feedback the positioning of the cloud in relation to the source is extremely important, hence the use of embedded and distributed intelligence within an IoT architecture.

The reason the network designers rely on embedded and distributed intelligence is three-fold; 1) a centralized approach to data collection and smart device and management does not scale well over the Internet. The Internet as a communication medium is non-deterministic and latency, jitter and even lost packets can cause severe delays. Therefore, it is best design practice to distribute the data collection points to minimize the distance data has to travel. An example of this is the principle of Fog rather than cloud computing, with Fog the resources, such as compute, storage and analytics are placed close to the assets producing the data to minimize response time especially in industrial scenarios. 2) Finite network resources such as available bandwidth can cause heavy traffic congestion over links attaching centralized resources. This can also seriously affect traffic throughput and network response times as traditional networks still route packets using algorithms that use best shortest path as the key criteria and do not take into account current congestion. SDN networks will remediate many of these legacy routing problems but for now they are still a rarity. 3) the unpredictable nature of a centralized intelligence network as demonstrated in 1 and 2, leads to reduced performance as the networks response and reaction time to alerts, alarms or application triggers are no longer, predictable, let alone deterministic so unsuitable for any real-time application. When we consider real-time, it is prudent to realize under which use cases we are using the term as its performance criteria is fluid depending on the scenario. In server/client or web apps we can consider real-time to be less than a few seconds, in IoT devices to servers we might consider real-time to be less than a second but real time communication between devices would be deemed to be in micro-seconds.

For instance, a sensor raising an emergency alarm on an asset that's main motor has exceeded its max safe RPM, needs that message to be conveyed to the intelligent system in as close to real time as possible. This is because industrial and many enterprise systems run on what is called closed loopback functioning and having the message traverse several hops in the network in order to reach the centralized intelligent system is only the first part of that loopback mechanism. The centralized system will have to analyze and respond to the sensor or its corresponding actuator in order to shut down the motor and this need to be done in an acceptable time frame without any unacceptable delays introduced by the network. It is for these principle reasons that IoT architecture relies on an embedded and distributed architecture, which places intelligent serves as close to the event/alarm source as possible.

Embedded and distributed intelligence is an important design constraint in IoT network, especially in industrial contexts where it is often termed Fog computing as opposed to the more popular term of cloud computing. However, they are not analogous terms or technologies, the difference, is that unlike with the cloud, fog resources are designed to be distributed throughout the network design in order to process data and events in a more efficient and deterministic manner than the traditional centralized cloud model.

Essentially the great strides forward in IoT technology has come about through the designers having greater choice and flexibility when choosing sensors, actuators and devices, which may contain several of each. These make up the new IoT type 'Things' and they differ from their predecessors by having compute, storage and networking functionality built into their design. Additionally, simultaneously to their empowerment they have also gone through the miniaturization process resulting in devices that have not only enough compute, memory and network to run lightweight OS, they also have extremely small form factor as well as low power consumption, which allows them to be deployed anywhere, as weight, size and battery life are no longer physical constraints.

IoT protocols

However, where designers may thrive on the new technologies available for use in an IoT network, the same is unfortunately not true for security practitioners. The problem that security practitioners face is that they cannot reuse security appliances and tools that they are familiar with in a traditional IP network. This is simply because an IoT network design will often be required to support a heterogeneous network comprising many protocols and technologies that are not compatible with one another. Consequently, security practitioners initially discover that deploying traditional security tools and functions does not work, as it is not a case of attempting to transpose enterprise security knowledge and skills onto an IoT network. The only way is for the security practitioner to analyze and research the strange new protocols required to get heterogeneous networks to seamlessly inter-connect, communicate and function.

As a result, many new technologies and devices required engineers to design, develop and standardize protocols at every level of the ISO model. One of the major requirements that engineers have to deliver is protocols that were energy efficient and required little in the way of compute and memory. This fundamental requirement rules out many of the traditional protocols, at both the physical, logical, network and transport levels. Furthermore, as we progress up the ISO stack it becomes clear that the higher-level session and application protocols, which handle important functions such as encryption and data presentation, such as HTTP, are also unsuitable. Consequently, if we consider a typical ISO stack for a traditional network against an IoT stack – (see Fig. 6) – we can see that at every level in the stack the traditional protocols have been substituted by a more energy efficient and lightweight IoT enhanced protocol.

So, what are the IoT protocols that we need to know about and how do we go about securing the IoT stack?

The IoT Stack

If we once again consider diagram (Fig. 6 – IoT Stack,) we can start to compare the relevant protocols one layer of the ISO at a time. The objective here is to understand why each of the tried and tested protocols have been superseded by modern equivalents and importantly how that will affect our views on security, privacy and trust.

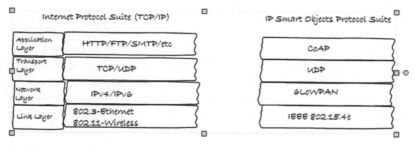

Fig. 6: The IoT Stack

If we consider the IoT optimized stack in figure 6, we can see the specialist protocols that have been deployed in order to meet the strict demands for energy preservation, addressability, routing, messaging and encryption for constrained devices operating over possibly lossy networks. A quick review of these protocols, which are just some of the most popular or generalist, as they perform well over a wide range of use cases, will demonstrate why they are necessary and importantly how they can be secured.

Link layer

At the link layer the requirement here is to deploy a protocol that can support small and cheap wireless devices on a common platform so that they can all communicate and share components in order to lower the overall cost. The 802.15.4 protocol describes wireless and media access for personal area networks, for example wearable devices. However, the IoT design community was quick to see the advantage of 802.15.4 s it is designed for hardware implementation on a wireless chip. This made 802.15.4 eminently suitable for a vast array of applications within IoT such as health and fitness, medical, HVAC sensors and actuators (transducers), in car telematics and entertainment systems as well as all those smart home devices.

What makes 802.15.4 so suited to the IoT is that the protocol is designed specifically to operate on devices without any human intervention. Furthermore, the protocol is designed to operate on small 8 or 16 bit microprocessors for long periods, which entails low power usage and robust and reliable software. As the largest consumer of power along with the microprocessor the wireless chip must conform to the strict design principles of energy efficiency and reliability.

As the 802.15.4 specification is deployed in security sensitive applications it must support the tenets of IT security – Confidentiality, Integrity and Availability. The 802.15.4 specification is capable of fulfilling the security requirements through a link layer API (application programmable interface). Developers interface with the 802.15.4 API, in two distinct ways. One method that developers favor is to use the API to access the features and functionality of the wireless chip directly. The alternative method is to interface with higher-level libraries that can use the 802.15.4 API in order to connect to their own higher-level services; one example of this is when deploying devices that run ZigBee.

The 802.15.4 specification provides link layer security features through four basic services:
- Access control
- Message integrity
- Message confidentiality
- Replay protection

Access control is performed at the link layer and its purpose it to prevent unauthorized devices from joining the network. This is an important security issue with WSN (wireless sensors networks) as many sensors and end node devices may be remote located and it is imperative that an IoT administrator knows that the devices visualized on the network are indeed their own legitimate nodes and not an unauthorized node that has joined the network via an automated neighbor discovery scan. Therefore, legitimate nodes must be capable of detecting messages from unauthorized nodes and rejecting them.

Similarly, message integrity is vital as messages traversing the network between legitimate and authorized nodes must be protected from man in the middle tampering. This is where a malicious actor may try to tamper with legitimate packets flowing between end nodes. The 802.15.4 specification enables message integrity protection by utilizing a MAC (message authentication code) which is a cryptographic secure checksum of a message. The MAC provides authentication and integrity as it is constructed using the secure crypto keys exchanged between senders and receivers of messages. The sender constructs the MAC using the secret key and sends the packet which includes the MAC to the recipient. The receiver upon receiving the packet computes the MAC using the shared secret key and then compares the result with the value in the original MAC from the sender. If the MACs do not match the packet is rejected.

However, an eavesdropper can easily collect genuine packets travelling between two authorized nodes and then replay the conversation at a later time. As the MAC and the secret shared keys were genuine at the time of the initial conversation the replayed packets will pass any security check based on the MAC comparison. In order to prevent this 802.15.4 uses replay protection which uses an incremental sequence number to label each packet, any packets turning up out of sequence with smaller sequence numbers are rejected.

In addition to integrity and replay protection the 802.15.4 specification addresses confidentiality through AES data encryption. Confidentiality ensures that no part of the message can be reconstructed from the encrypted data stream. Encryption is designed to prevent an eavesdropper capturing packets as they travel through the air – remember wireless is a broadcast medium, any one listening on the same channel and frequency receives the message – and retrieving the message contents.

With regards the security options in 802.15.4 specification it is important to understand that the application specifies the appropriate security settings through control parameter in the radio stack. What this means in practice is that if an application does not explicitly specify security options then no security will be enabled by default. There are eight security suite options that an application can specify. Each security suite provides different levels, options and guarantees so it is up to the developer to choose the most relevant and secure suite. As an example, the basic properties of each suite can be roughly classified by the level of protection; no security, encryption only, authentication only, as well as encryption and authentication. Each category of authentication, has three varieties based on the size of the MAC, for example whether it is 32, 64 or 128 bits long.

One interesting and very relevant point with regards the 802.15.4 security suites is that an application selects one based upon the source and destination addresses of end nodes. The wireless chip maintains an ACL (access control list) of each of these pairings and compliant devices support a list of 255 entries. However, what happens should the wireless chip lose power?

The problem here is that the ACL will be lost and upon the resumption of power the device may well end up functional and appearing to work but actually be running without any secure communications. It is therefore essential that application developers are aware of this and take into consideration the potential change of security states after a power interruption.

Adaption layer

The most appropriate protocol for the adaption layer is IPv6 as it is the version of IP that can scale to address the potentially hundreds of billion devices that will be connected to the Internet via the IoT. However, many small constrained devices do not have the memory to support a full IPv6 stack and that can lead to deployment issues. As a result, lightweight versions of the IPv6 stack have been developed to be fully compatible with IPv6 but have a much-reduced memory footprint, which can also run on the tiny OS's often found on these constrained devices. Additionally, if the network's link layer is running on 802.15.4 then it makes sense to use a light weight protocol designed to run on power efficient and resource constrained devices.

The result is the 6LowPAN specification that runs upon IP over 802.15.4, which in turn enables the use of existing IP network infrastructure. The pervasive nature of IP networks is due to their proven technology, there open specifications and the ease of deployment, integration and commissioning. Furthermore, IP networks have developed over several decades in enterprise and communication service provider networks so there is a vast body of knowledge as well as highly developed tools, to aide diagnostics and network management. Consequently, IP is well known and thoroughly tested and accepted by network designers, administrators and security practitioners.

6LowPAN therefore is very attractive as it is an adaptive layer protocol, which allows the seamless transportation of IPv6 packets over 802.15.4 wireless links. Additionally, 6LowPAN can use beacons for link layer device discovery, which can ease the administrative burden of neighbor configuration in even small networks. However, 6LowPAN also supports IPv6 over 802.15.4 by handling fragmentation and reassembly of large IPv6 packets as well as compression of IPv6 UDP or ICMP packet headers. Fragmentation and compression techniques improve the efficiency of the network which along with 6LowPAN's low processing and storage overheads and its inherent capability to support routing on mesh networks makes it a good fit with IoT network design.

With regards security option the 6LowPAN stack offers optional security functions that provide data authentication and encryption as well as device authentication and authorization. As we will see later device identification, authentication and authorization are keystones in an IoT network. 6LowPAN provides the necessary security mechanisms that re required to address identity and access management issues, such as authentication and authorization. The optional security mechanisms allow for end nodes to participate in full PKI (public key infrastructure) security schemes by supporting security protocols such as EAP, TLS1.2 SHA-256, ECC, X509.3 and PANA.

However, there are some security issues that we need to be aware of with 6LoWPAN and that is which security protocols to deploy. As we have seen 6LoWPAN utilizes 802.15.4 as its link layer protocol and to convey IP packets. In addition, 6LoWPAN can also benefit from the data encryption and integrity checks performed by 802.15.4 as these are currently supported by the hardware and are network protocol independent as they' re link layer mechanisms. The problem is however that these link layer security mechanisms only provide encryption and integrity checks on a hop-by-hop basis. The issue with hop-by-hop is that every device on the communication path must be trusted and any traffic leaving the 6LoWPAN WSN will no longer be protected.

The solution to this issue is to ensure end-to-end security and the most common method in traditional IP networks is to use SSL/TLS (transport layer security) – SSL is still commonly referred to but TLS has superseded SSL. TLS works between the transport and application layers in the ISO model in the session layer and it guarantees security between applications. TLS includes a secure key exchange mechanism in addition to providing security services such as authentication, confidentiality and integrity between Internet hosts. The problem is however that TLS relies upon TCP/IP to work and that is rarely used in WSN because of the session that must be built and maintained between communicating hosts. Over poor and lossy networks establishing a session might not always be possible let alone maintaining one reliably, as a result UDP is often preferred to TCP/IP. There is UDP adaptation of TLS, named DTLS and that can be used to circumvent the TCP/IP session problem.

IPv6 & IPsec

However, there is already a mandatory protocol in IPv6 that can provide end-to-end security for any IP communications and that is the inbuilt IPsec protocol suite. What makes IPsec suitable for WSN is that it can provide key exchange mechanisms, in addition to authentication, confidentiality and integrity. Furthermore, IPsec resides at the network layer so is independent of the transport protocol used for example TCP/IP or UDP or any other transport protocol even future ones. In addition, IPsec because it works at the lower media access level can provide for confidentiality and integrity of the higher transport packet headers, which is something that TLS cannot do.

However, TLS and DTLS are not without their fair share of deployments in working IoT networks. TLS because of its dependence on TCP/IP tends to be used in LAN and WAN topologies where TCP/IP's fault tolerance and error correction can be of use. For example, TCP/IP can resend lost packets, which makes it ideal for use over poor links. TCP/IP can also reorganize packets arriving out of sequence which is highly beneficial when dealing with packets crossing the Internet as packets can and often do take alternative routes. This reliable transport of IP packets however comes at a cost in initial session establishment and maintenance. UDP which is the unreliable protocol of the TCP/IP suite is often more suitable on networks that are extremely poor, as UDP is often able to continue working well after TCP/IP has failed to establish a session connection. However regardless of whether TCP/IP with TLS or UDP with DTLS is chosen as the transport and session protocols, one thing is certain, and that is they will be subjected to security threats and attacks.

Some of the more common vulnerabilities associated with SSL\TLS and DTLS are SSL Stripping, heartbeat, and many other exploits.

Routing

One common feature of IoT networks is that they often comprise constrained nodes with limited processing power, memory and very often energy resources are limited to battery, solar power or energy scavenging mechanisms. These nodes typically connect together in clusters which enable them sharing a router or a collection of routers that make up what is known as LLN (Low power and lossy networks). The characteristics of a LLN is that the routers interconnect across lossy links, that have low bandwidth capability are typically unstable and can only pass low data rates at the best of times. Another common feature is the topology of the network which tends towards a branch and leaf design where network communication patterns are often point to multipoint (downwards) or multipoint to point (upwards). Another feature is that these LLN consist of sometime very large numbers of constrained devices that are required to operate an IPv6 neighbor discovery protocol.

RPL (routing protocol for low power and lossy networks) was designed to meet the requirements and constraints of LLNs as well as to try to address the networking challenges. One of the main network issues with LLN is securing the establishment and maintenance of network connectivity between nodes.

At a conceptual level, security with regards routing protocols is concerned with ensuring that the protocol functions correctly, algorithms run, and network data regards the topologies, graphs and next-hop information are conveyed to neighbors and that these run without any external influences that could degrade routing performance. Additionally, when we consider security in the context of routing over LLNs using RPL in particular we are examining the nodes ability to perform the functions of authentication, access control, data confidentiality, data integrity and non-repudiation.

With regards RPL, routers use mutual authentication initially to establish routing peers prior to exchanging any information. The authentication process also attempts to authenticate the source of the routing information is indeed from that peer, this is called data origin authentication.

Confidentiality is required as LLNs require their routing updates and neighbor maintenance exchanges to remain confidential to prevent eavesdroppers viewing peer exchanges over shared medium.

Integrity is required as in other routing protocols to ensure routing updates and information is not tampered with as they traverse the shared medium network.

Non-repudiation, is the assurance that the transaction, transmission and or reception of message cannot later be denied. However, this is an interesting but somewhat worthless function as repudiation has no meaning in routing protocols. The practicalities of non-repudiation would require transaction logging and storing, digital signature verification for each transaction by each node participating in the transaction which for a LLN consisting of constrained devices is an onerous task that is more burden than benefit.

Availability, in an RPL context ensures that routing information exchanges are available and functioning. RPL also ensures that forwarding services are available and functional in order to maintain efficient routing information exchange as well as RPL neighbor discovery. However, routing protocols are obvious targets for malicious actors as they can influence how routers forward packets though a network. Similarly, routing protocols and RPL in particular are enticing targets for malicious actors as they are easily disrupted to provide for an effective denial of service attack leaving the network practically useless. Therefore, we will take a brief look at some of the potential threats that RPL and LLN networks face in the context of the IoT.

An attractive attack from the perspective of a malicious actor would be to impersonate an authorized and existing node. If successful, the impersonating node could interact maliciously with the other authentic nodes passing false reading or inappropriate control messages in the case of monitoring or control system applications respectively. Another potential target is the disclosure of routing information and neighbor exchange and state data. Routing exchanges can contain route metrics per link that may contain information such as bandwidth, available CPU power, and remaining battery life. Additionally, routing information will also contain reachability information that will allow an attacker to map the network and determine relative importance of each node in the network. The point here is that in RPL routing higher (north) nodes, for example, parent nodes have lower significance to (south) nodes. RPL forwards if possible from a higher to lower node in the network rather than between nodes of equal significance. This would make nodes higher in the topology more interesting targets as they have more information flows passing through them.

Attacks on the routing information are not always the result of a network attack, sometimes an attack will target a direct device, and this is a physical device compromise. The attacker's goal here is to expose the detailed routing information stored in the routing and forwarding database. If the attacker can expose this level of information, it would allow them direct access to the configuration and connectivity data of the network. This would in turn provide the intelligence to target high value nodes or links. The ways an attacker compromises a physical device is typically through remote network management or field support and upgrade interfaces.

Another common attack vector in LLNs and with RPL is node resource exhaustion. The goal here is simply to exhaust the processing, memory and energy resources. Typical methods deployed are to overload the node with neighbor peering requests, through hello flooding. A node requires using resource to establish and maintain neighbor relationships and the potential acceptance of multiple neighbors' peers can quickly exhaust the nodes compute and memory resources.

Messaging

The messaging protocols of choice for the IoT is typical down to two popular publish/subscribe messaging protocols, CoAP (constrained application protocol) and MMQ. We looked at MMQT earlier and now we will consider another popular messaging alternative. CoAP was developed specifically for the IoT so can naturally scale to support billions of devices. Additionally, it is extremely lightweight consuming only 10 KB of Ram and 100 KB of code space, which makes it ideal for low cost microprocessor, based devices. This is very fortunate as more electronic devices with very constrained resources are finding a place as sensors or actuators in the IoT. From a security perspective, developers have created CoAP to last for decades and security has been designed into the protocol. As an example, CoAP uses DTLS, as it uses UDP over IP as a transport protocol. Also, CoAP supports very powerful encryption parameters and its preferred security setting for DTLS equates to 3072-bit RSA keys. What is more it can run this on even the smallest nodes in the network.

CoAP however is also a good fit as a substitution for HTTP as they have much in common. HTTP like CoAP is RESTful, which makes published services available under a URL. CoAP consumes these services by using methods similar to HTTP, such as GET, PUT, POST and DELETE. This makes the transition from HTTP to CoAP very easy for developers as the methods and Rest based model is so similar to traditional HTTP web services. Additionally, because CoAP and HTTP are so similar and they both comply with the REST model, the integration of application between HTTP and CoAP is straightforward.

Another similarity is in the stack implementation whereas traditional enterprise networks using IPv6 look like diagram (Fig. 7 – IoT Application Stack), with the protocol layers: the MAC, Link Layer, network, transport, session and application layers corresponding to IPsec → Ethernet → IP v6 → TCP → TLS → HTTP. If we then compare and contrast the IPv6 protocol stack with the IoT protocol stack shown in Fig. 6 we can see that the corresponding network, transport, session and application layers directly map to IPsec → 802.15.4 → 6LoWPAN → UDP → DTLS → CoAP.

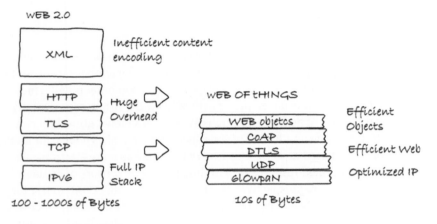

Fig. 7: IoT Application Stack

The advantages of using lightweight and efficient protocols in the IoT is that it provides greater efficiency, scalability, adaptability to low power and lossy networks and also it encourages energy preservation on small constrained devices.

Chapter 19 – Utilizing IPv6 Security Features

In this chapter, which follows on from the technical discussion on IPv6 and 6LowPAN we introduce the security features built into the IPv6 protocol and why we should make use of them. Additionally, we will look at TLS (transport layer security) routing and securing the IoT layers through the security tenets of CIA.

What the reader will learn in this chapter:
1. The built in IPv6 security features
2. 6LowPAN and where and how it can be deployed
3. Advantages of IPv6 through 6LowPAN
4. Securing the network for confidentiality, integrity and authentication

The introduction of 6LoWPAN allows for the compression of IPv6, which provides for a lighter weight protocol suitable for deployment in WSNs. This is a design requirement in most WSN as they comprise resource-constrained devices, which often need to be connected to the Internet. However, IPv6 is not always required, especially on non-Internet connecting devices or things. Indeed, in most implementations it may be more secure to only connect devices that required to be accessed directly and remotely to be configured with IPv6. Other devices that communicate only locally, with each other or through a gateway, could remain on IPv4, where NAT on the gateways would provide sufficient security from any Internet threats.

This hybrid form of network topology, a mixture of Internet connected IPv6 resource-constrained devices and IPv4 local\NAT connected devices form the modern IoT – or at least what we have at present. This has come about because unlike the enterprise or the Internet where devices are typically not lacking in resource capabilities, the devices\things in the IoT are extremely heterogeneous. An IoT device can be a just about anything, ranging from a passive sensor node, like a thermometer, pressure sensor, an accelerometer or a collection of sensors embedded in a single device such as a smartphone, a PC, a vehicle, a combine harvester. Even within the home we can find IoT things, which we prefix with Smart, such as light bulbs, thermostats, TVs and entertainment systems, fridges, toasters and kettles, and these connect via the Internet to a data base server or a cloud, which are also things. Hence, the plethora of potential devices that connect to the IoT are in hundreds of billions.

From a security perspective, the amount of smart devices being developed, is a concern as often consumers are unaware that their new acquisition is smart,

DOI 10.1515/9781501505775-024

and has the capabilities to auto discover a network and Internet gateway. The consumer is also probably blissfully unaware that the new smart TV they just installed has the default capabilities to spy on them as the microphone is typically always on, awaiting a voice command – this is also true in vehicles, especially with in-car entertainment systems.

However now that there are so many Internet capable things this requires the use of IPv6, which is a new Internet Protocol for IP addressing that increases the address size of IPv4 from 32 bits to 128 bits, which relates to 2^{128} unique addresses. In addition to the addressability, a number of protocols are being standardized to fulfil the specific needs of the IoT from a layers OSI perspective.

An example of this novel IPv6 style protocol is 6LoWPAN, which integrates IP-based infrastructures and WSNs by specifying how to route IPv6 packets in constrained wireless radio networks such as in 802.15.4 wireless chip networks. To achieve this, the 6LoWPAN standard proposes context aware header compression mechanisms: the IP Header Compression (IPHC) for the IPv6 header, and Next Header Compression (NHC) for the IPv6 extension headers, in addition to the compression of the User Datagram Protocol (UDP) header. Furthermore, the 6LoWPAN standard also defines a fragmentation scheme in which every fragment contains a reassembly tag and an offset this is necessary due to the limited payload size of the link layer in 6LoWPAN networks. Fragmentation is a necessity within 6LoWPAN networks when security is enabled as the 802.15.4 frame size may exceed the Maximum Transmission Unit (MTU) size of 127 bytes. This situation necessitates that packets are fragmented as needed. One way to try to prevent the max MTU being exceeded is to allow compression of headers in the UDP payload and the layers above, this is feature is called Generic Header Compression (GHC).

The problem with heterogeneous networks is that at some point typically a gateway or border router/hub some sort of protocol translation and traffic aggregation must take place. With 6LoWPAN networks, interfacing with full stack IPv6 networks this is relatively straightforward as the 6LoWPAN devices can connect to the Internet through a 6LoWPAN Border Router (6BR) that is analogous to a base station or sink node in a WSN. The 6BR, just like a base-station in the WSN is assumed to be secure, resource capable and with an unlimited energy supply – for example mains powered. The BR is responsible for compression/decompression and fragmentation/assembly of IPv6 datagrams and with the corresponding layer-to-layer translation – see Fig. 5.

Translation is a requirement because at the application layer, the Hyper Text Transfer Protocol (HTTP) is designed for TCP, which is unsuitable for use in WSN network where UDP is more commonly deployed. This is due to the low-powered and lossy nature of wireless sensor networks, as a result WSN typically implement connection-less UDP, instead of stream-oriented TCP. However, connectionless UDP does have some issues especially supporting other connection-orientated protocols such as MQTT which require a persistent TCP connection between clients and brokers. Consequently, there was a requirement to develop a light-weight HTTP version, which could operate over UDP and other connection-fewer protocols. The two most common implementations of this application level HTTP replacement are MQTT-SN (MQTT-Sensor Node) which is a variant of MQTT that supports publish subscribe over UDP and the Constrained Application Protocol (CoAP), which is text and method based with many similarities to HTTP. MQTT-SN and CoAP are designed specifically for resource-constrained devices and for machine-to-machine communication where small CPU and memory footprints are design criteria. Both MMQT-SN and CoAP are resident in software and can be compiled to run in 3-4KB of memory space. This is certainly light-weight, indeed suspiciously so, the catch being there is no native security. Both MQTT-SN and CoAP rely on other protocols such as TLS to secure connections and encrypt traffic.

In the network layer, IP routing is the predominant function and this can be problematic in CPU and memory constrained networks such as in the IoT. Routing is a CPU and memory intensive function, which stresses even powerful routing appliances and servers with unlimited energy and channel capacity. In resources constrained WSN networks, routing is achieved using the recently standardized, small, lightweight routing protocol with a big name, the IPv6 Routing Protocol for Low-power and Lossy Networks (RPL).

The RPL protocol creates a Destination-Oriented Directed Acyclic Graph (DODAG) structure that aims to optimize links by pruning sub-optimal routes based on path cost to the DAG root. RPL supports both unit-directional traffic to a DODAG root (typically the 6BR) and bi-directional traffic between constrained nodes and a DODAG root. Each RPL capable node has an IPv6 address, which serves as the node ID. The node maintains a list of DODAG neighbors and has one or more parents (except for the DODAG root). Nodes have a rank that determines their location with respect to the DODAG root. RPL nodes maintain routing tables that separate the traffic heading upwards, towards parents and the root, which are lower rank nodes, from the traffic heading downwards towards the higher rank nodes. (The rank should always increase from the DODAG root towards nodes.)

Securing the IoT

IPv6 provides the facility for interconnectivity of almost every physical object on the Internet. This has opened up the potential for tremendous innovation to develop new applications for the IoT, such as smart homes and cities, home security management, logistics with item and shipment tracking, personal health and fitness monitoring, connected and autonomous vehicles, the potential use cases and beneficiaries are endless. The potential is realized due to reliable global connectivity, large scale harvesting and storage of data with real-time streaming analytics performed in the cloud, which makes such operations financially feasible. However, to leverage the IoT technologies and infrastructure in data storage, computing and networking there has to be cloud based IoT aware applications, and high end security in real deployments in the IoT.

Security though at the conceptual level is no different from security strategy in the enterprise; it must comply with the three tenets of the CIA triad.

Confidentiality:

Messages that flow between a source and a destination could be easily intercepted by an attacker and secret contents are revealed. Therefore, these messages should be hidden from the intermediate entities; in other words, End-to-End (E2E) message secrecy is required in the IoT. Also, the stored data inside an IoT device should be hidden from unauthorized entities. Confidentiality services ensure this through encryption/decryption.

Integrity:

Ensuring the integrity of data is an important part of security. Data should be protected in flight as well as at rest. During data transmissions, it is imperative to verify that no third party has intercepted and modified the data payload. In order to achieve this common best practice is to use hash functions that take the packet and running it through a hashing function algorithm, which will return a value and this will be stored and sent along with the packet to the recipient. At the recipient node, the received packet will be run through the same hash function to determine a value, should the hash values match the integrity of the data can be assured. No intermediary between a source and a destination should be able to undetectably change secret contents of messages, for example a medical data of a patient. Also, stored data should not be undetectably modified. Message Integrity Codes (MIC) is mostly used to provide this service.

Availability:

Network availability is another important security function and this is to assure the services and assets of a network are available when required. Typical attacks on network availability are denial of service (Do's) attacks or more commonly on the Internet distributed denial of service attacks (DDoS). Attacks on IoT WSN would be very easy to accomplish as they typically have only very low bandwidth, and low power radio communication links so can be overwhelmed easily by a higher-powered frequency jammer. More sophisticated network attacks could result from reflection attacks such as DNS requests being sent on behalf on an IoT hub node, which connects a swarm of WSN nodes. As a DNS reflection attack consists of sending a tiny DNS request to several DNS servers with the IoT hubs IP address forged as the requestor. The DNS servers will return the DNS information, which is a very verbose and large packet to the unsuspecting IoT node which will be overwhelmed by such a sudden influx.

In IoT there are some other key security issues that must be considered in addition to the 3 enterprise IT tenets of C.I.A and these are source integrity and authentication, it is a necessity to check the identity of nodes that are communicating on the network. In addition, there is also a requirement for replay protection to insure against man in the middle attacks and eaves droppers.

Source Integrity or Authentication requires that communicating end points should be able to verify the identities of each other to ensure that they are communicating with the entities who they claim to be. Different authentication schemes exist. In addition, for the smooth working of the IoT and access to data whenever needed, it is also important that services that applications offer should be always available and work properly. In other words, intrusions and malicious activities should be detected. Intrusion Detection Systems (IDSs) and firewalls, in addition to the security mechanisms above, are used to ensure availability security services.

Replay Protection: Last but not least, a compromised intermediate node can store a data packet and replay it at later stage. The replayed packet can contain a typical sensor reading (e.g. a temperature reading) or a paid service request. It is therefore important that there should be mechanisms to detect duplicate or replayed messages. Replay protection or freshness security services provide this, which can be achieved through integrity-protected timestamps, sequence numbers, nonce, etc. In order to provide multi-faceted security, we need to ensure E2E communication security in the IoT, network security in 6LoWPAN networks, and also data-at-rest security to protect stored secrets and data.

Communication in the IoT should be protected by providing the security services discussed above. Using standardized Internet security mechanisms, we can provide communication security at different layers of the IP stack; each solution has its own pros and cons. broadly speaking, the communication security can be provided E2E between source and destination, or on a per-hop basis between two neighboring devices. Table 1.1 shows an IoT stack with standardized security solution at different layers.

Link layer:

IEEE 802.15.4 Security 6LoWPAN networks use the IEEE 802.15.4 protocol as a link layer. 802.15.4 link-layer security is the current state-of-the-art security solution for the IoT. The link layer security protects a communication on a per-hop base where every node in the communication path has to be trusted. A single pre-shared key is used to protect all communication. In case an attacker compromises one device it gains access to the key, and the security of the whole network is compromised. Per-hop security can detect the message modification on each hop unlike E2E where modified packets traverse the entire path up to the destination to be detected. Per-hop security with at least integrity protection should be used in 6LoWPAN networks to prevent unauthorized access through the radio medium, and to defend against effortless attacks launched to waste constrained resources. Though link-layer security is limited to securing the communication link between two neighboring devices, it is a flexible option and it can operate with multiple protocols at the layers above. For example, with link-layer security enabled we can run both IP and non-IP protocols at the network layer.

Network layer:

IP Security in the Internet and hence in the IoT, security at the network layer is provided by the IP Security (IPsec) protocol suite. IPsec in transport mode provides end-to-end security with authentication and replay protection services in addition to confidentiality and integrity. By operating at the network layer, IPsec can be used with any transport layer protocol including TCP, UDP, HTTP, and

CoAP. IPsec ensures the confidentiality and integrity of the IP payload using the Encapsulated Security Payload (ESP) protocol, and integrity of the IP header plus payload using the Authentication Header (AH) protocol. IPsec is mandatory in the IPv6 protocol meaning that all IPv6 ready devices by default have IPsec support, which may be enabled at any time. Being a network layer solution, IPsec security services are shared among all applications running on a particular machine. However, being mandatory in IPv6, IPsec is one of the most suitable options for E2E security in the IoT, as mostly only one application runs on a constrained device and the default security policies are enough for such scenarios. Furthermore, application developers require comparatively little effort to enable IPsec on IPv6 hosts, as it is already implemented at the network layer by device vendors.

Transport layer:

CoAP Security Although IPsec can be used in the IoT it is not primarily designed for web protocols such as HTTP or CoAP. For web protocols Transport Layer Security (TLS) or its predecessor Secure Sockets Layer (SSL) is the most common security solution. The connection-oriented TLS protocol can only be used over stream-oriented TCP that is not the preferred method of communication for smart objects; due to lossy nature of low-power wireless networks it is hard to maintain a continuous connection in 6LoWPAN networks. An adaptation of TLS for UDP called Datagram TLS (DTLS) is available. DTLS guarantees E2E security of different applications on one machine by operating between the transport and application layers. DTLS in addition to TLS that provides authentication, confidentiality, integrity, and replay protection, also provides protection against Denial of Service (DoS) attacks with the use of cookies. Though DTLS provides application level E2E security, it can only be used over the UDP protocol; TLS is used over TCP. The secure web protocol for the IoT, Secure CoAP (CoAPs), mandates the use of DTLS as the underlying security solution for CoAP. Therefore, it is necessary to enable DTLS support in the IoT.

Network security:

Even with the communication security that protects the messages with confidentiality and integrity services, a number of attacks are possible against networks mainly to breach availability security services. These attacks are aimed to disrupt networks by interrupting, for example, the routing topology or by launching DoS attacks. Intrusion Detection Systems (IDS) are required to detect impostors and malicious activities in the network, and firewalls are necessary to block unauthorized access to networks. In the IoT, 6LoWPAN networks are vulnerable to a number of attacks from the Internet and from inside the network. Also, 6LoWPAN networks can become source of attacks against Internet hosts, as it is relatively easier to compromise a resource-constrained wireless node than a typical Internet host. RPL [9], a routing protocol for low-power and lossy networks such as 6LoWPAN networks, is also prone to a number of routing attacks aimed to disrupt the topology. The IoT with 6LoWPAN networks running RPL, as shown in Figure 006, forms a network setup different from the typical WSNs. In the IoT, a 6BR is assumed to be always accessible, end-to-end message security is a requirement, and sensor nodes are identified by a unique IP address. In typical WSN there is no centralized manager and controller, security is usually ignored, and nodes are identifiable only within a WSN. Considering the novel characteristics of the IoT it is worth investigating the applicability of current IDS and firewall techniques in the IoT, or designing a novel IDS and firewall exploiting the factual and contemporary IoT features and protocols.

Part V: **Trust**

Trust: The firm belief in the reliability, truth, ability or strength of someone or something.

In this section, we will discuss a vital attribute of the Internet of Things and that is trust. The requirement for trust permeates through all layers of the IoT from its conceptual architectures through the entire manufacturing chain. Furthermore, trust is vitally important with regards security as inadequate products released to market that are insecure are eroding consumer trust and inhibiting IoT adoption. In this section, we will discuss the multi-facets of trust in the IoT and its relevance throughout the product lifecycle. We will discuss the requirement of trust and why we must preserve it through interaction at all levels. Further we will discuss where and who can assist us with developing trust models and providing trusted products and services in the consumer market.

DOI 10.1515/9781501505775-025

Chapter 20 – The IoT of Trust

This chapter introduces the concept and necessity of trust within the IoT ecosystem. We will discuss the necessity for trust in partner relationships and between manufacturers and the consumer. We will examine some pertinent examples of where trust was broken are damaged and how these situations can be avoided.

In this chapter the reader will learn:
1. What is trust and why is it so important
2. Why trust is necessary within the IoT and Internet
3. The Partners – partner trust model
4. How it can go badly wrong
5. The manufacturer – consumer trust model
6. How it has been eroded and how it was and is avoidable

Trust can also be defined as someone or something that we deem to be reliable, good, honest and effective, and will do me no harm. Trust is a very fragile emotion; it is extremely hard earned and easily lost. There are probably few of us that do not regret the loss of trust between ex-friends or partners. What is more, it can be seemingly innocuous words or actions that can lead to a loss of trust. The belief and confidence we share with one another can be destroyed all too easily if we do not live up to promises, expectations and behave predictably. We also need to show empathy with people as that instills confidence and promotes trust. Failure to foster and value trust has consequences that will lead to the loss of long term friendships and relationships both in business and in our social lives.

Trust is also a prerequisite for the concept of the Internet of things. Furthermore, the requirement for trust is pervasive within the IoT at almost every level. In business, it is a fundamental requirement for a manufacturer to the developer, partner to partner relationships. Also in the consumer IoT it is very important between the manufacturers and the end customer. Yet, all the evidence we see so far over the last few years lacks a concerted effort to build trust but instead an insidious erosion of trust between the major parties that is impeding the growth and consumer acceptance of the IoT.

The failure of trust between the major players has come about for a variety of reasons, some business orientated, others technical and others just because businesses are not managing the customer's expectations.

If we first consider the top level in the hierarchy the trust relationship between the manufacturer (OEM) and the developers (ODM) we will can see where

DOI 10.1515/9781501505775-026

conflicts arise and how trust is eroded leading to inferior products, loss of reputation and inevitably irretrievable breakdown of partner relationships between the manufacturer and the original design manufacturer.

Trust between partners – there isn't that much about

The concept of the IoT in business is all about trust, the feel-good relationship every business partner must have in order to work together under challenging situations. Trust enables partners to cooperate amicably, freely exchanging objectives, business models and enter into collaborative networks, which can integrate systems and share knowledge, information and experience. Trust fuels goodwill and team spirit, which is so vital when working under stressful and onerous conditions. Trust, also forges bonds between partners which encourages them to work co-operatively and share the collective responsibility rather than waste time and energy on toxic pointing the finger of blame. Finally, trust is a pre-requisite for knowledge sharing and mentoring as no one is likely to engage if they feel their positioned threatened. Therefore, we need the confidence that is instilled through feelings of mutual trust in order to disseminate information and as a consequence accumulate knowledge as a team of individuals to reach a common goal.

The theory of trust and teamwork is wonderful but the realistic obstacles are immense. As we have all probably witnessed even in symbiotic projects where both parties should be working together for a common goal and no conflict should be present, individual egos and internal politics can still raise their ugly heads and sour relationships destroying trust. From that moment onwards, teams work together but in partisan fashion unwilling to share, concede ground and worse sometimes deliberately obstruct.

Trust is a must for collaboration within a team, and this is where the hero workplace ethic must be discouraged. Individuals with egos or lacking self-confidence which results in shows of technical jousting with others are to be avoided. The IoT requires many skillsets and experience levels so team members are always preferable to those with an individual 'hero' approach. The relevance to security here is that IoT products cross many boundaries, the product could be a toy or a kitchen appliance so when brainstorming possible threats and vulnerabilities during the initial design phase of the project you never can tell when someone has unexpected operational experience and expertise.

Another major issue with trust between manufacturer (OEM) and the developers (ODM) can lie in the initial negotiation of terms and conditions of the contract and the finance. It is, if possible, a better strategy all round to keep those discussions to a separate team so that any frustrations and annoyances do not carry over into the project.

There is a common business term 'win-win' that is meant to indicate a willingness by the dominant party in negotiations to play fair. However, despite the term being bandied about so often by large companies there is little evidence to support their commitment to this ethic. Indeed, whenever a negotiator or senior manager comes out with this term, you know you are just about to be taken for an idiot, and it all goes downhill from there.

So, what can go wrong when there is an erosion or loss of trust between business partners, manufacturer's or third party service providers?

IBM Vs. Microsoft

Well let's look at trust within a supply chain. This is fraught with danger as can be seen through just a couple of examples, where trust is abused, or rather when one party's agenda differs from their partners. Way back in the early 1980's, IBM introduced the first business PC – the problem was that IBM's senior management had little faith in the product so instead of making their own OS they partnered with a small company called Microsoft. What IBM failed to realize is that because they were using a third party's components, notably Intel for the microprocessors and support chips their PC could be easily re-engineered and cloned. Microsoft, realized this and made binding agreements with Intel that every PC that used Intel's chips must ship with Microsoft's OS, at the time it was DOS, but later Windows. The result was that IBM the dominant partner in the alliance instead of dominating the PC market fell behind Microsoft, and the rest is history.

Apple vs. Samsung

Another more recent partnership that developed problems was Apple and Samsung. Apple came to the table with a design and an OS for their iPhone but it was designed on Samsung components. The iPhone became hugely successful and Samsung benefited from supplying the components such as the electronics and touch screens. However, it wasn't long before Samsung realized that they could instead of just supply components, build their own smartphone using Google's Android OS – which they duly did. This sparked years of acrimonious litigation and counter-litigation, but in 2016 Apple and Samsung are the top smartphone brands and still co-operate on many levels.

It is not only in technology that we can witness trust go astray within business partnerships. Camel a purveyor of high quality fashionable casual and outdoor clothing outsourced their manufacturing to a company in South East Asia. Of course, to be able to do this required that Camel issued the manufacturer with the templates, designs and material specifications with the understanding that the product would be made to high quality standards. The contract was to produce a run of a million or so products and true to their word the partner did produce the goods. What Camel probably didn't realize until it was too late was that now there were millions of their products being sold on the tourist night markets – not fake copies but perfect products.

As we can see, from only a few out of hundreds of examples of how business deals that should have been symbiotic and 'win-win' turned out to be anything but that.

Uber Vs Crowdsources drivers

Uber started a business, which had the vision of using a booking system (a taxi firm) to allow crowdsourcing drivers to apply for taxi jobs and drive their own cars and deliver the passengers to prearranged destinations. Uber became hugely popular and successful, yet strangely they then decided to invest in autonomous cars – for example get rid of the drivers that had made them successful.

The problem though is that there have been many crowdsourcing jobs such as retail delivery, logistics, and even shipment that have captured the imagination of the public. Initially this was a wonderful model; "if you have an empty truck or spare capacity on the ship, let us know, we can do a deal." The problem was that as soon as they could see ways to utilize autonomous cars and cut costs, the company planned to make the drivers redundant.

Manufacturer and customer trust model

Trust between the manufacturer of a product and their customer is paramount. Nothing is more important than creating a persistent feeling of well-being through providing a genuine quality customer experience. This is not just marketing talk a satisfied customer will be an evangelist for the product and importantly the technology. An example is a consumer that purchases a smart TV, if they plug it in and everything exceeds their expectations they will be delighted and tell their friends and associates. This by the way is also why managing customer expectations is so important, if the product or service exceeds their expectations then they will be pleasantly surprised. However, if the service or product is over hyped and it doesn't meet the customer expectations then expect a backlash. With the IoT today in 2016 we might just be slipping down that Gartner's 'trough of disillusionment' due to over-hype and the lack of quality products on the market that do actually interconnect but do not come anywhere near delivering the promised automated smart home that the consumer has been led to believe.

However, customer disillusionment and disappointment due to the product not meeting the products hype is the least of the manufacturer's concerns when we consider the loss of goodwill with the customer if the product betrays their trust. It is probably true that customers have become reconciled with the fact that buying electronic toys or devices on the Internet often do not live up to their advertising hype. Often they are like juicy burgers offered by fast food chains that when purchased rarely look anything like the advertising collateral, but we as consumers have come to terms with this. However what consumers have not come to terms with are when they buy products that come with incomprehensible instructions that are nigh on impossible to get working or need a technical degree in data communications and cryptography to configure.

Earlier in the security section the issue of why manufacturers' ship insecure products was covered in detail and how it was well intentioned. Also, this applied to the customer as their initial delight in having a device that worked as expected, out of the box encouraged that flawed strategy, which was ultimately irresponsible from a security perspective.

This is still a manufacturing conundrum for manufacturers as to how they can simplify the customer installation without jeopardizing the products security. The hard facts are that most manufacturers just do not care. They believe that they can always blame the consumer's home network, sometimes with justification, for their product being compromised. However, lately there have been a few products that have gone beyond consumer annoyance and caused a public outcry.

Dubious toys

The usual suspects are of course the child's web monitor, the interactive talking doll, and the Bluetooth locks. The children's products were always going to be a danger to the manufacturer's reputation as the threat of surreptitious surveillance of our children is a hugely emotive subject. The fact that this was being done within the security of the consumer's home and by a device that they had purchased only compounded the already massive collapse of trust.

Kids play

In late 2015, two security breaches revealed the private data of hundreds of thousands of children, their name, gender and age. However, the way the database schema was constructed it also indexed their parents, and so revealed their names, addresses and contact details and it was possible though awkward to correlate the two. Now what made these two hacks interesting and newsworthy was that they were very similar both used an SQL injection attack that returned a vast amount of records from the respective databases. The two companies were also both children orientated websites with one company, VTech, being focused on children's learning and online educational devices and the other, Hello Kitty, being the famous entertainment brand.

What was surprising was that these very large websites had severely lax security, and similar database schemas. Both these hacks which occurred in quick succession in the lead up to the holiday season, had severe repercussions for both brands as the newsworthiness of the topic made international news. The consumer backlash was certainly justified as the lax security showed an alarming indifference to the customers' data – in this case it was worse as it was also the child's personal identifiable data. It also didn't help that a spokesperson for one of the companies upon hearing the details of the hack, didn't seem to understand the seriousness of this data leak. Or perhaps they did. A skeptical view may be that they were trying to downplay the incident; by brushing aside the children' data as being inconsequential. Instead, the spokesperson tried to shift the focus to the fact that no credit card information had been misappropriated. Parents however, strongly disagreed with the company's assessment of the impact of the disclosure of their personal information.

This type of carelessness and disregard for the consumer's data was a breach of trust as the businesses that collect this type of data are responsible for storing the information. Furthermore, the public expects them to be the guardians of the information, and believe with merit that if they can't secure the information then they shouldn't collect it in the first place.

Chapter 21 – It's All About the Data

In this chapter on trust, we will examine the contentious issues revolving around personal data. Recently, data that was once considered worthless is now considered to have value and many companies are harvesting data wherever and whenever they get the chance. In this chapter we discuss why data has become to have value, why it is so important and how if it does have inherent value does the producer of the data – us – not get compensated when companies take it from us.

In this chapter the reader will learn:
1. Why data has value
2. Who are appropriating our data
3. Google & Facebook a fair barter
4. Data harvesting by stealth
5. Data appropriation an erosion of trust
6. If data has value should we not be compensated

Data is a valuable resource, and the common practices of data appropriation – which means capturing data from people without consent and compensation, is becoming a standard business model in the IoT. Some would argue that this practice should actually be treated as a form of theft – which means that companies that are capturing information from people without their consent or fair compensation are unethical to say the least.

But, how do modern tech companies view this? Data harvesting is determined to be one of the prime business objectives of modern technology startups. Previously, the capture and the refining of information through raw data were considered too difficult to be of value. It didn't really matter how much data was accumulated, the more that was collected made it harder to find the needle in the haystack. Indeed, the information was far more likely to be so hidden within the noise that it required intelligent analysis of the raw data streams and that was beyond the technology at the time. Also, mass storage was precious and expensive so it had to be rationed and not wasted. Furthermore, it was time consuming and expensive to determine what data to store and what to discard. As it is a skilled task to know what data to filter, it is no trivial task to recognize what specific data is required by algorithms to align processes with the business strategy. However, that has all changed with the advent of cloud storage, big data and online streaming and in-memory analytics. Now vast quantities of data can be seized and analyzed in real time, and it is cheaper to everything and throw

DOI 10.1515/9781501505775-027

nothing away, therefore data acquisition or appropriation is being looked upon as a new viable product.

But why are governments and companies dipping in to our private data with such a voracious appetite and why are they are so innovative and persistent in their methods? Why do they need to know what we do, where we go and what sites and content that we look at on the Internet? To realize the scale of this surveillance, just have a look at how many entities track you as you browse the Web. These trackers come from a vast number of entities that you may most likely have never heard of, so where do they come from?

Most are irritating infringements of trust, where partner apps have not declared third party interests, others are more blasé about it, including WhatsApp, sharing information that they promised they wouldn't, such as a name and phone number with Facebook. The only logical reason is so that Facebook's advertising machinery can kick into action, delivering to large businesses the targeted advertising opportunities derived from the very data they and WhatsApp have harvested.

Appropriating data

We know Google and Facebook have been harvesting our search data for years, but now we are tracked by many entities when we enter a website. We even get tracked by Geo-location in order for advertisers to target adverts with even more finesse. Lately, hiding GPS details is no longer enough to hide from the marketing houses as several startups are developing "fingerprinting" of our browser to identify us and track our movements. There are also technologies that allow fingerprinting of the Wi-Fi spectrums in the areas that you happen to be in so they can determine not only that you are in The Mall, but what floor and what department, and then target you with product specific details and offers. This might seem innocuous enough but those of us that remember the early 2000's and the cellular networks will only to quickly remember the scourge of Bluetooth marketing. But at least Bluetooth could be switched off.

Back in the early to mid-2000's most cellular phone came with early editions of Bluetooth installed and enabled by default. Bluetooth was and still is a fantastic cellular short range radio network technology. However, back then, Bluetooth was designed for convenience it enabled the phone to pair unauthenticated with any other Bluetooth device. What's more it managed this transparently and it was great for connecting devices in the home. Consumer's initially loved Bluetooth, especially teenagers that discovered that they could pair and exchange flirtatious messages with one another while in the shopping malls or cinema. However, it wasn't long until marketing realized they could do the same and send out unsolicited adverts and coupons to shoppers that had Bluetooth enabled on their mobile – which was just about everyone – as they passed by the shop. This was undeniably extremely successful. Well to begin with, however once ever shop in the Mall started copying the idea it became hugely frustrating – and consumers' suddenly disabled Bluetooth almost overnight by default. The point is if you abuse the consumers' goodwill and patience it erodes trust and they will take positive steps to severe the relationship even if it requires losing some beneficial features that they liked.

The Data Appropriators

There is an intriguing question as to what do these data appropriators actually do with our data. It is clear what Google and Facebook do, they feed the data into directed marketing algorithms and they sell this intelligent and focused advertising space on the open market. However, Google and Facebook are only two of the 30 to 40 trackers communicating with the browser. So, the issue is when or where did we sign up for these dubious services? Indeed, who or what are these data brokers that harvest and then distribute this personalized information profiles about each of us? Do we actually know about this and agree to it?

Unfortunately, we almost certainly do, as ferreted away within the ToC will be some ambiguous statement regards sharing data with third parties for some equally obscure reason. Are we as consumers actually expected to understand the ToC laid before us, the basis of which is the consumers' legal agreement with the manufacturer. Are we then sold products that the manufacturer knows are harvesting our personal data for financial gain but deviously hides the facts away within a TOC?

Further does the manufacturer brazenly uses this subterfuge to circumvent consumer protections meant to limit predatory and discriminatory practices. Unfortunately, it appears many do – so read the TOC and Privacy Policy!

These dubious instances of data harvesting are the techniques of Enterprises and Governments and they harvest data greedily. Their demand is for personal data, from all sources, irrespective of the means for extraction. It has created an industry for information, and the sole reason for collecting, and creating these massive reserves of data, is that it is an asset, which can be transformed into value.

Where is the fair barter?

People often do not even know how their data is collected and disseminated to third parties in a fragrant abuse of trust. Also, the user rarely knows or supplies the clear and explicit consent that the law requires. It became clear when mobile applications set about stripping users of their privacy by collecting by stealth geo-location data for example, that online data brokers were profiting. The data houses aggregated data from potentially millions of mobile app users without the consumers' knowledge let alone their explicit consent. These data houses were amassing troves of valuable data providing their services from the shadows, while amassing billions and trillions of data points about people worldwide.

What is far worse is that the government's intrusions and appetite for our data is shielded by laws, trade secrets, private courts, which prevent the public from knowing what data the analytics crunch and how it influences their liberty.

When companies do seek consent, it is typically through terms of service agreements – overly pseudo-legally worded contracts that a skeptic may claim was designed to be incomprehensible or at least ambiguous and that users are expected to "agree" to without understanding. Moreover, the ToC often are not presented to the consumer until they have bought or downloaded the product. Previously, this is how the sleight of hand worked with mobile apps. The developers would claim disingenuously that the consumer had implicitly agreed to share data through allowing access to their GPS and other sensitive sensors on their phone. This in itself was an unacceptable form of contract, yet it has become industry practice and become the standard model for obtaining the consumer's consent.

The trawling, collection and dissemination of personal information contributes to a lucrative data broker industry, which generates around $200bn in annual revenue. What is more they claim the data to be a residual waste product, which is of no value to anyone! So why collect it?

Consequently, some new technology startups actually have their business-case to generate profit through data acquisition. The harvesting and purveying of data is the prime goal and the product is little more than a façade an enabler for them to harvest the consumer's data. This is because there is a market for data, as information has value but the conflicting issue is that so does trust – perhaps in business more so.

Trust by design

The IoT depends on and is actually designed on concepts of unilateral trust it is a necessity not an option. The conceptual architecture of the Internet of things requires that all devices share the same trust level. What this means in design and practice is that all devices can interconnect, communicate, collaborate and share information at the same level.

Practically, that halcyon vision of the Internet just isn't feasible as we do not and cannot trust other people, devices or information. We trust but verify, and we require authentication, credentials, reputation and historical data to enable us to trust. The Internet is often displayed in conceptual animated diagrams where things simply connect with any other thing based on nothing more concrete than goodwill or perhaps naivety. However, in reality we are seeing silos of trust being designed into IoT deployments even within the private networks of the home.

One common security deployment for smart homes is to segregate IoT devices in their own VLAN (Virtual LAN) and keep the PC's, laptops and tablets in a separate VLAN. Indeed, in some security conscious homes the IoT devices may be segregated into functional groups such as the smart home thermostat being isolated from the smart TV and smart Light bulbs. The logic here being that a vulnerability that is exploited in one technology, say the smart TV will not provide a platform for an attack on the lighting or HVAC. The problem is though that by creating silos of trust we make interconnectivity more complex requiring not just gateways that can route between intranets but also controllers with the logic to manage the interoperability and communication between devices. This is not an ideal solution as it can lead to vendor-lock in whereby a consumer will prefer to buy devices from a single manufacturer rather than face the potentially onerous task of interconnecting devices from several manufacturers. The consumer should be able to purchase products on a best of breed basis and not be restricted to an existing a proprietary solution. This interoperability and the perceived threat of vendor-lock in have contributed to the ebbing of trust the consumer has in the maturity of IoT.

Trust in IoT is quite ambiguous depending on the point of view of manufacturer or consumer. As an example of this is that Gemalto an IoT security company believes that there are the three essential pillars required in order to deliver trust in the IoT ecosystem. The three fundamental pillars Gemalto refer to are:
1. Reliable connectivity
2. Reliable security
3. Agile monetization

Now if we consider each of these in turn we see that with regards connectivity, there are concerns. The Vason Bourne study, carried out for Brocade Communications revealed that 9 out of 10 senior executives have harbored doubts regarding their networks robustness and scalability for hosting IoT solutions. This concern may be well-founded as presently network failure is the biggest single source of IT downtime, which costs businesses around $700 billion dollars per year. As IoT interconnectivity is reliant on networks as the backbone of the IoT, the senior executives are perhaps right to be skeptical.

The second pillar is of course reliable security, and we all know the current status of IoT security.

It is the third essential pillar required to deliver trust in the IoT that is most revealing as it is agile monetization. What is illuminating here is that we are witnessing the manufacturer's perception of data, for its worth and its role in delivering trust – and none of them even mention the consumer.

Agile monetization consists of three stages of the IoT value chain:
1. Device monetization – suggests that manufacturers should charge a premium for enabling connectivity and upgrades on devices.
2. Service monetization – advises that manufacturers should look to PaaS (Products as a Service) to stimulate new revenue flows through innovative service-centric business models. Around 70 percent of IoT businesses are still failing to leverage revenue by providing additional services for their solutions, instead they are still reliant on the single sale opportunity.
3. Data monetization – proposes that manufacturers monetize the data collected from IoT devices for data analytics and here they quote a Gartner statistic that businesses that do not utilize software monetization tools have typically a 20 percent drop in revenue.

Of course, what we have looked at in the previous section is trust from the manufacturers point of view and it's all about providing trust in their business model. The model provides two trustworthy pillars for connection reliability and device security, to ensure the business has a product or services that are fit for purpose. The third pillar is about generating more income from their product, services and interestingly the data that can be extracted from the connected device. Therefore, we clearly see that for manufacturers' data collection and monetization is a part of the business model and isn't just a waste product service that some might lead us to believe.

Interestingly, Microsoft, which is moving more towards becoming a major data aggregator has a different philosophy to trust in a technological age and they propose a structure supported by four trust pillars; keeping data secure, transparency of data, for example the user will know what Microsoft knows about them, the ability to shut off data sharing and to opt out of data access schemes, and finally to be compliant with regulations.

Microsoft's official view is that, "We are just custodians of that data the only data the company has access to is when users allow it for the purpose of adding value to it."

This is of course very reassuring especially in light of Microsoft's 26.2 billion dollar acquisition of LinkedIn. Especially when we consider the vast amount of personal information stored in resumes and user profiles within LinkedIn data troves.

Interestingly, consumer trust issues with the IoT are maturing as the products gain more adoption and privacy matter are arising. For instance, many consumers how are indicating concerns over what they perceive to be lack of adequate security of the IoT. In a Fortinet connected home survey they revealed that 68% of respondents had issues that a connected device could lead to a breach of sensitive data. This is hardly surprising when they hear on the news with monotonous regularity about another hack that has lost millions of their customers' data records. It is believed by the Office of Civil Rights that in 2015 alone, 111 million health records were stolen, misappropriated or lost in just the top 10 security breaches. In addition, it's not just small companies with limited resources or even cloud service operators.

The latest shock being the web giant Yahoo who has admitted a loss of 5 million of their customers' records during a security breach back in 2014! One serious trust issues that Yahoo's customers and new corporate owner Verizon must be asking is why it took two years for Yahoo to come clean about this. Moreover, if a hugely experienced and wealthy company like Yahoo cannot secure customer data – apparently, Yahoo did protect the passwords but left the security questions and answers unencrypted as well as their contact details, alternate email and mobile phone numbers – then how can consumers trust startups that they have never heard of before. Finally, and most pertinently to the IoT, Yahoo is a huge empire of Internet service companies that use Yahoo services whether the consumer realizes or not.

Furthermore, trust is also further eroded when it was revealed that Yahoo also built a program to scan their users emails for specific signatures – a stream of words which the NSA decided were like fingerprints and could identify specific targets. Now let us not confuse this with PRISM or the like this was a request by the NSA for Yahoo to develop and deploy software to scan all Yahoo emails –

regardless of the user's nationality, which must have dubious legality in the U.S. – for a signature phrase within not just selected targets but ALL emails.

The result was that Yahoo did as they were legally obliged to do; though some question the legality of not just the NSA's request but also of Yahoo's action as they were practicing surveillance on US citizens. Regardless of the legality or not Yahoo has received a huge backlash from very unhappy subscribers, as many felt their trust had been betrayed, and Yahoo might never fully recover from the fall-out.

As an example, Sky TV consumers in the UK use yahoo mail even though it is branded differently as sky.com, so they too are affected by the breach, so too are Flickr customers and many more. The fallout from the Yahoo hack will not be known for a long time as the full ramifications of data breaches are felt fully in the future. However, the connivance and support for government agencies will hardly do them any favors. The danger for Yahoo and their prospective buyer Verizon is the hack and the consequent collaboration with security services, such as the NSA, has almost certainly caused irreparable harm in terms of customer trust.

However, the consumers' views on trust in the IoT are more difficult to ascertain and so we need to look at recent surveys to gain insights to this sometimes fluid and fast changing collective opinion. Indeed, consumer opinions differ around the globe and that is why the Mobile Ecosystem Forums survey of over 5,000 mobile users polled in the UK, USA, Brazil, France, Germany, China, India and South Africa is such an interesting study.

In the MEF study on the 'Impact of Trust on the IoT it was revealed that 60 percent of respondents around the global have concerns about the IoT. Perhaps, unsurprisingly privacy (62 percent) and security (54 percent) that were the largest single trust issues. Privacy is a major issue in the USA 70 percent and France 69 percent, which had privacy as the top threat opposed to a global average of 62 percent. With the IoT security issues, the UK had the highest concern with 67 percent versus a global average of 54 percent. Interestingly China (65 percent) and South Africa (61 percent) were the two highest countries with concerns over the lack of data transparency from wearable's providers, which is in contrast to a worldwide figure of 52 percent. Indeed, China's largest privacy concerns were around personal health data at 44 percent, whereas Germany and the USA were more concerned with location data as their main concern for privacy, returning figures of 50 percent and 52 percent, respectively.

From the MEF results, we can see that each country has different perspectives. The combined global figure of 60 percent was concerned and this was notably higher in the growth markets of South Africa, India and Brazil (66 percent) than in the UK (50 percent).

"The business opportunities surrounding IoT are clear, but only if industry heeds the lessons of the broader mobile ecosystem when it comes to the paramount importance of building consumer trust at the outset. Our 2016 Global Consumer Trust Report demonstrated the demand for transparency in mobile apps and services with 64 percent saying it's important to be told when an app is collecting and sharing personal information. This new report reaffirms the need for all stakeholders in the ecosystem to take action now to secure a viable future for such technologies."

"Nothing less than a technology evolution is underway, opening a world of possibilities to explore the Internet of Things (IoT)," said Todd Simpson, Chief Strategy Officer for AVG Technologies. "And yet, as the network of IoT devices grows, so, too, do consumers' understandable concerns about what this increased connectivity and data sharing means for security. If the IoT is to stand any chance of long-term, safe adoption that will benefit not just innovative companies but also the customers they're here to serve, we need to make secure by design a fundamental standard, no matter the device."

Despite the results, this is not the lessons that have been learned from social media. On social media platforms, we see that trust between humans is elastic. How many people do you know that are not celebrities, indeed are just average citizens leading normal monotonous lives like the rest of us, yet they have acquired hundreds if not thousands of Facebook friends?

The issue with social media is where did all these friends come from? More importantly, why do we accept them as social-media friends, when we have no clue to who they are? Yet, we trust these imaginary friends with our personal social information, our likes and dislikes, pictures of our children and family occasions, even our dreams and aspirations and even what we are thinking. The fact that most friends' identity was unknown, yet welcomed by the host anyway should have made the danger obvious.

Unfortunately, these new 'friends' became opaque to the individual as it didn't take long for companies to vet potential new employees by doing a Google search, then surreptitiously joining the social group of the prospect as a friend. This was an abuse of trust between employer and potential employee that could be hugely damaging to the individual as the potential employee knew nothing of this. Furthermore, the company rarely if ever declared this tactic which was somewhat unethical.

Presumably Human Resources when vetting a prospect deemed it ethical to spy on potential recruits without asking the prospect for their permission to invade and snoop into not just their private life but into their entire social circle. Of course, the company would argue differently claiming they were merely performing due diligence within the employment process and the information was freely published and accessible on the web so they are possibly correct. And it is this subjective definition of trust, what is acceptable and what is considered an abuse that makes it so difficult to define, especially when we consider the IoT.

Chapter 22 – Trusting the Device

In this chapter, we will examine the requirement for trust at the device – human level and how the original concept of the Internet of things has turned out to be fundamentally flawed and the name a misnomer. We will also see how blindly trusting in a device can have consequences that we did not anticipate especially if that device has surveillance capabilities. Also, we will cover the sometimes-problematic trust relationships with the media, their motivations and goals.

In this chapter the reader will learn;
1. Device trust model in the IoT
2. How it is not an Internet but more a collection of intranets
3. How trusting devices can have negative consequences
4. Some real-world examples, such as phone hacking
5. Trust and the media where is can go astray

The way that we have been sold the prospect of the IoT is through a vast network of devices that can communicate and share information, and interact to provide value. A definition and model of the Internet of things requires each autonomous device to communicate and collaborate with one another within a single flat hierarchy. The model requires each device to be able to unilaterally be capable to communicate with other devices in a democratic format. However, the current designs of the Internet of things, or more accurately the conglomeration of connected devices as we know them now, does not permit this. This is not the Internet of things, as we were led to understand by the early visionaries of the IoT. Instead, the IoT of today is developing into a model where we are presented with a wide array of autonomous devices connecting through a tribal network where every device within a closed group can intercommunicate. However, other devices despite being able to connect through mutual protocols still cannot communicate with one another in order to exchange information or cooperate in any meaningful way. In effect these devices exist only in invitational-only secure functional network silos.

As an example, how do we have such a thing as an Internet of things without global trust? An Internet would somehow require that every device was trusted, and what is more reciprocated that trust. This level of trust is just not feasible even between partners operating within business supply chains; therefore, it is still improbable within today's highly competitive commercial networks.

DOI 10.1515/9781501505775-028

Therefore, we are really speaking about an intranet of things! After all we are grouping devices and products into secure private intranets within even the private home network. This segregation is reinforced by using encryption and authentication as a form of membership in order to join the group. The issue is of course that by segregating functionality and purpose we are destroying the concept of the IoT.

The initial visionary, who had a utopian view of the concept, was for the IoT to have a flat-network infrastructure with everything interconnected hence the term Internet, where every connected device could interact and communicate with one another democratically. The potential and prospects were wonderful as each IoT device could harvest and swap information thereby accumulating knowledge and gaining a shared vision of the habitat in which they resided. This local intelligence raking and sharing could prove extremely valuable in intelligence gathering and decision making. The potential for having every remote device communicate with one another, exchange information and what is more come under a common command center in order to collaborate was revolutionary.

If we consider the status of the IoT today, it is not what was originally imagined, even in private networks such as the consumers home, that utopian dream of a trusted network is foolhardy. Proof of this comes from the Philips Hue 'Hack' discussed earlier, where a researcher compromised a PC with malware, the PC was situated behind the firewall so was on the local 'trusted' network. Because the PC was trusted the Philips Hue controller accepted and obeyed its commands, and subsequently turned off the lights – as you would expect. The problem was of course that the PC was running a malware script and it thereby compromised the operations of the Philips Hue controller.

Now this experiment had many far reaching unintentional consequences than were probably initially not envisaged. An unintentional consequence of the researcher's actions was it showed an important fallacy with regards trust within the IoT even in the smallest of networks. The point made was that clearly you cannot trust anything on a network explicitly. Trust but verify, is a common maxim but would it have made any difference?

If the Philips Hue controller had asked for authentication, or required a key exchange between the home PC and itself, that would only have prevented the attack if the PC was not trusted and was unable to communicate and command the Hue system. However, what this means is that to secure the Philips Hue system – which was not compromised by the attack, it just did as it was commanded – then the controller should obey only the smartphone running its paired application and ignore commands from all other devices on the 'trusted' private network. The alternative is to authenticate, encrypt data as well as run a virus scan and intrusion detection on every single device sharing the trusted network – and that isn't practical in a consumer environment.

The fall-out from this hack, was it illustrated that if the trust model for the IoT is already broken within the confines of a home network, then how on earth will this possibly scale to the enterprise, industry, and partner collaboration throughout a manufacturing supply chain?

Trust is essential, we require it from our partners, and we also demand trust as well. However, trust has to be reciprocated, we require to be trusted by our friends and family. Also, we need trust between the agencies that provide government, law enforcement and even immigration services, as this is necessary for them to protect us within a safe democratic society. Many citizens will claim with good reason that it is not an issue as they have nothing to hide. However, does the premise of, "well I have nothing to hide", actually work?

Well, let us take a look of how those trust assumptions can go terribly wrong.

Let us take for example an amateur author that is writing a thriller, for example, that requires knowledge of guns, bombs and the flaws, vulnerabilities and blueprints of nuclear power stations. Now unless the author is an expert in this field they will have to research all of this on the Internet. Therefore, will these web requests trip a wire? Do you believe that the NSA and GHCQ will not suddenly open a wary eye and start the process to hunt you down – and perhaps they should?

In the UK, a few years back journalists were struggling for a living due to falling newspaper sales and some took to embracing the modern technologies to get stories, work and income. The issue was that they were forced to undertake an almost photo-journalist or paparazzi role, that required hunting down interesting stories and clicking pictures of celebrities at the same time. Many very talented reporters were released from the newspapers that they had worked for most of their lives, covering decades, and had to find new sources of interesting newsworthy copy.

At the same time, the collapse of the village and local pub no longer became the source of gossip and news leads. Instead journalists were forced to raking information from the social media sites on the Internet. Journalists had become victims of the shift in media broadcasting. For example, it was now all about Twitter, Facebook, and other interactive social communities. Social media sites had become the main delivery of news to the latest generation of the population. Furthermore, the social media sites where not generating their own news but regurgitating the news generated through the reporters working for the traditional newspapers and TV news.

Strangely, social media news became focused on inter-communication within the online audience of common topics of interest, and the focus on popular interest was all it was about. Social Media news was no longer about current affairs but finely tuned and filtered and then targeted at specific groups of interest. News delivered to the populace was no longer as we knew it, bias and self-serving, delivered via experts, the thought deliverers of the new era of news had become just news delivery boys.

However, it did become clear that there was a flaw in the modern communication channels. There was still a market for high value content, though it was typically in the preserve of the photo-journalist that harassed celebrities. The opportunity came via phone hacking.

Hacking voicemail

Phone hacking is a misnomer as it is not hacking at all really it is simply using the default password to access the consumer's voice mail. Here we revisit default passwords and why they need to be done away with as it opens up the security to anyone that can find the person's phone number.

It became an issue, as journalists listened in to private conversations, but with little public concern as strangely most mobile phone users or consumers didn't care much about voice mail or rather how it could be abused. Indeed, if you were to ask the average mobile phone user how to access their mobile voicemail they could not have had a clue. And this was why it was such an innovative way to hack celebrity's phones.

Not being typically the brightest or sharpest tools in the shed celebrities would rarely it seems change the default password for voicemail from the default password of '0000' to something a tad harder to guess.

The result was that many redundant but now freelance journalists spent their time trawling through the celebrity voicemail boxes looking for a story, something that would put food on the table, or drinks on the bar.

Of course, this was never going to go unnoticed forever, and some brighter celebrities began to discover private conversations in the mainstream press and news. This resulted in privacy and trust actions, and journalists were rounded up and jailed for such privacy intrusions and misdemeanors.

The public however never really caught on to this, after all it was simply more celebrity information being spread about the Internet or front pages just like any other day. After all the freelancers arrested were just hired hands doing a job. Yes, they had undoubtedly broken the law in harassing famous people – just like the annoying paparazzi but was that a crime, when it produced such juicy gossip?

Furthermore, the cases were hardly publicized. That was until the phone hackers really made a huge mistake.

Unethical phone hacking

You see, trust with the public was destroyed when the journalists shifted their focus from arrogant self-publicizing celebrities to a missing child. They used the same tactics used to eaves drop on celebrities to listen into the missing child's mobile phone voicemails. The huge problem was that the police investigation team realized that the voicemails were being accessed and the local community stepped down their search and rescue efforts believing the child to be alive, perhaps a runaway. When her body was discovered days later and she was found to have died days previously to the voicemails being accessed, then there was hell to pay and rightly so.

Therefore, we must realize that trust is a multifaceted thing, we demand trust but we should also reciprocate trust. Our relationship with the media is certainly a flawed trust model after all we expect them to promote news about our products and deliver the good news into the home, which is the consumer marketplace. However, we cannot also expect the media to only market and promote good news, and sweep under the carpet any bad news, when that is not in their interests. To the media, news sells, whether that is bad or good, it all depends on the circumstances. Therefore, media outlets court popular stories, and with technology just like with fashion topics they tend to have a very short lifetime.

Consequently, the IoT became extremely popular and the futuristic Sci-Fi potential was great news. However, after a decade or so it is beginning to lose its appeal, after all there are only so many enthusing stories regarding intelligent fridges that the public can endure. Therefore, the media has to respond and it does so through scare stories and sometimes they cross over into irresponsible reporting.

As evidence of irresponsible reporting that damages not just individual and perhaps culpable brands is the way the media dramatize security issues. For instance, 60-Minutes a highly reputable news program, which is broadcast throughout the US at prime time, delivered a study of IoT devices and their security vulnerabilities.

The program was wonderful viewing and entertainment at its best, it showed how a skilled drone operator could in-flight lose control of their vehicle to a devious hacker. What is more the hacker could demonstrate their control by making the drone, on request, go up, down, wiggle from side to side and then the drone spectacularly crashed into the ground. This was wonderful TV as it demonstrated how an advanced hacker could not only commandeer your drone - Amazon watch out, – but also destroy it unintentionally.

However, it was the next program segment that caused concerns with trust. The 60-Minute presenters' flush from the excitement of witnessing a drone hijacked now took to the wheel of a Chevrolet Impala. The purpose of this demonstration was to make the consumer believe that a connected – not an autonomous car – but I doubt that distinction was noticed – was open to hackers. It was actually quite comical to see the 60-Minute presenters, without any safety gear, drive around in a vehicle under the control of a security researcher, and fake their surprise when the brakes didn't work.

Chapter 23 – Who Can We Trust?

In this final chapter on trust, we examine further some of the trust issues that have sprung up lately and why they have proven to be so toxic. We will see why businesses give us products and services for free and how we have become to expect this online. Further we will also see the self-destructive nature of the security industry as analysts strive to be the first to hack new and popular devices – sometimes rendering them irreparably damaged in the eyes of the consumer. Finally, we will close with an introduction to the neutral Online Trust Association and a brief discussion on their goals and aspirations.

In this chapter the reader will learn:
1. Why trust is such an issue between business and consumer
2. Why businesses give us free online services, tools and products
3. How we are doing ourselves harm by hyping security failures
4. How we should be hyping the security success stories
5. Gain an understanding of the OTA and its purpose and goals

The public and the media (popular and trade editions) have major trust issues with the general public, it used to be that the mainstream media was trusted – 'it must be true, it's in the newspaper' – was a common maxim.

Despite this common misbelief, we are now witnessing a shift in trust between consumers and the media. The media today see themselves and importantly so do consumers that the media are simply tools of business and commerce as profitable marketing outlets. After all, subscriber rates have plummeted and advertising is the only revenue keeping on the lights with most newspapers. Therefore, the media need advertising revenue so they initially promote and hype up products in this case IoT devices, forcibly promoting them onto a gullible consumer market. Using marketing skills and the marketing practices they are drumming into us as to why we need these products and why we cannot do without them.

The relation to the IoT is that the media have like Gartner found that the IoT has peaked in the interest of the public. Furthermore, over the last few years the hype on consumer IoT and the smart home has now lost focus, it is old news to the mainstream media and the focus has shifted to autonomous vehicles. However, even the latest news of technical revelations, advanced research and successful trials with regards autonomous vehicles is jading the publics' appetite, now the media is hungry for failure. Where is the trust there?

The real problem with the trust within relationships between business, media and the consumer, is that we all want to believe what we want to believe and if

DOI 10.1515/9781501505775-029

one business or media outlet tells us it is so then we are happy. We believe, we trust, that their products stance, their image, will reflect and even cement our beliefs, choices and actions as they share our common ethics. They share our life-goals, evangelize, and even offer advice as to how we should conform if we wish to remain in this social group.

Companies and service providers therefore want to build loyalty; they want the consumer to sign on long term and stay with them. Mobile communication companies especially go down this route as they want subscribers to move to pre-paid long term contracts perhaps with the lure of subsidized latest model smartphones. However, has it ever crossed your mind that the reason mobile phone operators offer incentives to join their networks through cheap handsets is they are actually supplying an onerous long term contract deal.

It is actually no surprise that they want to get as many subscribers as possible signing up for contracts that ties them into long term financial commitments – it makes perfect financial sense. Yet the majority of the people do not understand this as they will see, for example an iPhone 7 in a shop priced at say $900 dollars and laugh as they procured theirs from the mobile operator for next to nothing albeit they most likely unwittingly signed up for a three-year contract at exorbitant rates. If they actually took the time to read the Terms and Conditions and pricing of the contract it would probably wipe the smirk from their face. The business has abused their naïve trust they are actually being charged more for the phone than if they had bought it retail.

But how does this sleight of hand work? Well one of the things we the Internet generation have become accustomed to are that everything should be free on the Internet!

However, even before this avarice attitude inflicted the Internet generation, things had become free. The early exponents were Mosaic web browser, and then Yahoo, Google and Facebook provided all those free services. But to these web giants you were a subscriber, just a number. The goal was to generate a preposterous amount of connections and subscribers, that in itself was considered value – they would figure out how to monetize it later – although it is doubtful if any of them even thought about consumer data and direct marketing at the time.

However, as the Internet matured during the 2000's more and more free items became the normal model of releasing new products. Indeed, it was annoying to have to even register for a free product before download, let alone register your credit card. Most thought that companies were using the business model of initial free giveaways to generate usage, word of mouth and then latterly to introduce premier features through paid for licenses. However, that never happened, for decades now we have been subjected to and become accustomed to free services and products on the Internet. The result is that the millennium generation expects everything on the Internet to be free, but why did business germinate such an attitude in their consumers?

Free is an Earner

Well, it soon transpired that these Internet giants were way ahead of the game. They may have started of thinking that to build trust and loyalty was to give the product away for free and reap the benefit later was a viable business strategy, but it is unlikely. What they had realized, was that if the product is free, then the consumer becomes the product.

This understanding was a seismic shift in trust but was opaque and yet also transparent to the consumer, suddenly they were the product not the email service or the Map services. The consumer was the user of the service or product but to the provider the consumer had become the product. What is more, it wasn't just going to be in subscriber numbers, it was going to be their personal data that created value and even today in 2016 most people do not understand this – it is their personal present and historical data that is worth money and not them as an individual.

Pissing into the Tent

If you are a security practitioner, designer or even a manufacturer of an IoT product, it is highly unlikely that you would deliberately put a shoddy insecure product to market as it destroys trust in the brand and the industry. In a similar vein, let us consider why security analysts go to such great lengths to destroy trust by finding improbable flaws within consumer products. This phenomenon can be witnessed in a desire to preorder toys in order to be the first to cyber-exploit or electronically re-engineer them. Their own rush to market in order to find technical exploits outside the device's operational parameters. Now the failure in trust we are addressing here is that most analysts are going looking for flaws that are highly improbable to be exploitable under normal usage. For example, one researcher did make a valid point, when asked about electronically re-engineering a toy and for what purpose could it have been used. He suggested I doubt with a straight-face, that the doll could have been repackaged and sent to the CEO of a presumably unfriendly company as a gift for the children and hence delivered a snooping device into their home. It is this ludicrous belief that all smart devices are designed to spy on us is why the consumer will not buy them. The fact that so many analysts are searching for highly technical flaws in devices that cost only $75 is eroding trust for all devices within the IoT.

IoT Trust is Essential

Security analysts do have a duty of trust they cannot just turn a blind eye to a technical flaw or potential vulnerability – that would be them being complicit in the failure of the product and they would suffer a loss of trust in their professional reputation. And this is where there are huge conflicts of interest. For example, there is a difference between independent security analysts and hired security analysts, the former is unconstrained and can experiment and report as they feel fit and this freedom of expression is wonderful they have no product bias or immediate financial gain. Their conflict is a bit different, do I exploit the vulnerability or do I report it to the manufacturer? The dilemma is not always so straightforward, as it seems as sometimes the manufacturer is hostile to revelations of lax security, but other times they may be grateful and pay a bounty.

The reason for this is basically not all hacks are the same, but are so often treated as such, causing a lot of unnecessary damage to a product. If we revisit the poster boy product of the consumer IoT the smart light bulbs we can clearly demonstrate this paradox.

The Osram debacle

Osram, a major player in the smart home lighting field were found to be vulnerable to a host of security exploits which could leave users open to attack. The Osram Lightify product was found by security firm Rapid7 in 2016 to have nine vulnerabilities, some of which could be used to attack the home network. Worse some of the flaws were so basic that it is doubtful any competent security review of the product could have taken place with any sort of diligence.

The security firm released their findings in a security advisory and disclosed that one of the flaws allowed the injection of persistent JavaScript and web-based HTML code into the web management interface. This could allow an attacker to "take control of a product" in order to launch drive-past attacks against a user's browser.

In addition, Osram had another severe security flaw in that the smart bulb's mobile application, stores unencrypted copies of an owner's Wi-Fi password. This flaw flies in the face of all elementary security practice, as everyone in the business should know that passwords are not stored like that. Because of this major flaw, hackers could easily obtain this information via the app, which would grant them control of the Wi-Fi network.

A further weakness in the Osram Lightify product allowed an attacker to identify the wireless network's password. This was due to the password using short, eight-character codes, which were susceptible to brute force password attacks that could be cracked within a matter of minutes.

Osram were clearly lax in implementing sufficient security and these issues were rightly brought to the publics' attention through the media.

However, another attack – or security analysis – on a competitor the LIFX connected smart bulbs, also declared the product to be insecure and duly hacked and this too made the headlines.

Despite the lurid headlines what the researcher had found was that the company made the mistake of transmitting most bulb-2-bulb communications in clear text, which made analyzing traffic sent between master and slave bulbs a trivial exercise. However, despite the fact that the security researchers found they could inject packets into the network and mimic the behavior of a bulb requesting Wi-Fi credentials from the master bulb. They soon discovered that the sensitive information sent between the bulbs was encrypted.

The task of breaking the encryption wasn't easy. The researchers' first approach was to download the firmware by extracting it from the micro controllers embedded within the LIFX bulbs – however this entailed smashing the bulbs open in order to gain access to the printed circuit board (PCB).

Despite this the researchers still needed to be able to analyze the PCB, and then figure out the manufacturer of the System on Chip (SOC) integrated circuits that control the 6LoWPAN and Wi-Fi communications as well as the underlying architecture of those circuits.

Once they reverse engineered the PCB, the researchers had to get access to the memory on the chips in order to extract and begin reverse engineering the firmware. That effort required using a JTAG (Joint Test Action Group) debugger and then software for extracting the firmware.

LIFX's another Hack?

LIFX's security model certainly had some flaws such as the failure to encrypt all intra-bulb communications. However, the point is that not all hacks are equal. While the headlines share the same common message, that these products are insecure and open to hackers, the truth is rather different. In the case of Osram the researcher's may well point to a smart home devices that was vulnerable to casual hacking. But with LIFX the researchers tell a less sensational tale of a company that had diligently secured its product, and that only was victim to sophisticated and persistent attackers.

Balancing Security and Trust

If you are a contractor or part of an in-house security analyst team things are far more complex than life as an independent freelancer. To explain this further, a professional security analyst works very similarly to a lawyer or a judge. Legal types know the scope of the argument is potentially vast and the repercussions are not palatable. So, what do Legal types do? Sensibly, they restrict their focus within the parameters of the legal argument in order to concentrate on the finer points within clearly defined limits. As do security analysts working for a manufacturer, they will determine the products market its usage and then ask for the limits of the security boundaries to be defined. The rationale here is that you can't possibly mitigate every possible threat – to paraphrase Donald Rumsfeld: there are known threats, the things we know and understand, and of course there are also the unknowns, these are the threats we recognize but just do not have current information, and then there are the unknown-unknown, and these are the inexplicable threats that we have never imagined. Subsequently, security professionals, working professionally have to limit their scope. They will diligently test and verify a device within those usage boundaries, and then can say with professional confidence that under these 'restricted' circumstances that the product is secure or it is not. To expect anything else is rather wishful thinking. Therefore, who or what can we trust?

So, Who Can We Trust?

The trust that we require in IoT is only going to come about through standards and best practices that come about through companies adhering to ethical practices. These needs to come from neutral organizations which consumers can relate to and trust. Regardless of how we evaluate and deploy trust within our own environments it just is not going to happen alone. Consequently, a neutral organization the OTA has developed a framework to help IoT businesses build and develop trust as it is beneficial to all in the industry. Some of the OTA's suggestions within their guidelines are based upon their model of the IoT ecosystem. The OTA model of the IoT is based upon a few classic criteria for example the persistent, highly personal and dynamic collection of data. They also put a strong emphasis on a lack of defined standards, best practices and industry guidelines for the new breed of untraditional manufacturers to follow. In addition, they also recognize that the vast array of diverse devices, products that are connecting to applications, smartphones, and cloud infrastructures makes each individual use-case a plethora of diverse touch points, interfaces, threat maps, attack surfaces and potential data disclosures.

Open Trust Alliance

The OTA also recognizes the threat of what they term ambient data, which is all the information collected through the array of devices and transferred to the cloud. The OTA's concern is what happens to this ambient data, where does it get stored or where is it forwarded. The concern is that ambient data may well be shared with undisclosed or unknown 3rd parties, which is an erosion of trust and breach of privacy.

The OTA trust frameworks consists of three major sections that address, security, user access and credentials, and privacy, transparency and disclosures.

These major functional groups cover topics such as:
1. Device security, which entails ensuring that all PII (personal identifiable information) data is stored (at rest) and transported (in motion) securely using acceptable industry standards of encryption – this may be through specific IoT device certificates that have lately started to come to market.
2. Vulnerability reporting – IoT solution providers must understand the unique end-to-end security issues, risk and vulnerabilities of IoT applications – the problem here is a lack of vendor testing and lack of a vehicle for vulnerability reporting for example through bug bounties or just feedback forums, this is now being pushed by the FTC in the US the idea is to encourage feedback via vulnerability and bug reporting.
3. Upgrade and lifecycle patching – All software and firmware updates must be authenticated and verified as coming from a trusted source and be cryptographically signed to ensure the integrity of the patch, file or update and test and verify, patches, upgrades and firmware code as this is a common source for breaking a products functionality.
4. Privacy disclosure – ensure that privacy, security and support policies are easily obtainable, clear, concise, understandable and available for review prior to purchase or download. Disclosure of what data will be collected,

stored and with whom it may be shared and for what purpose is a legal requirement in the EU and many US states so should not be underestimated or simply ignored.

5. Data storage and sharing – conspicuously display and make consumers aware of what PII data will be harvested and stored externally for instance in the cloud and specifically for what purpose.

6. PII data can only be shared to third parties if the consumer has given their explicit consent on the basis of clear transparent disclosure that they can reasonably be expected to understand.

Consequently, the OTA have come up with a set of working objectives and goals aimed at producing a Trust framework and this is based upon security, privacy and sustainability. The individual working group goals are to provide:

1. Guidance to reduce potential vulnerabilities and adopt responsible data and privacy practices
2. Drive the adoption of best practices through a voluntary but enforceable code of conduct
3. Provide recognition to companies that adhere to the code of conduct
4. Think globally to adhere and apply to international standards and practices
5. Encourage collaboration to share vulnerability intelligence and share best practices
6. Evaluate a gating system, via voluntary code of conduct and a seal or certification program

Yet, every IoT exploited device, analyzed with the power of hind-sight has perhaps fallen below the OTA's expectations. They have quite correctly identified the basic security and privacy mechanisms that manufacturers and developers have consistently missed when delivering trustworthy consumer products.

Let's look at what they feel as being the major failings, by manufacturer's, developers, and even consumers as to why these IoT devices are so insecure?

What is notable is that over that last year there is shown to be a serious disconnect between the OTA and researchers/hackers of the IOT.

Where on that list do you see firmware hacks, UART or Trust is essential, it is the key stone to the IoT, and without trust the IoT concept cannot feasibly work.

Part VI: **Privacy**

Developers, manufacturers and certainly marketing people must understand that privacy is extremely important to the design of IoT products. Certainly we must understand that lax security is the major inhibitor to IoT uptake. Indeed, lax security, and poor privacy models will only ensure that our designs fail in the long run. Unfortunately, designers and manufacturers have come to believe that the public have no concern for privacy, so are unwilling to pay for it .

Privacy is often described by the internet giants, Facebook, Google, and the like as being redundant or a waste of time. They will claim that consumers will willingly submit their personal details and are only too happy to read those of others via social media.

However privacy is far more complex than just social media. Privacy for an individual is deemed to be a human right, a social requirement, and something that we all cherish. It is just we express it in different ways.

So why have we so readily forsaken our privacy? Or have we?

DOI 10.1515/9781501505775-030

Chapter 24 – Personal Private Information (PIP)

"Privacy is the claim of individuals or group or institutions to determine for themselves the when, how and to what extend information about themselves is communicated to other."

Alan Westin, 1968

"Privacy is the subjective decision that people enjoy when they have the power to protect information about themselves and when they use this power consistent with their interests and values."

Jim Harper, 2013

Privacy with regards to the two quotes from Alan Westin and Jim Harper is the people's subjective claim to protect information about themselves and control what, and to what extend information can be communicated to others that are consistent to their interests and values.

Why is the Privacy of our Personal Information Important?

The word subjective is very important for understanding the anomalies of privacy. For the decision to exercise the power of privacy is subjective to the interests and values of each individual. It must be our decision as to when, how and to what extend we communicate information about ourselves to others.

Subjectivity is very important when considering privacy because we are seeing diverse levels of tolerance towards what is considered acceptable and what privacy infringements are. Some may claim that privacy is dead, or as Mark Zuckerberg said in 2010 that 'Privacy was no longer a social norm.'

Although, to be fair to Mark Zuckerberg, he did also say in a Times interview also in 2010 that, "What people want isn't complete privacy. It isn't that they want secrecy. It's that they want control over what they share and what they don't."

This is interesting because Mark Zuckerberg's words echo the profound statements of Allan Westin back in 1968, which were made long before the Internet or social media were imaginable.

Notably, Allan Westins' prophetic observations back in 1968 seem to have captured the US population's view of personal information privacy in 2016. There is no clear consensus and definitive viewpoints with regards the people's claims to privacy, it is a shifting, fluid emotion depending on benefits and circumstances. The scenarios determine what, how and to what extent we are willing to release our private information and importantly in the benefits the person receives in return.

DOI 10.1515/9781501505775-031

In a very interesting survey performed by Pew Research Centre in the U.S. revealed a strange anomaly. Of the 461 U.S. adults and nine online focus groups consisting of 80 people, the results indicated that many respondents were receptive to the offer to trade personal information for tangible benefits. Although, saying that, many of the respondents were often cautious as to what would happen to their data after the companies had hold of it.

However, the real surprise was not that the U.S. adult would trade personal information for tangible benefits it when and to what benefit, which seemed to fly in the face of popular wisdom. To summarize the report, it consisted of six hypothetical scenarios that reflected an opportunity to exchange personal information in return for free service or use of a product. The respondents were then given three choices; acceptable, it depends, not acceptable.

In one scenario, which reflects many of the Internet service models that are common online the respondents were offered free access to a social media site in return for creating a profile with a real name and photograph. The use of the service would be free but the website would collect information on your activity on the site for directed advertising purposes. This model of providing a free service in exchange for personal information is how Facebook, Google and Yahoo have built vast business empires. However only 33 percent found it acceptable, 15 percent said it depends, and 55 percent of respondents said it was unacceptable. What this appears to imply is that the very successful social media and Internet business model of exchanging personal data for free service is very benefit dependent. After all, 55 percent rejected it outright as the benefits were simply not attractive enough so did not outweigh the risk of surrendering their anonymity online and being targeted by advertisements.

In another IoT related scenario, respondents were offered a new smart thermostat product that could control the temperature within the home in exchange for basic information of the residents' movements and activities such as what rooms were occupied and for how long or when rooms were unoccupied. This is all the basic data that smart thermostats collect. Yet, only 27 percent found this an agreeable deal, 17 percent said it depends, and 55 percent found it unacceptable. Again, this is surprising as the data requested is the typical data required and harvested by smart thermostats, which would cost them in excess of $250 yet they 55 percent were against the deal – that doesn't look too promising for Nest and the others. 17 percent were reticent as they too found the service not as attractive as the risk of the loss of personal information.

Over the six scenarios tested, Pew Research came to the conclusion that the American public's mood favoring privacy or information divulgence was – it depends.

This appears to be because the respondents perhaps now understand that the Google's and Facebook's of the Internet are not providing free service they are bartering with them for their private information. Therefore, the respondents realize that their information has value.

If that is true and data does have value, then a problem the IoT manufacturers will face regards their products collection by stealth of personal information when seemingly collecting it without the owner's consent or in most cases their knowledge. Google and Facebook can with some merit point to providing unpaid quality services as barter for personal information. Similarly, we can say the same of media such as online news, who supply us with a quality product as barter for our browsing history and site activity – hence the deluge of trackers that latch onto our browsers as we brose their sites. But, with IoT products how does the manufacturer of a $150 dollar video camera or a fitness tracker for $250, manage to convince the consumer that their data, which is streaming out back-doors on their own devices, which they have bought and paid for, to many third party ODM developers, is actually inconsequential. These third-party links have been built in during the many iterations of the products development but the third parties have no association with or partnership no matter how tenuous the link with the future owner of the device. So how are they to convince themselves or the owners that this data is actual just a waste product of no residual value, especially now that the truth is out there.

There are many manufacturers complicity working with third parties who are taking advantage of the situation and cultivating a lack of transparency as to when, how and to what extent our information is being monetized through a deliberate loss of privacy.

For if the manufacturers are selling us IoT products that they know are harvesting data that is a function neither documented or declared to the owner when they know that data has value to both parties then the appropriation of data by stealth must be considered theft. Therefore, it's not a question of whether we have anything to hide, it wouldn't matter these businesses are likely to burgle the information anyway.

For this reason, it should be the government agencies, such as the FTC, that should be strenuously enforcing acceptable trading practices and ensuring that the consumer is treated fairly and have either their privacy enforced or are suitable reimbursed for their product, their personal information.

Collecting Private Data

If we consider the quantity and the relative value of personal data being collected today by data aggregators within technology, then it is vast. Huge amounts of PPI (Personal and Private Information) from our social media profiles, our personal information and even the demographic data from our bank accounts, medical records or even employment data is being swept up by our service providers, governments and god knows who else. Furthermore, some of the providers are providing little explanation, justification or no compensation for appropriating our data and selling it on to third parties.

After all, our entire personal yet innocent web browsing is to be recorded by the UK Government, why when we are not suspected of any crime or misbehavior?

The purpose of this appears to be simply is to record the actual sites that we visit, what we view and which political parties that we may support. The government will also record our likes and dislikes, personal history as well as our purchase histories. Furthermore, tweets, texts, emails, phone calls and photos as well as the coordinates of our real-world locations will be noted and recorded.

Amazingly, the state-of-the-art data mining technologies that help to analyze and combine these massive amounts of personal, but probably mostly useless data, also result in the invasion of our privacy. The emerging agencies, businesses and also those in social media and mobile applications make commercial and profitable use of the collected data.

Data is the New Oil, or Is It?

It has been stated before that personal data is the new oil of the Internet and the new currency of the digital environment. After all everyday services on the Internet are relying on aggregated data and are becoming more and more complex and difficult to analyze. However, most IT people and even data scientists have insufficient knowledge about what may happen to their personal data when using smartphones or the Internet. This of course leads to fear, uncertainty and a decline in trust. We only have to look to the World Economic Forum, who stated in its report, when rethinking Personal Data (2012) that privacy is no longer believed to be a natural function of the IoT.

However, is collecting vast quantities of personal data from citizens that are unsuspected of any wrong doing and storing it in the cloud actually beneficial. Funnily enough we saw how GHCQ came to the conclusion that not all data is good and valuable data when they surreptitiously stole unencrypted Yahoo video chats, just because they could.

Hilariously, GHCQ discovered that Yahoo transported Yahoo Video Chats unencrypted, so they decided to intercept each and every one, because it was easy to do. As a result, GHCQ captured and watched every Yahoo Video Call, this we know for a fact due to Snowden's NSA revelations. Incidentally, GHCQ have never refuted the claim.

It appears that GHCQ became aware that Yahoo video calls were unencrypted and so where easily captured and watched. Unfortunately for the spooks that were participants in the Yahoo video project they discovered that subjects had a penchant for showing each other their bodily parts and nudity was a major issue. Perhaps this was against the UK's intelligence service's code of acceptable behavior, sitting about watching porn all day. Certainly, they were worried about their agents being subjected to this nudity, and perhaps in danger of falling foul of GCHQ HR rules regarding pornography on work computers, so this was not acceptable at all. Consequently, they promptly dropped the escapade as a bad idea.

Therefore, it appears that not all data is good data.

Attacks on data privacy at Internet scale

It isn't just the regulatory authorities or IoT manufacturers that have issues with privacy and fair business practices. Indeed, the web giants are hoovering data and personal information from us all using practices that are also beginning to come to the attention of Internet regulators. Consequently, because of this escalating appetite for consumer data and third party interest in trawling and hoarding the value and resale of consumer PIP, regulations and compliance are becoming enforced.

Facebook is of course an interesting subject when investigating the concept of privacy in the Internet, social media and IoT world. After all Facebook's goal is about connecting as many people as possible within a vast social Internet of interconnecting friends willing to share more, and in Facebook's view a more connected sharing world, is a better world. Facebook started out just over a decade ago and gained 4,300 subscribers in the first few months. Today its global subscribers exceed 1 billion active users that share nearly 5 billion items, and click 'Likes' 4.5 billion times.

However, it appears from Mark Zuckerberg's interview at the Web 2.0 summit in 2008 that despite Facebook's stellar growth users were initially reticent about loss of privacy and that been a formidable barrier to adoption.

"Four years ago, when Facebook was getting started, most people didn't want to put up any information about them on the Internet. ...So, we got people through this really big hurdle of wanting to put up their full name, or real picture, mobile phone number."

Mark Zuckerberg is addressing the launch times back in 2014, over a decade ago but it is still interesting to note how the public's perception of privacy has changed fundamentally. The social-media generation has apparently different values regarding the distribution of their personal information and how it is shared with others. Many young people certainly do appear to believe that privacy is an impediment in the socially-connected world and would agree with Zuckerberg that privacy was no longer a social norm.

Young and Carefree

However, we seem to accept the younger generations lack of privacy awareness as a given, and by all accounts teenagers and young people seem to be less reserved about what they post up on social media. Or has growing up constantly in the presence of cameras within their mobile phones, which are pervasive amongst their social peers given them a celebrity like acceptance and even desire for publicity. Just over 92 percent of today's generation of teenagers post online photographs of themselves up from 76 percent in 2006, a study by Pew Research Center in the US revealed. Despite this people deny that the craze for 'selfies' is egotistical and narcissist, instead most claim that they do not expect their self-portrait to be viewed by anyone out with their close circle of social media friends.

The younger generation's shift in attitude to sharing information about themselves with others through social media broadcasting to a wide net of friends may seem enlightened and liberating but it isn't really. It is simply that they are exercising in Jim Harper's words; their subjective claim to protect information about themselves and control when, how and to what extent information can be communicated to others that is consistent to their interests and values.

The major problem with our expectancy of privacy is whether we can compare our private lives and that to the extent that law enforcement and intelligence agencies can intrude on our daily existence. Strangely, privacy is often disregarded yet anonymity, the right to remain anonymous is considered to be sacrosanct.

After all some Internet users and IoT consumers take an alternative view, they consider privacy as being irrelevant and yet they do hold their online anonymity dearly. As individuals or groups, they also wish to exercise their claim to freedom of speech. They wish to be protected from the divulgence of information about themselves and also to control when, how and to what extent information can be communicated to others that is consistent to their interests and values.

Of course, privacy is not a digital concept and many of us will have privacy values that fall somewhere in between the two bookends of being sharing averse and having sharing rapport. However, what this does mean is if we accept privacy as being an individual's subjective claim then it cannot be regulated for by a third party so we must have our own controls and mechanisms to publish or embargo information.

Can we Control our Privacy?

Do we have the power to control our information on the Internet? Many proponents of the information sharing culture will say we already do. If we wish to opt-out of tracking, then there are mechanisms to do so. If we wish to opt-out of receiving directed advertising, then we can install an ad-blocker into our browsers. Similarly, we can detect and block tracker cookies using browser plug-in such as Ghostery, which will list all trackers on each site and the user can block individual trackers or by group category.

However, using ad-blockers results in being blocked access to many sites, which is fair enough as there is a refusal to barter fairly. In this case one party is not accepting the other party's revenue generating adverts but expects to browse the product without paying anything. Of course, this type of retaliatory action is out of the question for the big Internet companies, if Google refused to accept web searches from every user on the Internet using an ad-blocker it would only hurt itself, so how does it deal with the ad-blocking conundrum?

Ad-blockers – They're Not What They Seem

Google makes approximately 90 percent of its revenue through advertising and marketing through their AdWords advertising programs. Therefore, it is detrimental to Google to have users running ad-blockers as it restricts the number of potential customer's seeing their personalized adverts let alone clicking through on the adverts. The scale of the problem is also significant as globally the usage of ad blockers increased by 41 percent Year on Year from 2013 to 2015.

Google and the dubious ad blockers

So how does Google deal with this threat to is main source of revenue?

Currently it is looking into ways to limit the damage done by unrestricted ad-blockers. The way Google is approaching the problem is through an acceptable ads initiative where it can use its massive research data into what users find acceptable forms of ads, and which formats they do not. The problem is that they cannot be seen to be running the initiative as that would be unacceptable to competitors.

In the meantime, Google has instead done something a bit devious. They have paid the owners, Eyeo of the most popular ad blocker application, Ad Blocker Plus, the conveniently most prominently placed application in the ad block category within Google's Chrome extensions, $25 million per year to white-list Google ads.

Those figures are unsurprisingly neither confirmed nor denied by either party but as Google created $74.5 billion in revenue from advertising last year it's hardly an onerous payment. Indeed, it is actually a bargain if Google did manage to reclaim almost one billion in lost revenue by appearing in the white-list as was suggested by anti-ad blocking firm Pagefair.

The lessons learned from Google and Ad Blocker Plus's connivance is not just the cynical betrayal of the consumer's trust. But that even when the consumer does take the initiative to opt-out of the marketing program in order to preserve their privacy, the mechanism is still often surreptitiously loaded against them. Indeed, as most customers see a significant drop in ads appearing on the browser page, which frees up real estate and letting their pages load quicker they simply accept the remaining ads as perhaps being local to the site they are visiting.

Whatever the case Google has once more circumvented by stealth the consumers – claim to determine for themselves the when, how and to what extend information about themselves is communicated to others – namely their privacy.

After all it is the individual or group or organization that should have the power of control, not Google and Ad Blocker Plus and this is one of the issues with privacy on the global Internet.

Privacy Laws Around the Globe

The problem with the IoT, trust, privacy and the like is that we are not living in a vacuum and the Internet is a global utility that is governed by no-one as every nation reflects their own culture, views and laws upon their regulators and citizens. This is why it is near impossible to standardize the IoT as each country has their own flavor of security, surveillance, trust, cryptography, data transport, third-party data sharing, marketing and manufacturing regulations. And so it is with privacy. There are many diverse attitudes towards an individual's privacy rights around the globe and it is not always predictable. As a result, we will look at certain major countries that have relevance through influence to the IoT and examine their privacy laws and regulations.

United States of America

The United States has about 20 sector specific national privacy or data security laws and hundreds of state specific data and privacy laws among its 50 states. There is also the Federal Trade Commission ('FTC') and the Federal Communication Commission ('FCC') and they cover a wide range of companies that are subject to enforcement if they engage in materially unfair or deceptive trade practices. The FTC & FCC have previously used this authority to pursue companies that fail to implement reasonable minimal data security measures, fail to live up to promises in privacy policies, or frustrate consumer choices about processing or disclosure of personal data.

Privacy requirements

The States of California and Delaware require commercial online websites and mobile applications to post a relatively general online privacy policy. Liability for failing to post the privacy policy may only be imposed if the website or mobile app is notified of its non-compliance and fails to post the policy with 30 days of receiving notice of non-compliance.

There is no specific federal law that regulates the use of cookies, web beacons, Flash LSOs and other similar tracking mechanisms. However, the Children's Online Privacy Protection Act (COPPA) applies to information collected automatically (e.g. via cookies) from child-directed websites and other websites and third party ad networks or plug-ins that knowingly collect personal information online from children under 13, COPPA also regulates behavioral advertising to children under 13.

In addition, undisclosed online tracking of customer activities poses class action risk. The use of cookies and similar tracking mechanisms should be carefully and fully disclosed in a website privacy policy. Furthermore, it is a best practice for websites that allow behavioral advertising on their websites to participate in the Digital Advertising Alliance code of conduct, which includes displaying an icon from which users can opt out of being tracked for behavioral advertising purposes. Under California law, any company that tracks any personally identifiable information about consumers over time and across multiple websites must disclose in its privacy policy whether the company honors any 'Do-Not-Track' method or provides users a way to opt out of such tracking; however, the law does not mandate that companies provide consumers a 'Do-Not-Track' option.

The same law also requires website operators to disclose in their privacy policy whether any third parties may collect any personally identifiable information about consumers on their website and across other third party websites, and prohibits the advertising of certain products, services and materials (including alcohol, tobacco, firearms, certain dietary supplements, ultraviolet tanning, tattoos, obscene matters, etc.).

California law requires that operators of websites or online services that are directed to minors or that knowingly collect personally identifiable information from minors permit minors that are registered users of their sites to remove any content the minor has posted from the site or online service. The law does not give minors the right to remove information posted by third parties. Minors must be given clear notice on how to exercise their right to removal.

Privacy requirements of location based apps and services are in flux and are a subject of extensive interest and debate. Federal Communications Commission regulations govern the collection and disclosure of location information by telecommunications carriers, including wireless carriers. Further, any location service that targets children under the age of 13 or has actual knowledge that it is collecting location information from children under age 13 must comply with the requirements of the COPPA Rules including obtaining prior verifiable parental consent in most circumstances. Both the Federal Trade Commission and California Attorney General's Office have issued best practices recommendations for mobile apps and mobile app platforms, and the California Attorney General has entered into an agreement with major app platforms in which they promise to prompt mobile apps to post privacy policies. Furthermore, a Department of Commerce led multi stakeholder negotiation to develop a code of conduct for mobile app privacy is well underway.

Germany

Germany has one of the most stringent privacy laws and regulations. The main legal source of data protection in Germany is the Federal Data Protection Act, which implements the European data protection directive 95/46/EC. Additionally, each German state, like the U.S., has a data protection law of its own. In principle, the data protection acts of the individual states intend to protect personal data from processing and use by public authorities of the state.

These will remain the legal sources until the European Data Protection Regulation comes into force in 2018. The Data Protection Regulation will then completely replace the BDSG and the European Data Protection Directive 96/46/EC.

Russia

In Russia, there are some fundamental provisions of data protection law, which can be found in the Strasbourg Convention for the Protection of Individuals with regard to Automatic Processing of Personal Data (Convention) ratified by Russia in 2006 and the Russian Constitution. These laws are establishing the right to privacy of each individual (articles. 23 and 24). There is also specific legislation, including the Data Protection Act. In addition, the Russian Labor Code contains provisions on the protection of employees' personal data other laws may also contain data protection provisions which implement the provisions of DPA in relation to specific areas of state services or industries.

Russian law however does not specifically regulate online privacy. The definition of personal data under the DPA is rather broad and there are legal views that information on number, length of visits of particular web-sites and IP address could be considered personal data.

China

Currently, there is not a comprehensive data protection law in China and instead, provisions relating to personal data protection are found across various laws and regulations. Generally speaking, provisions found in laws such as the General Principles of Civil Law and the Tort Liability Law may be used to interpret data protection rights as a right of reputation or right of privacy. However, such interpretation is not explicit. A draft Personal Data Protection Law has been under review by the government for many years, but there is still no indication as to if and when such law will be passed.

The purpose of the law is to protect Internet information security, safeguard the lawful rights and interests of citizens, legal entities or other organizations, and ensure national security and public interests.

However, Chinese citizens do have some recourse, for example once citizens find network information that discloses their identity or breaches their legal rights, or are harassed by commercial electronic information, they have the right to require that the network service provider delete related information or take measures to prevent such behaviors reoccurring.

India

There is no specific legislation on privacy and data protection in India. However, the Information Technology Act, 2000 contains specific provisions intended to protect electronic data

India's IT Ministry adopted the Information Technology and their Privacy Rules, which took effect in 2011, which require corporate entities collecting, processing and storing personal data, including sensitive personal information to comply with certain procedures. It distinguishes both 'personal information' and 'sensitive personal information'.

There is no regulation of cookies, behavioral advertising or location data. However, it is advisable that user consent is obtained by inserting appropriate disclaimers.

Brazil

Currently, Brazil does not have a single statute establishing data protection framework. For instance, the Brazilian Internet Act which establishes general principles, rights and obligations for the use of the Internet, has some relevant provisions concerning the storage, use, treatment, and disclosure of data collected on-line.

Most, aspects of data privacy are still regulated by general principles and provisions on data protection and privacy in the Federal Constitution, in the Brazilian Civil Code and in laws and regulations that address particular types of relationships in particular sectors and particular professional activities (e.g. medicine and law). Additionally, there are laws on the treatment and safeguarding of documents and information handled by governmental entities and bodies that have privacy implications.

Australia

The data privacy/protection in Australia is currently made up of a mix of Federal and State/Territory legislation. The Federal Privacy Act 1988 applies to private sector entities with an annual turnover of at least A$3 million and all Commonwealth Government and Australian Capital Territory Government agencies.

The Privacy Act was last amended by the Privacy Amendment these additions significantly strengthened the powers of the Privacy Commissioner to conduct investigations and to ensure compliance with the amended Privacy Act and, for the first time, introduced fines for a serious breach or repeated breaches.

Unfortunately, there are no laws or regulations in Australia specifically relating to online privacy, beyond the application of the Privacy Act and State and Territory privacy laws

However, if the cookies or other similar technologies collect personal information of a user the organization must comply with the Privacy Act in respect of collection, use, disclosure and storage of such personal information. App developers must also ensure that the collection of customers' personal information complies with the Privacy Act.

Japan

Japan has a law that requires business operators who operate or host in Japan a personal information database which consists of more than 5,000 individuals in total identified by personal information on any day in the past six months to protect personal information.

The Act on the Protection of Personal Information ("APPI") as it is known applies to all companies operating within Japan.

There is no law in Japan that specifically addresses cookies and location data. However, if the information obtained through cookies may identify a certain individual in conjunction with other easily-referenced information (e.g. member registration) and it is utilized (e.g. for marketing purposes), such Purpose of Use of information obtained through the use of cookies must be disclosed under the APPI.

UK (Under review)

Different Laws in Countries – What Possibly Could Go Wrong

Facebook's EU Opt-out Scandal

Just how much power of control do we have on for example social-media sites such as Facebook that tracks people around the web regardless if you are a subscriber or not unless you explicitly opt-out of the tracking scheme? But how can you opt-out of an advertising mechanism that you, as a non-subscriber or visitor to Facebook would in all probability know nothing about.

Researchers in the EU discovered that due to the way that Facebook plugins such as the 'Like' button worked they tracked all visitors to any non-Facebook site which hosted any of this plug-ins. As a result, Facebook tracks users whether they are logged in to Facebook or not, and this is for advertising and marketing purposes. Furthermore, Facebook even tracks visitors if they are not registered users of the site or that they have explicitly opted out of tracking. Facebook's cookie policy states that the company still uses cookies if users do not have a Facebook account, or are logged out, to "enable us to deliver, select, evaluate measure and understand the ads we serve on and off Facebook".

However, it appears that Facebook not only disregards their user's privacy wishes when they explicitly indicated that they did not wish to be tracked they were actually flawed in their reasoning regarding the opt-out option in the first place. It appears that under EU regulations the opt-out option is not an adequate mechanism to gain a user's informed consent especially due to the opt-out mechanism being hosted on a third-party site. This is because under article 29 of EU law Facebook and others cannot infer consent due to a user's in-action.

However, as can be seen from the Facebook privacy opt-out mechanism, it not only was insufficient for Facebook users the company had clearly no business tracking non-Facebook subscribers and visitors under any circumstances. The fact Facebook could do this was through cookies that were used on non-Facebook sites that hosted any of their plugins.

However, not only did Facebook's opt-out mechanism have no legal basis. It actually unbelievably worked in reverse in so much as it entered people against their express wishes into the Facebook tracking program even though they had explicitly requested to opt-out!

The way this happened was due to the way the opt-out mechanisms are deployed for the big web giants such as Facebook, Google and Microsoft amongst circa 100 other large companies. Users wanting to opt out of any behavioral tracking are directed to sites run by the Digital Advertising Alliance in the US, Digital Advertising Alliance of Canada in Canada or the European Digital Advertising Alliance in the EU.

But the researchers from Cosic in the EU discovered that far from opting out of Facebook's tracking program, the third-party site proposed for the EU, did something entirely different. It seems that when people who were not being tracked by Facebook make use of the 'opt out' mechanism Facebook instead placed a long-term, uniquely identifying 'Datr' cookie, which can be used to track them for the next two years.

Furthermore, the researchers found that Facebook does not place any similar long-term identifying 'Datr' cookie on the opt-out sites suggested by Facebook for US and Canadian users. This anomaly of practice was confirmed by a researcher at Princeton University that verified the different behavior between opt-out mechanisms, and long term cookies in the UK compared to US and Canadian versions of Facebook.

Facebook hotly denied any wrong doing and attributed the behavior to a bug. However, they did take the opportunity to explain how Facebook is offered free of charge, and it is monetized by showing ads that they think are relevant to people's interests. This is no different to the funding method used to support many other services including those from Google, Microsoft, and Yahoo.

Interestingly, Facebook initially lost the case, but won on appeal against an earlier EU order to stop tracking non-Facebook users of websites. The appeal victory was not however legal recognition of the validity of Facebook's working practices, far from it. The appeal court dismissed the case due to the Belgium regulator was deemed to have no authority over Facebook which has its European headquarters in Ireland. Consequently, nearly a year later in May 2016 Facebook resumed tracking non-Facebook users in the EU but this time without the 'Datr' cookie bug and with prominent banners displayed warning non-Facebook users.

Chapter 25 – The U.S. and EU Data Privacy Shield

What the Facebook privacy issues in the EU, and specifically within Belgium and France, brought to the fore was the swift divergence of attitudes between the U.S. & EU on information privacy. Previously, the huge global behemoths like Facebook, Microsoft and Google had done business within the EU single market under a data privacy agreement termed a Safe Harbor that had been agreed back in 2000.

The EU however was undergoing a sea change in its views on data privacy and was in the process of rewriting their current legislation to make it more relevant and unified across all 28 states as the legislation at the time dated back to 1995.

The European Union's intention to toughening its data privacy laws, would apply to all Internet companies doing business with EU consumers. The key issue was the degree of control individuals would claim over their digital data. However, this was far reaching with potentially severe issues for large scale Internet companies operating in the EU. One issue was that individual data defined was ranging from pictures on Facebook to web searches and surfing habits stored by Google.

The EU wanted to allow it citizens as individuals and groups the power to restrict the movement, and divulgence or delete their data, which Internet companies were collecting, storing and monetizing through targeted ads. However, by providing EU citizens with control over their own information data would have a profound effect on the business models of the U.S. Internet companies, which made significant profit from tracking individual's online habits and activities. Furthermore, these proposed changes in EU laws would create a wide gap between existing U.S. data privacy laws and EU data privacy laws and raise concerns as to how multi-nationals were expected to do business whilst complying with multi-regulatory bodies.

There are many notable differences between the laws regarding data privacy in the European Union and the United States. However, generally in the E. the individual has more rights under a single data privacy directive. The U.S., however, takes a more ad-hoc approach to data protection, often relying on a combination of public regulation, private self-regulation, and legislation. This is not to say there are not any individual privacy rights, far from it. California alone has over 25 privacy and data security laws. It just means there is no single law providing individual data privacy protection.

DOI 10.1515/9781501505775-032

However, the EU has moved swiftly over the last decade and this has brought about friction between The EU and Internet companies as they see themselves with some justification as being primarily the targets of the legislation. Despite, their uncommon show of self-awareness as it is their resistance to deleting individual's data in the case of Facebook and Google's voracious appetite for every scrap of individual behavioral data that it can hoover up are only two of the motivators for privacy protection. There are many other factors, one was the far reaches of the Patriot Act and its implications for U.S. intelligence agencies to access cloud data storage. Others were more mundane, such as EU individuals demanding that Google, Microsoft and Facebook amongst others show more transparency with their intentions regards storage and usage of the individual's personal data. However, not all privacy activists were interested in the technological aspects; there was within Europe a growing concern regarding the powers of these global companies. The question being raised was who actually is running the world, governments or these vast corporations?

In the U.S., the data privacy laws protect specific types of data, and they have over 20 sector specific or medium-specific national privacy and data security laws. Specific laws such as the Health Insurance Portability and Accountability Act (HIPAA), which deals with individual's medical records, are one example. Another is the Payment Protection II which protects individuals financial and credit card transactions. Additionally, and very importantly, there is also the Bill of Rights which does provide an implicit right to privacy, but it is weakened by its lack of relevance to the Internet and especially to the concepts of social media and willing sharing of data. Under the Bill of Rights an individual cannot expect protection for information willingly shared. An example is a consumer's utility bills, with traditional utility bills there was a requirement for the police to seek permission before they could seize the information as it was considered private. However, if the consumer has a utility meter installed then the police do not need to seek permission as the individual has already willingly shared the data in question with the service provider. Therefore, in the age of social media, where data is shared by some naturally, and willingly without any concern then the Bill of Rights is severely diluted. Furthermore, large businesses seem to have little appetite for further insights into the Bill of Rights so lobby against any calls for revisions to bring it up to date with today's modern technology.

When privacy laws collide

What the Safe Harbor agreement of 2000 provided was a way to bridge the gulf between the U.S. and EU's values and laws on the individual's privacy. The EU's requirements were that EU citizens' data would be protected from U.S. data laws that might not provide a similar level of data protection as under EU law. Furthermore, the Data Protection Directive of 1995 insisted that both the individual and the regulator had to implicitly agree to the transfer of data out with the borders of the EU. This was very difficult to implement in practice for all parties so the Safe Harbor agreement provided a self-regulated opt-in program that all participating companies would have automatic permission granted for all data transfers.

Losing a Safe Harbor

The Safe Harbor agreement worked well, possibly to well for the opt-in self-regulated participants became severely lax with compliance. Indeed, one research study in 2008 urged the EU to renegotiate the Safe Harbor agreement as they discovered an appalling lack of compliance despite the requirement barriers being so low. The researchers revealed there were only 1109 companies registered out of 1597 listed by the US Department of Commerce once, duplicates, triplicates and not current organizations were removed. Further out of that 1109 only 348 met even the most basic requirements for compliance. Also, another 206 falsely claimed to have been members for years despite no evidence of them being subject to US enforcement. A further 421 had no links to their privacy policy, and that for those that did some was only a few sentences of virtually no substance or betrayed a complete lack of understanding of the concepts and principles of the Safe Harbor program.

Nevertheless, the Safe Harbor survived that 2008 mauling and continued albeit under closer scrutiny especially from the EU. This growing version to the agreement was exacerbated in 2011 when it became clear that the US had every intention of ensuring data stored in the cloud came under the Patriot Act. Indeed, in 2012 independent research supported the notion that current U.S. policy did not exclude or protect cloud data regardless of whether it was stored in the world from the Patriot Act. Alarmed, European businesses and citizens became seriously concerned and ruled out U.S. cloud companies from bidding for government projects.

After the subsequent Edward Snowden in 2013 revelation regarding the U.S. intelligence services, specifically the NSA practices and interpretations of the laws the European Court of Justice in October 2015 invalidated the Safe Harbor Agreement.

After the closure of the Safe Harbor

For the huge US Internet companies and businesses trading in the EU single market the ECJ court's decision to invalidate the Safe Harbor threw their operations into turmoil as they were now effectively operating illegally. Furthermore, the EU was even considering whether companies like Facebook's transference of data out with the EU should be suspended. Also, the EU regulators stipulated that if there was no agreement between the ECJ and the U.S. within three months then US companies could face action from EU privacy regulators. This deadline was later extended from Feb 2016 to July 2016.

Model and Standard Contractual Clauses

In the meantime, many Internet companies determined to find another legal method to continue their operations within the EU. Microsoft for example decided on using model clauses, which are standardized contractual clauses used in agreements between service providers (such as Microsoft) and their customers to ensure that any personal data leaving the European Economic Area will be transferred in compliance with EU data-protection law.

Model clauses and the subsequent standard contractual clauses issued to their customers required a large investment in time and operational process to prepare. The standard operational clauses offered to customers provide the specific guarantee that transfers of personal data out with the EEA would be in compliance with EU law.

The new EU – US Privacy Shield

On July 12th, 2016, less than a year after the closure of the Safe Harbor, the EU commission adopted its decision on the EU – U.S. Privacy Shield.

The Privacy Shield is based upon – and some critics say too closely – the Safe Harbor agreement. However, proponents claim there are significant alterations that strengthen the privacy policy framework, which will protect the fundamental rights of anyone in the EU whose personal data is transferred to the United

States. Further, they will claim that as well as bringing legal clarity for businesses relying on transatlantic data transfers the Privacy Shield also includes:
— Strong data protection obligations on companies receiving personal data from the EU
— Safeguards on U.S. government access to data
— Effective protection and redress for individuals
— Annual joint review to monitor the implementation

New shield or old failings

The European Commission formally adopted the Privacy Shield framework in July 2016 and US companies could begin the certification process on 1st August 2016. It is less nine months since the Safe Harbor was deemed to be invalid so creating or amending new legislation in this time period is an impressive task for two legislative slowcoaches as the EU and the U.S.

It should come as no surprise then that Privacy Shield is merely a revamped Safe Harbor with some additions to address some of the original frameworks shortcomings.

The with regards compliance, problem resolutions and safeguards on how US authorities can access the data of European consumers,

However, not everyone has found the improvements of the EU-U.S. Privacy Shield too their liking. Indeed, Austria, Slovenia, Bulgaria and Croatia abstained feeling that the Privacy Shield did not go far enough to satisfy them that the new agreement would protect their citizens from U.S. surveillance.

The concerns regarding how well protected European citizens' data is from the analysis of the US intelligence agencies, regards the less than precise language and undefined terms, that provide no meaningful legal protections just promises made today which could just as easily be reneged tomorrow. After all, if we discovered one thing in all the data and documents released by Edward Snowdon it was the absolute shamelessness the U.S. Intelligence agencies have for mangling the definitions of words when justifying their actions. The NSA cannot really be blamed for this after all the government sets the rules, the boundaries of their activities and it is NSA's task to do their duty. If that means testing the elasticity of those boundaries, then that has to be expected. The explosion in new Internet technologies, processing power and vast storage capabilities have given the NSA the skills to not just make seemingly concrete boundaries elasticated but transform them simultaneously into opaque membranes. However, these flexible boundaries, the rules, work both ways and it is also the duty of non-US intelligence agencies and governments to make sure these boundaries, the agreed and unambiguous rules remain concrete and impervious to fickle changes in circumstance.

Despite concern from civil and privacy activist groups, the business communities on both sides of the Atlantic hailed the agreement. As did the European Commission, which clearly disagreed with the accusations of bogus security reassurances, claiming that the Privacy Shield agreement provided, "clear limitations, safeguards and oversight mechanisms" which would govern how law enforcement and federal agencies access the data of Europeans, and that bulk data collection would only be carried out "under specific preconditions and needs to be as targeted and focused as possible."

Contradictions on privacy

Notably, these observations seem to have captured the U.S. population's view of personal information privacy in 2016, with there being no clear consensus and viewpoints shifting fluidly depending on circumstances, the scenario and importantly in the benefits the person received in return. For in the MEF survey of mobile users worldwide it was the consumers in the U.S. (70 percent) and Germany (69 percent) who declared privacy to be the major threat of the IoT. Furthermore, with regards their privacy the U.S. and German respondents stated it was the dissemination to third parties of information regards their location that they considered the biggest threat to their privacy. Whereas other nations such as China and South Africa said the misappropriation of their personal health records were their major concerns with regards loss of privacy.

A very interesting survey performed by Pew Research Centre in the U.S. revealed a strange anomaly. Those only 461 U.S. adults and nine online focus groups consisting of 80 people the results indicated that many respondents were receptive to the offer to trade personal information for tangible benefits. Although, saying that, many of the respondents were often cautious as to what would happen to their data after the companies had hold of it.

However, the real surprise was not that the U.S. adult would trade personal information for tangible benefits it when and to what benefit, which seemed to fly in the face of popular wisdom. To summarize the report, it consisted of six hypothetical scenarios that reflected an opportunity to exchange personal information in return for free service or use of a product. The respondents were then given three choices; acceptable, it depends, not acceptable.

In one scenario, which reflects many of the Internet service models that are common online the respondents were offered free access to a social media site in return for creating a profile with a real name and photograph. The use of the service would be free but the website would collect information on your activity on the site for directed advertising purposes. This model of providing a free service in exchange for personal information is how Facebook, Google and Yahoo have built vast business empires. However only 33 percent found it acceptable, 15 percent said it depends, and 55 percent of respondents said it was unacceptable. What this appears to imply is that the very successful social media and Internet business model of exchanging personal data for free service is very benefit dependent. After all, 55 percent rejected it outright as the benefits were simply not attractive enough so did not outweigh the risk of surrendering their anonymity online and being targeted by advertisements.

In another IoT related scenario, respondents were offered a new smart thermostat product that could control the temperature within the home in exchange for basic information of the residents' movements and activities such as what rooms were occupied and for how long or when rooms were unoccupied. This is all the basic data that smart thermostats collect. Yet, only 27 percent found this an agreeable deal, 17 percent said it depends, and 55 percent found it unacceptable. Again, this is surprising as the data requested is the typical data required and harvested by smart thermostats, which would cost them in excess of $250 yet they 55 percent were against the deal – that doesn't look too promising for Nest and the others. 17 percent were reticent as they too found the service not as attractive as the risk of the loss of personal information.

Over the six scenarios tested, Pew Research came to the conclusion that the American public's mood favoring privacy or information divulgence was – it depends.

This appears to be because the respondents perhaps now understand that the Google's and Facebook's of the Internet are not providing free service they are bartering with them for their private information. Therefore, the respondents realize that their information has value.

If that is true and data does have value, then a problem the IoT manufacturers will face regards their products collection by stealth of personal information when seemingly collecting it without the owner's consent or in most cases their knowledge. Google and Facebook can with some merit point to providing unpaid quality services as barter for personal information. Similarly, we can say the same of media such as online news, who supply us with a quality product as barter for our browsing history and site activity – hence the deluge of trackers that latch onto our browsers as we brose their sites. But, with IoT products how does the manufacturer of a $150 dollar video camera or a fitness tracker for

$250, manage to convince the consumer that their which data is streaming out backdoors on their own devices, which they have bought and paid for, to many third party ODM developers, actually inconsequential. These third-party links have been built in during the many iterations of the products development but the third parties have no association with or partnership no matter how tenuous the link with the future owner of the device. So how are they to convince themselves or the owners that this data is actual just a waste product of no residual value, now that the truth is out there.

There are many manufacturers that are complicity working with third parties who are taking advantage of the situation and cultivating a lack of transparency as to when, how and to what extent our information is being monetized through a deliberate loss of privacy.

For if the manufacturers are selling us IoT products that they know are harvesting data that is a function neither documented or declared to the owner when they know that data has value to both parties then the appropriation of data by stealth must be considered theft. Therefore, it's not a question of whether we have anything to hide, it wouldn't matter these businesses are likely to burgle the information anyway.

For this reason, it should be the government agency, such as the FTC, that should be strenuously enforcing acceptable trading practices and ensuring that the consumer is treated fairly and have either their privacy enforced or are suitable reimbursed for their product, and their personal information.

Leveraging the value of data

Many IoT manufacturers have recognized the value of big data in the opportunities it provides to learn more about the product, how it is used and about the customer. Additionally, big data analysis can also provide key product differentiators that are derived from device data, such as identifying desirable features or predicting reliability issues. In this respect, most technology companies are competent and re taking advantage of data opportunities. However, some IoT technology companies have taken this a step further and are utilizing data that was previously thought of being a side effect of the products activity. By unlocking this opportunity and utilizing data as being a product they have managed to develop new innovative business models.

There are several types of data-driven business models, such as product providers, that use the data generated by their product to create an additional value proposition via data analysis. However, a new breed of IoT manufacturers is adopting a data provider business-model, which sells data which is a byproduct of their operations to other companies. An example of this is a mobile telephone company that sells crowd analytics to retailers based upon the local network activity of their subscribers.

Data Brokers on the other hand do not typically produce their own data but source it from others. This is very relevant to the IoT as so much data is generated by devices as a side effect of their functionality. So, data obviously has value than other data but brokers can aggregate and analyses data looking for knowledge which they can monetize and sell on. In addition to brokers there are the better-known delivery network collaborators, which share data in order to optimize the delivery of products, the classic example is advertising. Delivery network collaborators are traditionally companies that track customer's online using cookies and sell that information to advertising houses. However, the IoT has provided these delivery network collaborators with a vast new source of prime data via IoT product manufacturers selling on their data collected as side product. By selling on their hopefully anonymized customer data to data brokers and delivery network collaborators IoT manufacturers can create a very profitable additional source of revenue. Indeed, analysts from Gartner forecast that 30 percent of companies will be trading or selling their data by 2016.

However, in the U.S. data, brokers that deal in personal customer data are coming under increasing scrutiny from not just the public but also the Federal Trade Commission. The FTC wants to see greater transparency regards data sources, for example where they have acquired it and what they are doing with it.

In the EU where privacy law is consolidated and therefore stricter, data brokers are required to get actual permission before they can use personal customer data for advertising.

The public though are becoming better educated to direct advertising and data brokers, aggregators and network collaborators have to ensure that they maintain trust with their customer base – and source of data. Therefore, they must stipulate within their privacy policy why they collect and use the customer's data and how they will secure, anonymize, store and perhaps distribute the data to third parties. Still the misuse of customer data is one of the major privacy and trust concerns that IoT consumers face. Indeed, customers in particular are uneasy about the capture and distribution of geo-location data despite its functional benefits as they see it as potential surveillance. This is particularly true in the U.S. and Germany where there is a growing unease within the consumer base about data brokers and advertising houses tracking their movements and keeping them under constant surveillance particularly when in or around their home. Despite this many new startups are using the data trading model to not just supplement and create new revenue streams but as their main revenue source and this can result in a real conflict of interest, whereby the product is only a means to extract and appropriate the consumer's personal information.

Part VII: **Surveillance, Subterfuge and Sabotage**

If the lack of privacy is the consumer's greatest fear, then the treat of surveillance cannot be far behind. The IoT delivers a vast potential for surveillance on a scale never seen before. IoT devices can track and spy on our every movement, detect what we read, watch, do and even what we may be thinking.

As a result, many have compared the current state of the internet and the potential threat of the IoT to the Panopticon.

The **Panopticon** was a conceptual design for an observation tower in a prison environment by Jeremy Bentham in the late 18th century. The concept of the design was to solve the problem of how to observe all the prison inmates without requiring hundreds of security guards. The Panopticon was Bentham's elegant solution. The Panopticon was to be a tower that overlooked the entire premises, it could see everyone but no one could see the watchman within, therefore the inmates were unable to tell whether or not they were being watched.

Although the inmates would know it was physically impossible for the single watchman to observe all cells at once, the fact that the inmates did not know when they were being watched meant that all inmates acted as though they were being watched, which effectively controlled their own behavior.

DOI 10.1515/9781501505775-033

Chapter 26 – The Panopticon

The good, the bad and the ugly

Surveillance within the context of the IoT has become something of a dirty word, which conjurers up chilling threats of devices spying on their owner, or being used as conduits for snooping and voyeurism by nefarious characters lurking in the shadows of the Internet. Recently, since 2013, surveillance has also come to popularly be associated with the mass collection, tracking and monitoring of communications, social contacts and the behavior of citizens by their own intelligence services, most notably the NSA and GCHQ. However not all surveillance is intrusive of privacy or a bad thing. Take for example, tracking the whereabouts of workers in dangerous locations, such as on an oil platform out in the sea. In case of an emergency, it is necessary to know where everyone is so that emergency drills can ensure safe evacuation of workers as quickly as possible without having to go looking for people. Similarly, surveillance in public places is not considered an invasion of privacy as we have no expectation of privacy when in a busy shopping mall, train station or airport. Instead we are willing to trade any illusion of privacy for the security benefits that we receive in return.

Therefore, we can see that people are happy enough to undergo surveillance in publicly designated areas or even in the workplace if they can see a justification for its use and that it is non-intrusive to their personal privacy. For example, they will accept surveillance cameras in retail areas in a store but not in the changing rooms. It is when the line is crossed between where the subjects have no expectancy of privacy to a place where they feel that privacy is a given, a bathroom for example, that general surveillance become unacceptable and becomes snooping.

Home surveillance

Privacy is the main concern of many consumers and it should be as the Internet of Things is so pervasive and although it may enthrall manufacturers, entrepreneurs and consumers alike it is also insidious and will creep into our lives perhaps undetected. One concern that keeps being raised by consumers is that of pervasive surveillance especially if it can extend to within the home. As we saw earlier in the Pew survey where respondents were offered a free home thermostat service in exchange for their home activity data, for example sharing data that

DOI 10.1515/9781501505775-034

tracked their and their family's movements around the home. This was not video or audio surveillance simply presence detection and recording of which rooms were populated, which were empty and at what times as well as the movement of people between rooms which is a requirement for smart home energy efficiency solutions. This for many respondents (55 percent) was an unacceptable deal and just over a quarter (27 percent) of them found it acceptable. The primary reason for their dissatisfaction with the terms of the deal was that many considered this surveillance within the home and as such an intolerable invasion of privacy.

On the other hand, many homeowners are installing home surveillance cameras and physical security equipment such as movement and presence sensors, and things like smoke alarms which can bring peace of mind at relatively little investment. The advantages of IoT home security systems is that expensive installation is typically avoided as new miniaturized and innovative designs allow for multi-purpose devices to fit into light sockets from which they derive their power supply but also their camouflage. These multi-purpose devices are built around a smart light bulb, which are also fitted with speakers, presence detectors, a microphone, and camera. This is more for aesthetic reasons than for covert operations, as everything now resides on one device that can be hidden away within the light fitting recess in the ceiling.

Now there may be several valid reasons why a homeowner might wish to install covert cameras throughout their property, such as for home security, or the remote surveillance of the elderly or infirm for care givers. The problem though can arise when they are used for covert purposes such as remotely checking on a nanny or babysitter. If the subject of the surveillance is unaware they are being monitored, then it can create some legal issues.

Often the law and regulations are ambiguous regards personal surveillance as it lags several years after technology. Even today, before the forecasted public adoption of IoT products has become reality, there are many legal issues, which need addressed, for example, the rights of privacy. The issues are complex and will take years of legal consideration to reach a conclusion especially when the concepts of the requirements and necessity of personal privacy itself is often questioned.

The smart home is an example, products such as web cams and presence-monitoring devices are often required for the whole ecosystem to operate efficiently. However, in the home does the homeowner have the permission of guests to have their privacy invaded? The law as it stands today (2016) in most states in the US says no, that as a guest you could have no expectation of a right to privacy. The homeowner can place surveillance equipment throughout their property, with the only caveat being where a guest has an expectation of privacy such as a bathroom/toilet. This though does not extend to bedrooms, so a house-owner can quite legally video their guest's activities, even though the guest does have an expectation of the right to privacy. Additionally, it doesn't just affect guests it can be used legally and submitted as evidence against babysitters, or nannies suspected of abuse, theft or other wrong doings. The homeowner though must tread carefully because they must have a good reason for the surveillance of their guest, babysitter or nanny, for if the court suspects voyeurism was the original intent then they might be found liable.

Liability is also a major concern for manufacturer's as it provokes legal questions that are intriguing. IoT products are by their nature purposed to interact with other manufacture's IoT devices, such as the cloud for analytics and data storage or more mundanely the consumer's smartphone, tablet or PC. Sometimes, in the case of the smart home or especially in a smart home security system, many manufacturers' products will be expected to interconnect and operate but who is responsible if something goes wrong. If a consumer is harmed by an IoT device's action or failure to act, it may not be so simple to apportion liability. For example, an IoT device by its nature is not a stand-alone product, and may even be deployed in an environment or for a purpose never envisaged by the manufacturer. Furthermore, IoT devices may form ad-hoc networks with other manufacturers IoT devices within the home. These ad-hoc network devices may well provide inputs into the device's own machine-learning algorithms that could affect their performance and ability to perform as designed. Therefore, we can see that although manufacturers must be responsible for carrying out appropriate assurance testing on all reasonable use-cases for their products, they cannot be expected to carry out testing on all possible deployment scenarios. To further muddy the liability issue, what if the input fed into the device was from the consumer rather than an environmental sensor or ad-hoc device, a simple case of user error rather than a malfunction of an internal algorithm. Where do liability laws current address complex issues where consumers can have little expectations of knowing let alone understanding a devices workings and algorithms.

Law enforcement – going dark

Snooping and spying have unfortunately become the currency of mobile apps and that potential revenue has been inflated as smartphone technology and services have forked many IoT solutions. Mobile app developers have for years harvested location data, and requested camera, and microphone access under the most tenuous of excuses. The geo-location data they could sell to data brokers, along with standard behavior data this would make them a profit. The data brokers in turn would sell on the geo-location and behavioral data to advertising and marketing houses. However, they were not the only ones using the smartphone for surveillance.

The traditional mobile (cellular) phones never mind the smartphone is a vast source of surveillance information. The cellular networks enabled geo-location through triangulation of a mobile phone between base stations within a cellular network. Additionally, there were law enforcement interfaces built into the cellular network equipment that allowed law enforcement access to voice calls, SMS, texts and data transfers such as web browsing or any other Internet activity. Indeed, it wasn't just law enforcement that could access and read SMS, anyone in the SMSC (SMS Center) could also read the clear text messages, even though some of these were used for confidential transactions such as eBanking. Of course, this weakness in SMS wasn't common knowledge to the customer and it was neither in the mobile operator, the banks nor law enforcements interests to see that change.

The popular and pervasive smartphone further enhanced the surveillance capabilities of law enforcement. Now the public were willingly paying to carry around the most invasive surveillance kit that law enforcement could ever have envisaged possible. Now law enforcement agencies could use all sorts of telemetric data such as GPS for more detailed outdoor positioning where ever the subject roamed, though they still would use mobile triangulation when the subject went indoors. They could plot a subject's journey and know how fast they were traveling even at what altitude. They could intercept and collect metadata on every call, chats, Internet access details and Wi-Fi locations. In essence the smartphone was a surveillance dream for law enforcement.

Lately law enforcement agencies have been complaining about data encryption and how things have gone dark, making it ever more difficult for them to solve crime. As a result, they are canvassing for backdoors to be built into encryption running on networks and smartphone devices. This request has come about partly due to the demand for end-to-end encryption from consumers to their web service providers such as Facebook, Yahoo, Google and Apple. Demand has escalated after the revelations by Edward Snowden in 2013 regards the highly dubious activities of the National Security Agency (NSA) and its UK counterpart Government Central Head Quarters (GCHQ). Alarmed by the unauthorized bulk collection, storage and analysis of potentially their private and confidential information, consumers have taken action. Angered by the growing encroachment on their online privacy consumers have pressurized for encryption services that are genuinely secure and that cannot be interfered with by a man in the middle. As a result, some applications such as WhatsApp use end-to-end encryption over their messaging service, which means they have no way of decrypting the conversation. Consequently, even if law enforcement demanded access to the information it is useless as they have no way to decrypt it anyway. This approach though is not universally acceptable and Brazil amongst other countries have been riling against WhatsApp, indeed blocking their services on a number of occasions.

In the U.S., the response to this trend towards encryption led to complaints from the FBI, CIA and NSA about going dark, which is their term for the growing gap in their capabilities and the technical barriers that end-to-end encryption would bring about. The position of law enforcement agencies with regards encryption is strange as it shouldn't really affect law enforcement anyway. After all it is the metadata that they collect – or so they claim – and that is mostly unencrypted as it is required within data communication to forwards packets to the correct destination, user and application – it is the content that is encrypted. In a recent report by the Berkman Center for Internet and Society, surveillance and cyber security experts disagreed with the "going dark" metaphor, saying that it; 'does not capture the current state and trajectory of technological development.'

The Berman reports grounds for their disagreement that law enforcement and intelligence agencies were going dark were threefold. First, they believed that most of the web giants actually monetize the unencrypted data flowing through their services so were unlikely to encourage mass end-to-end encryption as it would not be in their financial interests. Secondly, networks and application software ecosystems are typically fragmented which makes applying widespread end-to-end encryption difficult. Thirdly, and most disconcertingly, the very companies that are supplying their customers with end-to-end encryption services are also providing governments with data that is used for surveillance analysis.

Furthermore, the IoT has just opened up a whole new world of possibilities for surveillance which is far more intrusive than law enforcement has had previously. So, working in the dark is unlikely to be the problem they are far more likely to be concerned with their capabilities for shifting through the vast oceans of data they are collecting under the bright glare of the legal and media spotlight.

Dragnet Exploits

The IoT will change the way surveillance works and make consumers potentially vulnerable to getting caught up in a dragnet of mass snooping, dirty tricks or malicious attacks. This is because the potential for harm to innocent people is great if the NSA, FBI in the US and GHCQ in the UK deliberately keep consumer communications and tools vulnerable. This can be seen in the recent spat between Mozilla and the FBI.

In the spring of 2016 the makers of the Firefox browser and the basis of the TOR browser entered into a contentious battle with the FBI over a vulnerability that the law enforcement agency had exploited against a child porn site to track down anonymous users.

The background to the case is that in 2015 the FBI used an undisclosed vulnerability in Mozilla's browser to target a dark web child porn site, Playpen. However instead of closing the site down, the FBI used an exploit to download malware to over 1,000 users of the site which disclosed their location.

This is of course nothing new as the FBI used the malware Cornhusker and Torsploit during operation torpedo back in 2012-13. They also used similar malware to exploit the Silk Road servers in Operation Silk Road. However, the difference this time is their reticence to come clean about the vulnerability they exploited. Consequently, they have been left in a legal quandary.

The problem is that one of the people caught up in the dragnet challenged the case and demanded to see the malware. The position the defendant's legal team took was they believed that it was the malware that introduced the illicit material onto his computer. The FBI duly refused to hand over the exploit even when the judge ordered them to, they even refused to expose the vulnerability to Mozilla behind closed doors in the judge's chambers. Indeed, such was the FBI's determination not to reveal the vulnerability or the source of their malware that it looked as if they would prefer to drop all charges rather than comply with the court order.

Now what is of interest in this case is that it seems to fly in the face of conventional wisdom of how the law operates. Why on earth would they be willing to let a suspect walk free rather than divulge a vulnerability that exists in Mozilla browser. Furthermore, the Obama administration policy is that when the government learns of a new flaw or zero-day-exploit then it must be submitted first to an interagency group. The understanding that was generally accepted and promoted by the White House is that the group had a strong bias towards disclosure to the vendor rather than allow the security services to keep and exploit it. This policy was intended to allow vendors' time to fix their products before the vulnerability became available in the wild and this ensured the security of their customers. However, it doesn't appear to be working in practice.

The 5-Eyes (FVEY)

However, what is certainly working in practice is the 5-Eyes, which is the spying coalition consisting of the five major English speaking nations, Australia, Canada, New Zealand, United Kingdom and United States. The 5-Eyes or FVEY as they are abbreviated have been around since WWII so have extensive history and experience working with one another. The 5-Eyes are joined by the multi-lateral UKUSA agreement a treaty for joint cooperation in signals intelligence. But why should the IoT be of interest to national intelligence, haven't they more important things to do?

> "In the future, intelligence services might use the [Internet of things] for identification, surveillance, monitoring, location tracking, and targeting for recruitment, or to gain access to networks or user credentials,"
>
> James Clapper the U.S. director of national intelligence

It really would be foolish to believe that the NSA and their partners in the 5-Eyes would not be looking into using IoT devices for identification, surveillance and especially location tracking. After all they have exploited just about every other possible method to get the public's data whether they are under suspicion or not. Indeed, over the last decade or so the 5-Eyes consortium have spent a lot of time and effort becoming masters of the Internet, they are unlikely to give up such a golden opportunity as this.

However, the IoT rides upon the Internet so we have to consider the threats that national intelligence can bring. As IoT products will be sold globally we will need to trust that these devices have not been tampered with during 'customs opportunities' or given security backdoors in order to comply with domestic laws and regulations. Unfortunately, these rules have become very fluid lately as our laws fail to match current technologies and lifestyles. The laws are hopelessly inadequate for addressing privacy and restraining those that wish to exploit the massive capabilities of bulk collection, storage and analysis, especially when they are our governments. However, it is not just our own governments that we need to trust as there are alliances of intelligence agencies that operate so closely that national boundaries no longer appear to exist, one such group are the 5-Eyes.

The basic philosophy of the 5-Eyes requires that they share all information within the group, and don't spy on one another. This sharing of data is and resources is inherent to the system and it has proved to be an extremely fortuitous arrangement as it allows partners to circumvent their own countries laws and regulators interference. For example, in the U.S., the NSA has relatively strict regulators, rules and guidelines compared to the UK's GCHQ which has comparatively lax and co-operative regulators. Indeed, in a training document released by Edward Snowden, GCHQ actual boast of this lack of oversight.

This agreement to share between the 5-Eyes members means that regulations can be circumvented. For example, the U.S. is not allowed to spy or carry out bulk surveillance on U.S. citizens, but there is nothing stopping the UK's GCHQ – despite the no spy pact – doing it for them and then sharing the data – and vice versa.

Of course, both the NSA and GCHQ will deny such an arrangement, with the NSA standard response being, we would never ask another country to do an illegal act, or words to that effect. GHCQ, don't even bother to lie, they just retort, we do not comment on security matters and always work proportionately and within the law. But, of course the NSA doesn't ask GCHQ to spy on Americans, it doesn't have to ask, the 5-Eyes partners share everything anyway.

The relationship between the NSA and the GCHQ is very close with considerable co-operation and even close integration of staff, training and projects and this has been evident for many years. What was not evident before the documents released by Edward Snowden was just how close all the 5 Eyes, United States National Security Agency (NSA), the United Kingdom's Government Communications Headquarters(GCHQ), Canada's Communications Security Establishment Canada (CSEC), the Australian Signals Directorate (ASD), and New Zealand's Government Communications Security Bureau (GCSB) worked together. In fact, so closely do they co-operate that almost all of the documents include the classification "TOP SECRET//COMINT//REL TO USA, AUS, CAN, GBR, NZL" or "TOP SECRET//COMINT//REL TO USA, FVEY." These classification markings indicate the material is top-secret communications intelligence (aka SIGINT) material that can be released to the US, Australia, Canada, United Kingdom and New Zealand.

New Zealand is a particularly interesting FVEY partner as it is from a direct request for assistance from GCSB to the NSA that we have documented evidence of the first civilian victim of PRISM. The extraordinary covert operation against ironically a Pro-Democracy campaign in Fiji reveals the extent of the global surveillance apparatus available to the NSA and its partners.

The release of more than 190 pages of top-secret NSA logs regarding the pro-democracy group's surveillance reveals the NSA intercepted communications between May and August 2012. The logs show that the agency used the controversial Internet surveillance system PRISM to eavesdrop on pro-democracy members' Gmail and Facebook messages. One target was a New Zealand citizen, and pro-democracy advocate Tony Fullman, and he has the distinction to be the first person in the world to be publicly identified as a confirmed PRISM target. And yes, he thought he had nothing to hide.

PRISM

Revelation by NSA whistle blower Edward Snowden regarding PRISM in 2013 was met around the world with a mixture of outrage and awe. The NSA shouldered most of the flack as it was their 41 slide PowerPoint presentation on the PRISM program that explained how the scheme operated. Unfortunately for the NSA and the rest of us, the Washington Post and the Guardian only posted a handful of the slides (5) which created the wrong impression. Initially despite Snowden's request that all 41 slides be published the Washington Post and The Guardian published only a select few – as to why we do not know. The ones that they did choose to publish showed the PRISM project in the worst possible light leaving the NSA with some explaining to do. By publishing a misleading slide naming the nine companies who had deemed to be collaborators with the NSA, such as Microsoft, Yahoo, Google, Facebook, PalTalk, AOL, Skype, YouTube, and Apple, amongst others, meant these companies also had some serious questions to answer.

Technically it still isn't clear how PRISM worked due to conflicting accounts. The leaked NSA presentation clearly states that the NSA had backdoors into the servers of the nine collaborating web service providers and they even show a timeline of when each came online. For example, the slides show that Microsoft was the first compromised back in 2007; followed by Yahoo 2008, Google & Facebook in 2009, YouTube 2010 and even Skype in 2011, later they were joined by other major technology players such as Apple in 2012. Despite this seemingly damning evidence the technology companies strenuously denied any backdoors into their servers, and refused to admit any wrong doing. Just about every one of the nine put out a spokesperson to emphatically deny, on record, that NSA had no direct access to their servers and to unequivocally state how they valued their customers' privacy and would never allow such practice without a legal court order. Some, Apple for example, even went as far as to total deny ever having heard of the name PRISM let alone them allowing the NSA or anyone else for that matter having direct access to their systems. So, something clearly wasn't right.

The direct access anomaly caused confusion but it could be explained simply by semantics or perhaps imprecise language used in the NSA presentation to describe the actual interface between the NSA and the Service Providers. Another explanation is that PRISM was simply a way to streamline the warrant process in order to expedite court-approved data requests. This actually made a lot of sense as the PRISM program was a product of The Protect America Act (2007), which allowed the attorney general and the director of national intelligence to collect intelligence on foreigners overseas. However, it does not require specific targets or places to be named. Once the plan is approved by a federal judge sitting in a secret court and issuing a secret order, the NSA can require companies such as

Microsoft and Facebook to send data to the government. The problem with this theory is that the court order would not be legal in the EU or anywhere else for that matter as the subsidiaries operating and registered in those countries would be the ones collecting and forwarding the data.

The actual issue though with the reporting of PRISM was the withholding of the full presentation deck of slides. By releasing only a few selected slides out of context created unnecessary confusion because later released slides showed that there was no direct access between the nine service provider servers and the NSA. Indeed, one slide that wasn't for some reason published initially shows clearly that the request for data interception flows from a lawful request from the NSA to the relevant service provider via the FBI. Similarly, another slide that was released much later, and more damningly, showed a clear distinction between the Upstream Programs and PRISM.

The Upstream projects deal with cable tapping and direct access interception of data via the flow through domestic telecoms companies. PRISM deals with automated streamlined requests through the established FBI interface and protocols called DITU (Data Intercept Technology Unit). By selectively releasing some of the slides out of context from the full 41 slide presentation, the two newspapers involved created confusion and the wrong conclusions arose. Worse the wrong questions were asked which enabled the nine companies involved to deny any direct involvement with the NSA. Because it was true the nine companies involved gave the data requested of them to the FBI, not directly to the NSA.

If the full deck of slides had been published as a complete set initially, as was Edward Snowden's request, then this would have been clear and the nine service providers could have been asked more pertinent questions regarding their cooperation, such as was the DITU located onsite and connected to the network?

When this question was eventually raised with the nine technology firms not one had a direct link to the DITU either on premises or remotely. All preferred to install their own monitoring equipment and deliver subpoenaed data as ordered by a warrant. Google for example used manual secure FTP transfers to deliver the subpoenaed data, and used a secure drop box, or even handed delivered the data. Neither the FBI nor the NSA collected, intercepted or obtained directly by their own actions data from any of the nine service providers.

Instead the PRISM protocol required that the NSA requested through the legal process of a warrant, retrieval of specific target-selectors, such as email, phone numbers, and the technology company was legally bound to deliver the subpoenaed data to the FBI. This can clearly be seen in the slide in Figure 8.

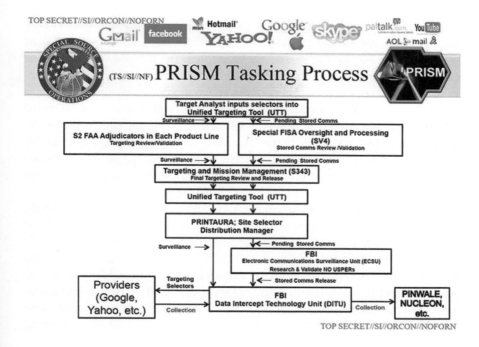

Fig. 8: PRISM Tasking Process

Therefore, from an IoT perspective U.S. citizens should have nothing to fear from PRISM as it is a suspicion and warrant based legal framework where the NSA must supply the technology company with specific target-selectors. The evidence of this is also amongst the recently released slides, which highlight the differences between another NSA project codenamed Upstream, which is a cable tap bulk interceptor and PRISM. The key differences by looking at the slide are;

1. PRISM has no access to telephone records (DNR) where Upstream does access DNR
2. PRISM has access to stored communications, it can request historical data, Upstream only sees what flows by at the time
3. PRISM has no ability to collect 'Abouts'; Upstream has that ability
4. PRISM has no direct relationship with the comms provider, any contact is through the FBI), Upstream on the other hand has direct contact

These technical capabilities highlight the nature of the two programs with PRISM being limited to Internet records from nine US based Service providers and being request/deliver warrant based system where as Upstream is a cable-tap directly into service provider networks to intercept warrantless and suspicion-less bulk data. This is why Upstream cannot access stored communications whereas PRISM can request historic emails, messages, and the like. However, the most telling difference is with the 'Abouts' collection. 'Abouts' means anything connected to the target-selector, for example an email address. With Up-stream, it can filter every occurrence of that target-selector as the data flows passed on the wire, this is regardless whether it is in the metadata or in the content. With Upstream if the target-selector is in the bulk data flow it will intercept that record. For example, if the target–selector is a name, let's say, Joe Bloggs, then Upstream will hoover up every record that contains the term Joe Bloggs regardless of any other criteria.

Now, originally we were led to believe that this is how PRISM worked but we can see here from the slide that this isn't the case. PRISM does not collect 'About' Collection, it can only request collection of the target-selector that is in the metadata for example the 'To:' or 'From:' fields but not if it is mentioned in the message content and that includes the subject field. So, the NSA must make requests using PRISM through due legal, albeit streamlined process, a warrant request for a specific target-selector. The comms provider must return all records that specifically and directly address that target-selector in metadata and nothing else.

Therefore, PRISM is not the program or the tool that the NSA utilizes in mass warrantless and suspicion-less surveillance of Internet users – because as we will see in due course they are certainly not averse to that tactic, it is just not through the PRISM project. Therefore, with IoT domestically in the U.S., it is UPSTREAM that should be feared and not PRISM.

Due to understandable prejudice towards the PRISM project, and the fact that Upstream somehow managed to have flown below the media's radar, PRISM resulted in massive political fallout around the world. The Snowden leaks caused mass embarrassment to the U.S. government as it became clear that the NSA had been spying on all the customers of the nine largest technology companies. Anger was also directed towards the nine technology companies who had aided the NSA with or without their direct connivance, but certainly their knowledge. Furthermore, it became clear that not only did the other 5-Eyes partners know about this but they actively participated and benefited from the trove of data being collected.

Mastering the Internet

Back in the mid 2000's, GCHQ the UK's intelligence agency was in some trouble as it was beginning to be seen by its US partner the NSA to be not pulling its weight. The NSA was troubled by the seemingly one way flow of sigint (signal intelligence) across the Atlantic. The issue that GCHQ had was that new technologies were outflanking them. The turn of the millennium had brought in an exponential growth in mobile phones, VoIP and general Internet usage, such as email, chat and social media, which made it harder for their analysts to get access to the information they required.

For GHCQ, these new technologies provided them a problem because all the tradition technologies were rapidly being abandoned, such as the tradition telephone landlines, the postal service and were being replaced with new Internet versions that were out with their reach. To compound the problem, the Internet was by its nature global and therefore it was dominated by a new breed of internationally owned service providers that were located abroad out with the jurisdiction of UK law. This was a major problem as GCHQ could no longer access data through legal warrants. There was however a glimmer of hope, and the problem soon was to turn into an opportunity as GCHQ came up with the initiative to Master the Internet as it first began life back in 2007.

A year later in 2008 an experimental project was initiated from GCHQ's outpost in Bude in Cornwall. The projects goals under the name TINT was to provide a method for retrospective analysis for attribution – which basically was a storage system that provided a buffer to hold Internet data long enough to enable analysts to review it. Initially the source of this data came from Satellite links from GCHQ monitoring stations but soon GCHQ decided to plug into the submarine cables that conveniently came ashore in the UK. In Cornwall where they had a vast listening station several international submarine cables came ashore. Two of these were the Internet backbone cables carrying traffic into and out of the UK. By tapping into the Internet's sub-sea fiber-optic cables GCHQ could harvest vast quantities of raw data which they could feed into their TINT buffer storage for analysis and this was the beginning of Project TEMPORA.

Project TEMPORA

Project TEMPORA went live in 2011 and is a mass surveillance program run by GCHQ in partnership with the NSA to tap into the international subsea fiber-optic cables running into the UK or located around the globe. The TEMPORA program works by placing optical taps on the sub-sea cables or their landing stations as they enter the UK or in foreign territories where they have influence. The TEM-PORA program's aim is to covertly mirror and bulk collect the Internet backbone traffic entering or passing through the UK or over any backbone link which they can gain access.

How GCHQ gains access is a matter for debate because they would certainly need the cooperation of the subsea cable owners. Some analysts believe that GCHQ pays the companies that own the cables or they somehow compel them to become intercept partners. Whatever, the intercept partners are forbidden to disclose the existence of warrants compelling them to allow access to their infrastructure cables.

TEMPORA collects the Internet backbone signals through an optic-tap, which allows the GCHQ to mirror the data stream transparently without any degradation of the original signal. The mirrored traffic is then buffered in temporary storage for later analysis. In 2011, GCHQ had 201 Internet links each carrying 10Gbps of Internet backbone traffic. It has since been expanded to cater for high-speed 100Gbps links. This vast amount of Internet traffic requires huge storage capabilities so TEMPORA has a volume reduction component called POKERFACE which strives to reduce the burden by blocking or filtering certain categories of data. At this stage POKERFACE filters and discards traffic of low value such as P2P streams in order to optimize storage capacity. As a result, POKERFACE typically reduces the amount of data collected by 30 percent. Despite this the quantities of data are still so huge that the TEMPORA program only keeps content data for typically three days and metadata for 30 days.

The way that TEMPORA works is that it consists of two main components, "Mastering the Internet" which is concerned with Internet data and the "Global Telecoms Exploitation" for telephone information. As a result, TEMPORA consists of both recordings of telephone conversations, and the contents of emails, chats, video, social media entries, Facebook profiles, and the Internet usage profiles of users. The problem that TEMPORA had was that the raw data being captured was growing at astonishing rates. At one point during 2010 GCHQ recorded 39billion Internet events in a single 24-hour period, which they claim dramatically improved their ability to produce unique intelligence from their targets use of the Internet.

GCHQ needed a way to categorize valuable data into groups such as emails, VoIP, chat, video, VPN, web browsing, and dump low value high volume traffic such as torrent downloads, which can reduce the bearer's load by 30 percent. The solution was to use their partner the NSA's existing search and retrieve tool, XKEYSTORE to chop and dice the data.

XKEYSTORE

The NSA and GCHQ work in partnership on TEMPORA and the program includes several NSA tools such as the XKEYSTORE search and retrieve tool, which is used for searching and analyzing Internet data on huge horizontal databases. XKEYSTORE is best described as a data search and retrieval system that provides a variety of user interfaces through a frontend web server. The backend data bases of which there are over 700 are categorized dependent on their function, for example there are

- **F6** – which is a database on clandestine operations between the CIA and NSA typically on foreign territory, diplomats and leaders
- **FORNSAT** – which is a database of intercepted data from foreign satellites
- **SSO** – the Special Source Operations database is for data that is collected through cooperation with telecom providers
- **Overhead** – this data is derived from U.S. spy planes, drones and satellites
- **Tailored Access Operations** – which is data derived from NSA special operations such as hacking, malware and cyber-warfare
- **FISA** – this database hold all the data related to FISA warrants and surveillance approvals from the FISC (Foreign Intelligence Surveillance Court)
- **Third Party** – This data comes from third party sources that work with the NSA but out with the 5-Eyes, these countries are typically EU countries that make up the signal intelligence services of friendly states.
- **MARINA** – This is the main NSA Internet metadata and it is integrated **with XKEYSTORE but it remains a separate entity**

As GCHQ was now producing the same or even more metadata as the NSA a close working relationship between GCHQ and the NSA was proposed. The proposal was to work together on the analysis with GCHQ analysts exploiting NSA metadata for intelligence production, target development/discovery purposes and the NSA analysts would work on GCHQ metadata to the same purpose, thereby ensuring the same data wasn't processed twice. Incidentally, it also conveniently meant they were not analyzing their own citizens' Internet traffic they were all foreign national to them. This worked around a sticky point of law for the Americans as they are forbidden to exercise surveillance on American citizens in the United States without a warrant and suspicion.

It appears by 2013, the two agencies had come to rely on one another, NSA for the GCHQ's TEMPORA data buffering technology and GCHQ for NSA's XKEYSTORE search and retrieve capability to make sense of it all.

However, GCHQ and the NSA realized that much of the traffic of interest crossing the Internet backbone was being encrypted by SSL which was useless to them. The plan was to use the new cable tapping expertise and technology and work together on several other joint initiatives under an umbrella program called Windstop. One of the sub-projects was aimed at gaining access to the new foreign based data centers being used by Google and Yahoo for cloud storage. This new initiative was how the MUSCULAR project came about.

Windstop

MUSCULAR

In the MUSCULAR joint sub-project between GCHQ and the NSA the project goal was to defeat the encryption used by the web giants when they sent traffic across the Internet backbone. To do this the 5-Eyes partners would need to tap into the networks of Yahoo and Google in order to gain access to the unencrypted data. This was to prove to be a very attractive proposition for a number of reasons. First, Google and Yahoo's data centers were scattered around the world in order to be close to their customers. This would mean tapping into the fiber links connecting the foreign cloud centers of the web giants. The advantage with this approach was as they were based on foreign soil and used foreign connections to the public network no warrants would be required as FISA considered that it could be assumed that no significant amount of U.S. citizens would be using foreign network links. Therefore, the NSA were free from the requirements to gain FISA approval and warrants as was the case with PRISM's albeit very streamlined approval. Therefore, the tapping of Google's and Yahoo's foreign private networks would be much less problematic from an approval perspective. Secondly, the chance of collecting all the Yahoo and Google email, messages, video and sundry data before it was encrypted was a tantalizing prize and this was the rational for the MUSCULAR project. The issues were though that Google and Yahoo now used encryption by default when sending data across public Internet links and interconnects between major data centers were private fiber WAN links. These sometime long distance links were privately owned so were off-limits to GCHQ and the NSA, so they would have to find another way to grab the unencrypted data.

As it happened, it turned out to be technically rather straightforward as both architectures used encryption only between data centers traversing the Internet. Internal WAN communication within the Google network for example passed over the private fiber-optic links unencrypted. Similarly, Yahoo's network was designed in the same manner with external data on the public Internet encrypted but left unencrypted inside the private network. Therefore, GCHQ and the NSA needed to tap into the private network area where all the data would be discovered in the clear.

The way they did this was to tap into the Gateway Front-end routers that performed the SSL encryption/decryption process. By tapping into the public Internet facing gateway router the MUSCULAR project could access all the data traversing the WAN link before or after the SSL encryption engine thereby defeating the encryption process. By tapping into the router hosting the SSL engine MUSCULAR had access into all the unencrypted customer data stored in the web giants' data centers and it was all available in clear text. The evidence of this was a hand sketched drawing by a GCHQ or NSA employee of how the breach was done, embellished with a cheeky smiling face just to rub salt into the wound.

Google network engineers for example reacted with fury when it was later revealed that the NSA had entered through a network gateway router which terminated SSL encryption. It was little wonder they were furious because this was a surprisingly aggressive attack on two American companies by a friendly party at the behest of their own country's intelligence agency and they were astonished that FISA allowed and condoned the action.

What they had to understand, was that outside U.S. territory, statutory restrictions on surveillance seldom apply and the FISC has no jurisdiction. Congress conducts little oversight of intelligence-gathering under the presidential authority of Executive order 12333, which defines the basic powers and responsibilities of the intelligence agencies.

Because digital communications and cloud storage do not usually adhere to national boundaries, MUSCULAR has amassed content and metadata on a previously unknown scale from U.S. citizens and residents. The joint operation with GCHQ has not been publicized or debated in public or in Congress because the existence of the operation was classified.

The Google and Yahoo operations do however call to attention a problem in U.S. surveillance law. Although Congress has lifted some restrictions on NSA domestic surveillance on grounds that purely foreign communications sometimes pass over U.S. switches and cables, it has not added restrictions overseas, where American communications or data stores now cross over foreign switches.

MUSCULAR though was based in the UK and relied on a foreign access point DS200-B to breach the networks of Google and Yahoo and this was achieved through the cooperation of an unnamed telecommunications company. MUSCULAR managed to collect over 181 million records and at times was unable to keep up with the vast amounts of Yahoo mail it would intercept, for example when

Yahoo was reconciling or backing up entire data centers of email to other locations within the private network.

However, no matter how successful MUSCULAR was deemed to be it was dwarfed by its sibling project also under Project Windstop and that was called INCENSER or DS-300.

INCENSER

Strangely, the INCENSER program, which is one of the bulk feeds into TEMPORA's buffer and analysis system, which is rarely mentioned yet it is far larger in terms of capturing bulk information than MUSCULAR or TEMPORA. Initially little was known about INCENSER other than some mentions in Boundless Informant, which is a NSA graphical presentation and reporting module. However, the information was quite fascinating as it showed the performance figures for a monthly period for the Windstop program – Windstop is an umbrella program for 2nd party data sources (5-Eyes) in this case GCHQ. What stood out was that the MUSCULAR program – the tapping of Google & Yahoo cables – showed 181 million records, but this was dwarfed by a sister program called INCENSER, which had a staggering 14 billion records over the same period.

With just over 14 billion records collected in a month, INCENSER is the NSA's fourth-largest cable tapping program. INCENSER by these figures accounted for approximately 9 % of the total amount of records collected by Special Source Operations (SSO), the division responsible for collecting data from Internet cables.

So, what was this program that remained almost anonymous and with little reference in other documents.

INCENSER came to light through a combination of sources, initially as with most secret revelations the source was Edward Snowden. However, only a fraction of the documents that Snowden passed to the Washington Post and the Guardian have been released. This is because many have been either heavily redacted or self-censored for legitimate reason, for example to protect U.S. security. Consequently, in the documents that were released there are many frustrating fragments of information and INCENSER is a good example. Fortunately, Channel 4 (UK TV Station) in conjunction with German regional TV channels WDR & NDR, and newspaper Süddeutsche Zeitung released a documentary on GCHQ that brought together many of the fragments into a complete view. The program detailed how INCENSER tapped all its information from a single source, a submarine cable running from the UK through the Middle East and South East Asia to

Japan. Furthermore, it provided a view of the entire interception chain from the parent program through to the interception stations and systems involved.

From what we learned from the researchers, GCHQ were keen to build on their cable tapping programs that had proved so successful in the recent past however they had a problem in getting hold of enough data as they simply didn't have the resources. The solution they came up with was to get the Telecommunication companies to do the work for them. GCHQ were able to do this by using loopholes in the existing Telecommunication laws to get warrants that they used to compel the Telecommunication companies or submarine fiber-cable owners to cooperate. This was of course nothing new and had been the basis of the TEMPORA project.

Typically, the Telecommunication companies took a dim view of being compelled by legal notice to cooperate but were unable to refuse as they had to operate within the constraints of the law. So typically, they would do what was required by law in order to keep their operating license. As a result, they would reluctantly cooperate but in this case GCHQ seems to have discovered an interception partner, that was not just compliant but helpful. Indeed, so helpful was the telecommunication company that it would provide technical assistance and even suggestions to improve the interception techniques. This technical assistance would include advice on which fiber cables and wavelengths would likely produce the most optimal results. In return for such intensive cooperation, GCHQ paid out tens of millions of pounds for their expenses. For example, in February 2009, six million pound was paid and a 2010 budget references was a 20.3 million pound payment to the company.

The company, Cable & Wireless, which was a British telecommunications operator, codenamed Gerontic, handled 29 international cables entering the UK, either as a direct owner, by lease or by indefeasible right of use. Of the 29 cables, GCHQ had an interest in nine of them, which went to such diverse locations as, Holland, France, Ireland but their real interest was in the premium cable runs, Flag-Atlantic1 and Flag Euro-Asia.

The Flag-Atlantic1 connects the east coast of North America to the United Kingdom and France (6.000 kilometers) and it has a capacity of 2.4 Terabits/s. In order to connect the US to both the UK and France there is a cable landing site in Cornwall and it serves as a terminus for the two ends of a submarine optical cable: one from across the Atlantic which lands at the beach of nearby Sennen in West Cornwall, and one that crosses the channel to Brittany in France.

Fortuitously for GCHQ, Cable & Wireless (Gerontic) also took their clients data from the Middle East and Asia ashore over the Flag Euro-Asia sub-sea cable, which was now owned by Reliance communications. Conveniently, Flag Europe-

Asia came ashore at a landing point at Porthcurno beach in south west Cornwall and the terminus for that cable was a few miles west of Skewjack Farm. Figure 9 shows how the two major Internet backbone cables, Flag Atlantic 1 and Flag Europe-Asia were intercepted, connected, and then tapped using the Cable & Wireless backhaul network.

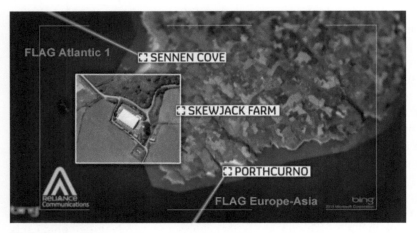

Fig. 9: Skewjack Farm

The Flag Euro-Asia connects United Kingdom to Japan through the Mediterranean, with landing points in Egypt, the Saudi Peninsula, India, Malaysia, Thailand, Hong Kong, China, Taiwan, South Korea and Japan (28.000 kilometers) and has a capacity of 800Gigabit/s.

The importance of Skewjack Farm is it is the designated backhaul point for both Flag-Atlantic1 and Flag Euro-Asia into the UK and this is where Gerontics using their own backhaul network intercepted the traffic from both the Cable & Wireless and the Reliance submarine cables. The audacity of this was that Gerontic were not only giving GCHQ all their traffic but all the traffic on the Reliance Communications cable, who were a competitor.

We know that Cable & Wireless, code named Gerontic collaborated with GCHQ but Reliance Globalcom – now Global Cloud Xchange -were not part of the cooperating partnership. We can infer this from the fact that GCHQ felt it necessary to hack into the Reliance network using one of their Computer Network Exploitation (CNE) or hacking operations codenamed PFENNING ALPHA. GCHQ needed to do this so they could get additional router monitoring and performance statistics for their GTE (Global Telecoms Exploitation).

The result of location of this audacious interception place (Skewjack Farm) codenamed Nigella suddenly makes sense, as GCHQ how had access to not just Cable and Wireless data but all of Reliance Globalcom clients at the landing point in Egypt, the Saudi Peninsula, India, Malaysia, Thailand, Hong Kong, China, Taiwan, South Korea and Japan. Hence the INCENSER projects performance figures of 14 billion records a month.

Despite the INCENSER program's success, in so much as the NSA collect almost $1/10^{th}$ of all the data collected from all their Internet access points combined came from a single cable tap NIGELLA, it still ranks only 11th in the presidential daily reports. The Presidential report is an indication of how helpful a program is, as it shows typically how many analysts have cited the program as a source of useful information in their security reports. Furthermore, INCENSER is only the fourth largest special source operations (SSO) Internet cable tap program. INCENSER, with its 14 billion records is still way behind a NSA program codenamed DANCINGOASIS, which tops the SSO charts with a staggering 57.8 billion records a month, the total SSO records collected for all sources in that month was a total of more than 160 billion metadata records, which were counted, divided into 93 billion DNI (Internet) data and 67 billion DNR (telephony) data.

Despite all the 5-Eyes efforts around the globe to tap into the Internet backbone and collect hundreds of billions of records each month it doesn't appear to be terribly efficient. For example, DANCINGOASIS is only fifth in the most cited sources for analysts' reports, with the much-maligned PRISM topping the useful information charts and the primary source of information for almost four times the number of analyst reports in a month.

Encryption in the IoT

You may be wondering what this all has to do with the IoT. Well the issue is that the 5-Eyes did not become masters of the Internet to just concede that the golden age of surveillance may be coming to an end. More and more people and service providers are switching to end-to-end encryption and even rerouting Internet backbone routes to avoid the UK and U.S. wherever possible. But the intelligence agencies especially GCHQ in the UK are looking for more powers, as they can see the interception techniques of their INCENSER and the NSA's DANCINGOASIS days are numbered. Hence their lobbying for the additional security requirements for mobile telephone and Internet service providers to store every one's Internet browsing history, emails and call record for one year. It also explains the ridiculous stance that the former Prime Minister David Cameron took when proposing to ban encryption unless there was a backdoor for law enforcement. It is little wonder business, commerce and industry leaders joined with technology CEO's to rightly condemn the idea, but it wouldn't be hard to guess who was pushing him down that blind alley.

Just this summer in 2016 we witnessed a similar incident in the U.S. where Apple and the FBI found themselves in a standoff over encrypted devices. Apple despite a court order compelling them to assist the FBI refused pending an appeal. The FBI determined to break the encryption and gain access to the iPhone instead paid what is believed to be a seven-figure sum to a third party to hack into the phone. The fact that the hacker duly obliged and the FBI got their data brought the legal spat to a close, but for how long. The legal issues revolve around the security vs. privacy topic that will become more intense and contentious as more IoT devices have security and privacy in the design. The only way at present this can be realistically achieved is through secure boot devices with onboard cryptography capabilities such as presently used in smartphones. By using strong encryption of data at rest and in motion designers can provide the consumer with the confidence of confidentiality. Similarly, if boot and vital OS files are digitally signed and verified at boot time, as currently happens with Apple iOS phones then designers can provide assurance of integrity. Therefore, the way ahead, the path out of the laughable state of IoT device security must entail embracing strong cryptography throughout the system starting at the IoT endpoints or at the hub that perhaps resource-constrained devices connect too right through to the data at rest in the cloud.

To provide security and Privacy the IoT will require designers to implement not just end to end encryption across the communication channels but also deploy encryption on files and data on the device itself and importantly on files at rest in the cloud. The failing of so many secure encrypted end-to-end messaging services for example, WhatsApp, is that the communication channel is encrypted, and the message when stored on the phone may also be encrypted but there is a weakness. Typically, the consumer forgets that when they backup their phones messages and data to the cloud via Google, Amazon or Apple then it will no longer be stored encrypted and will be freely accessible to anyone that hacks the cloud provider network or to the FBI, NSA or anyone else with a warrant.

When considering the IoT it could be argued that using end-to-end – where the consumer does not share the keys with anyone – strong encryption of data in the cloud or in transit is overkill but we have to remember that governments are already addressing the shortcoming in the law to deal with the latest technologies and encryption is high on their list. In the U.S. draft legislation is already underway which will enable judges to order technology companies to assist law enforcement agencies break into encrypted devices or data. What this means in practical terms is that technology companies would have to provide the technical assistance to access locked devices or provide the data requested in an intelligible format. This is of course the outcome of a long-standing feud between, on one side the technology community, who believe strongly in encryption as being a necessity in the fight against hackers and those intent on breaking the security, trust and privacy of the Internet. On the other side, we have the law enforcement agencies such as the police and the FBI who strenuously claim that the use of encryption denies them access to evidence in their investigation of a crime.

The U.S. draft bill under proposal authored by, Senators Richard Burr and Dianne Feinstein was leaked back in February 2016 turned out to be an overtly vague measure that would in effect ban all strong encryption. The bill received a strong backlash from the tech community and only lukewarm reception in the senate. That bill seems dead in the water for now but equally well-meaning but technically and security naïve bills will surely follow.

Similarly, in the UK in 2015 the government also strenuously but ill-advisedly wished to ban strong encryption but worse in 2016 they managed to re-launch The Investigatory Powers Bill nicknamed the 'Snooper's Charter', which had previously thought to be sunk without trace. The purpose of this bill is to legitimize the bulk surveillance, interception and storage of UK data communications.

The concerns for the IoT in the UK are grave indeed. For under the snooper's charter service providers must keep metadata of all Internet activity for a period of one year. Now, that may not sound too bad that your communication service provider stores metadata records or information of your emails, chats, messages, presence, location, IP address, phone number, call records, VoIP call, browser history and a thing called Internet Connect records for one year. Additionally, if you happen to use a VPN or worse the TOR network then that will certainly raise a red flag. Now if you are still not concerned, then think again, that includes everything that goes through the Internet via an Internet Service Provider or a Mobile Telecommunications Provider any data that transits their Internet, telephone or data networks and which comes from your router, Wi-Fi, mobile devices, all the IoT connected devices, such as your car, smart home and wearable's such as your Fitband, everything!

The Snooper's charter

Now, many will perhaps rightly say that most of that data the service providers are collecting will be unusable for fighting crime or terrorism and will in most probability never even be looked at. But do you honestly believe that GCHQ who of course have access or the NSA, who they share everything with, will discard metadata as potentially invaluable as this sort of information. After all, an analyst can tell remotely from the comfort of their desk when a target is walking about the house, when the target goes through a door, what the temperature is in the room, what they are watching on TV or music they are listening to. Furthermore, they can tell when the target leaves the house, start their car, where they are going, and the speed they are travelling. Importantly, because spies think this way, who they meet with or at least who else happens to be at the same location as them at the same time. From their fitness band, they can tell their physical state, their exertion or stress level, they can tell how well they slept the previous night, when they woke and from their online actions and physical behavior even infer what they are thinking.

And you think GCHQ and the NSA are going to forego that opportunity?

The UK government has driven this albeit trivial opposition on the emotive concerns but, for example, there is a trove of metadata hidden inside of the tweets sent from a Twitter app. The message, the 140 characters are content and that doesn't matter. It is what information is held within the metadata that counts. For that is what the Snoopers Charter wants to collect and store. If we take a Tweet as an example in the metadata header, there is a wealth of potentially confidential information contained within the metadata; the number of user mentions, geolocation, URLs, profile statistics, friend counts and dozens of other metadata fields.

The Internet Connect Records (ICR) that the Communication Service Providers are being instructed to collect and store for 12 months consist of metadata that includes your customer account information, detail of the device you are using, phone number, IP address (source and destination), the date and time of your connection, how much data you download or shared, who you are connecting with and what devices you connect to.

As far as the IoT is concerned it will mean service providers will store all a consumer's Internet and Internet connection records so they can trace when you are roaming or switch service providers. This is required because they intend to build a request filter, basically search-engine, which would be similar to the NSA's XKEYSTORE, which is used by GCHQ. This national search engine could poll all the databases of the service providers simultaneously to search for key attributes, or in NSA/GCHQ parlance selectors. The importance of the Snooper Charter is that the government is now openly doing what UPSTREAM, TEMPORA, INCENSER and all the other covert operations carried out by GCHQ and their 5-Eyes partners have been doing for the last decade!

Somehow, 444 Members of the UK Parliament voted for this only 69 abstained or voted against.

When the Snooper's Charter becomes Law in the UK in January 2017, which it certainly will as the MP's voted it through 444-69 with the only resistance coming from the SNP based on Privacy and Civil Rights concerns. Both the major parties the Conservatives and the socialist Labor Party supported and voted the bill through. Of course, being politicians, they did vote this through without any due concern – albeit the honorable members did insist that they the MPs were exempt from the snooper's charter. So, what the UK has now is a nation subjected to the most intrusive surveillance laws in any western democracy.

Depending on democratic views and those of the public's beliefs in western society – on the proportionality between privacy, civil rights and national security this will be seen as either a good or a bad development. Strangely, in the view of the esteemed politician Kenneth Clark a senior Conservative MP, who it must be noted pushed for the Snooper's Charter but stressed the need for tighter operational controls.

Ken Clarke did come out in favor of restricting access to data to only issues of national security. 'Under the current wording, data access will also be allowed if it is in the "economic well-being" of the country.'

He added that *"I've known some very strange things go on under the banner of 'economic well-being'"*

Ken Clarke, MP Conservative Party.

Unfortunately, Ken Clarke then went on to claim that those opposed to the Bill did not understand that previously the UK intelligence services had the legal right to intercept a phone call or to steam open an envelope traversing the postal system. Ken Clarke perhaps didn't understand the difference between targeted and suspicion based surveillance and bulk suspicion-less and warrantless interception of private communications. After all there is a huge operational difference between a GCHQ agent steaming open a letter and a router hoovering up data from an Internet backbone cable.

Ken Clarke who has lengthy experience at the top levels of government, and he is said to be the best prime minister that the country never had, knew full well that the snooper's charter left the UK public wide open to government mass surveillance. However, he like the senate member for California in the US, and even the US President Obama, seem to believe 'if you have nothing to hide, then you have nothing to fear'.

Nothing to hide nothing to fear

It is commonly believed that the phrase, 'nothing to hide nothing to fear', came from Joseph Goebbels, the propaganda minister for the Nazi Party. However, there are earlier examples of the phrase being used such as back in 1918 in *The Profits of Religion: An Essay in Economic Interpretation*:

Not merely was my own mail opened, but the mail of all my relatives and friends—people residing in places as far apart as California and Florida. I recall the bland smile of a government official to whom I complained about this matter: 'If you have nothing to hide you have nothing to fear.'

Such nonsense and hypocrisy has been revealed through our government's fearful reaction to the Internet and more pointedly social media. The interactive, social groups and at times tribal platform of social media has provided a channel for not only for those requiring confirmation of their strongly held beliefs that makes the Internet act as an echo room to compound participant's bias. The Internet also sometimes allows alternative yet radical views to surface. The Internet generation often does feel safe in the assurance that anonymity and the scale of the Internet will keep them out of harm's way. What we are seeing though is not just an erosion of privacy but the stripping away of anonymity. Therefore, it is very important for those that feel that they have nothing to hide to understand that they should no longer require anonymity, because they have lost that as well. After all it would take a trivial amount of effort for law enforcement or even service provider staff to match an Internet alias or pseudonym with a real name and a street address. However more importantly, it is not you as an individual that the machine learning algorithms are searching for, it is what you resemble.

One of the major problems with IoT security, trust, privacy and surveillance is the almost daily incidences that occur that highlight the seeming incompetence of our technology providers. In September 2016, a reporter from the news agency Reuters, Joseph Menn reported that Yahoo had in May 2015 agreed to secretly collaborate with the NSA to scan and search every email entering Yahoo's mail service. The plan was to actively search each mail for a selector which was a string of keywords. What made this different from PRISM was that it was done in real time and every email entering Yahoo was scanned for this selector regardless of whether the sender or recipient were U.S. citizens or not. This was a clear violation of the law as we understand it at present, however no doubt the NSA will come up with some elasticized definition of email or U.S. citizen.

The troubling aspect of this though is Yahoo's claim that all email is encrypted. Yahoo is not being economical with the truth, the email is encrypted and inaccessible from anyone but them, and this is notable of all the other cloud storage providers as well. However, if the service providers are served with a warrant, or should they lose their encryption keys then all the end-to-end encryption counts for naught. It is essential therefore those end users storing sensitive and confidential data in the cloud should use their own encryption and keep hold of their own encryption keys and not share them with anyone least of all the cloud service provider.

Its only metadata

An interesting angle on the encryption banning/backdoor debate that is still going on between privacy groups and law enforcement agencies, which has relevancy to the IoT as well as the Internet in general, is the NSA's ambivalent response. Notably, the NSA seem to have no public stance on the matter they seem to not care either way, so why is that. Well, it appears that metadata which is the information about communications rather than the content of the communications is what they are interested in, and metadata for technical and practical reasons – call, email or packet routing – is not typically encrypted.

However, we must not underestimate the importance and power of metadata, despite President Obama repeatedly using this key-phrase in the same speech, just so that it was abundantly clear to us all, 'it's only metadata'.

Interestingly, it appears that the NSA and CIA do not agree with President Obama regards the importance of metadata

> *"We kill people based on metadata."*   Michael Haydon, the former head of
> the NSA and CIA

Presumably, Mr. Haydon was referring to the relationship between signal intelligence and the CIA drone operations, of "We track 'em. You whack 'em!"

Certainly, in the coming years there will be a plethora of ways to track suspects and targets using the IoT's 50 billion or so sensors and communication devices, even before we consider the power of analytics on the oceans of data that these sensors will be collecting. Consequently, we must be careful how we allow this technology to be utilized. Indeed, it will be vital to ensure that society polices the police, and restrains our sometime overzealous politicians. Importantly, society can start by containing the voracious appetite of our intelligence services for our information. Only by doing so can we send a clear message to our governments and law enforcement agencies that they are here primarily to protect and serve us, not spy on us. If we do not make, as a democratic society, the acceptable boundaries of state surveillance clear to all concerned then the IoT does have the awesome potential for delivering more damage than good.

Index